ADVANCE PRAISE FOR

Depletion *and* Abundance

Depletion and Abundance offers a vivid portrayal of where resource and energy scarcity is taking us, and with calm, incisive logic disassembles the too-easy answers and the panicked proposals offered on all sides of the energy debate. What's more, the author gives us a path having both heart and reason toward a sustainable and appealing future.

— Toby Hemenway, author of
Gaia's Garden: A Guide to Home-Scale Permaculture

This thoughtful, passionate book breaks away from the conventional wisdom of doomsayers and cornucopians alike to offer a deeply practical vision of survival through family, community, and personal responsibility in the age of peak oil. Highly recommended.

— John Michael Greer, author of
The Long Descent and *The Archdruid Report*

Sharon Astyk has given us an exquisite roadmap describing where we are now, where we are likely to find ourselves in the next few years, and how to prepare on myriad levels for the journey. This book is both brilliant and beautiful, reverberating with her insight, wisdom, and compassion. At the same time that she pours a tall glass of hard reality for the reader, she sits beside us with her hand on our shoulders while we drink it. I will enthusiastically use this book in every college class I teach.

— Carolyn Baker, Ph.D., author of *U.S. History Uncensored: What Your High School Textbook Didn't Tell You*, and blogger, Speaking Truth To Power, www.CarolynBaker.net

You come out of an *Inconvenient Truth* and you're lost. You can hope that technology will figure it out. Or, like Sharon Astyk, you can take the situation into your own hands. You can lead your family away from dependence on fossil fuels and stuff and towards a joyful vision of simplicity, self-reliance, planetary stewardship and strong local community. If that is your bent, this is your handbook.

— Colin Beavan, author and blogger at NoImpactMan.com

A smart book that will get you thinking about what the world might look like if it changed — which seems altogether likely. Sharon Astyk has all kinds of suggestions for individuals and families, but never forgets that real resilience lies in working communities.

— Bill McKibben, author of *Deep Economy*

This is a wonderful book about a terrible subject; situation — we're screwed. If it doesn't kill us, the coming depression could be the best thing to happen to Americans in a long time. A marvelously funny, compelling, passionate and practical book about how to survive the hard times ahead, written by a farmer and a mother of four for anyone who loves their family. More common sense than anyone deserves to find between the covers of a book. Buying it would be a good use of your last $25.

— Peter Bane, publisher of *Permaculture Activist*, www.PermacultureActivist.net

Many of us can see the ruins of our society for what they are, and understand that we have to make some other arrangements if we are to survive. Fewer of us seem able to make the switch to serving best those who matter to us most: the people in our lives. Sharon lifts the curse of the lost and lonely individual by pointing us toward family and community and giving us all work to do.

— Dmitry Orlov, author of *Reinventing Collapse: The Soviet Experience and American Prospects*

Without Sharon Astyk's courage and style, the converging crises that headline the daily news would indeed seem ominous. But Sharon has ventured off into our worst dystopian nightmare and experienced it, personally, and then come back to report to the rest of us, "Hey, it isn't all that bad!" She has seeded abundance from scarcity and happiness from despair, and is willing to share that secret.

— Albert Bates, author of *Climate in Crisis: The Greenhouse Effect and What You Can Do* and *The Post-Petroleum Survival Guide and Cookbook*

Depletion *and* Abundance

Depletion *and* Abundance

LIFE ON THE NEW HOME FRONT

Sharon Astyk

NEW SOCIETY PUBLISHERS

CATALOGING IN PUBLICATION DATA:
A catalog record for this publication is available from the
National Library of Canada.

Cover photos: iStock/Wael Hamdan
iStock/Sam Sefton

Printed in Canada. First printing June 2008.

Paperback ISBN: 978-0-86571-614-8

Inquiries regarding requests to reprint all or part of *Depletion & Abundance*
should be addressed to New Society Publishers at the address below.

To order directly from the publishers, please call toll-free (North America)
1-800-567-6772, or order online at www.newsociety.com

Any other inquiries can be directed by mail to:

New Society Publishers
P.O. Box 189, Gabriola Island, BC V0R 1X0, Canada
(250) 247-9737

New Society Publishers' mission is to publish books that contribute in fundamental
ways to building an ecologically sustainable and just society, and to do so with the
least possible impact on the environment, in a manner that models this vision. We
are committed to doing this not just through education, but through action. This
book is one step toward ending global deforestation and climate change. It is printed on Forest Stewardship Council-certified acid-free paper that is **100% post-con-
sumer recycled** (100% old growth forest-free), processed chlorine free, and printed
with vegetable-based, low-VOC inks, with covers produced using FSC-certified
stock. Additionally, New Society purchases carbon offsets based on an annual audit,
operating with a carbon-neutral footprint. For further information, or to browse our
full list of books and purchase securely, visit our website at: www.newsociety.com

NEW SOCIETY PUBLISHERS
www.newsociety.com

To Eric,
undepletable.

Contents

Acknowledgments

THIS BOOK IS A PRODUCT OF ABUNDANT INTELLECTUAL GENEROSITY, KIND-NESS and support from a host of people. I couldn't possibly name them all, nor could I ever thank them enough.

First of all, the seeds of this book grew up as I was training for an entirely different career, in English Literature. The critical thinking skills and work I did on population and disaster helped both make me a writer and prepare me to think about the same issues in the present context. Thanks to all of those who so patiently read and critiqued material that they never imagined would appear in this particular form. Thomas Brennan, John Burt, Mary Campbell (who I owe special thanks to for first introducing me to the concept of Hubbert's Peak), William Flesch, Thomas King, Jennifer Lewin, Rebecca Potter, Laura Quinney, Judith Wilt and Laura Yim all contributed to this text.

Navigating Peak Oil and Climate Change requires knowledge of a host of fields not covered in the education of a Shakespearean. I'm grateful to Richard Heinberg, Dmitry Orlov, Stuart Staniford, Robert Waldrop, Jeffrey Brown, Peter Bane, Keith Johnson, Colin Beavan, Albert Bates, Thomas Princen, Rob Hopkins, Gail Tverberg, Matt Savinar, Julian Darley, Linda Wigington, Dale Pfeiffer, George Monbiot, Tom Philpott and a host of others who got there first and helped me understand where I was going.

Hundreds of people on the Internet offered comments and critiques of various ideas as I worked through them. Members of Running On Empty 2 and 3 and the Riot for Austerity Yahoo Group, as well as kind readers who commented on my blog immeasurably improved my work. Thank you all.

Working with the endlessly encouraging Ingrid Witvoet was wonderful, and thanks to all at New Society who did so much to midwife this book into the world. Audrey Dorsch enormously improved the manuscript — I feel lucky to have had her guidance.

Special thanks to Pat Murphy, Megan Quinn and Faith Morgan at Community Solutions. Without them, I would never have had the public role I do, and all three provided enormous help and support. Kathy Breault read the health care chapter and gave me insights from her perspective as a midwife. Roel was a one-man research institute and an honest critic. Pat Meadows sent me articles, read several chapters and always gave good advice. MEA kept me honest and made me laugh. Larry Halpern modeled the low energy life. Miranda Edel was game for anything. Matt Mayers, Steve Balogh, Deanna Duke, Edson Freeman, Kyle Schuant, Philip Rutter, Bat Tzion Benjaminson, Melissa Norris, Brian and Robyn Morton, Harvey Winston and Sally Odland all helped me think things through. And Aaron Newton unfailingly gave me wise, honest and funny advice, was kind and supportive and a wonderful friend — I couldn't have done it without him.

Then there are the people who are stuck with me and couldn't avoid hearing about this. Bess Libby, Jon Libby, Alexandra Schmidt, Joe Shiang, Susan Sharfstein, Sandy Lawrence, Angel Schultz, Laurie Cybulski and Jesse Wertheimer put up with endless discussion and offered good advice. Steve Schmidt, economist extraordinaire, would probably like to disavow everything in this book, but taught me a great deal about economics nonetheless. My in-laws, Nancy and Marty Neschis were incredibly kind and encouraging, and made it possible for much of this to happen. Inge and Cyril Woods, Eric's late and much missed grandparents treated me as their own granddaughter, and shared their stories of hard times past.

My parents started all of this. All three of my parents — Naomi Astyk, Suzanne Lupo and Robert Astyk modeled many of the things that have led me to believe this is possible. My father had no car most of our growing-up years, and taught us to get around without one even in the 'burbs. Sue and Dad both provided from scratch meals every day after work. Mom and Sue gardened and taught me the value of DIY. And all three were unfailingly supportive, helpful and wonderful, as were my wonderful sisters and brothers in law Rachael and Sander McCauley and Vicki and Bill Baxter. Abby and Coco Baxter and Molly Read provided a great deal of inspiration to work on a better future.

Finally, I literally couldn't have done this without my husband, Eric Woods, and my four sons, Eli, Simon, Isaiah and Asher. Eric did everything in the world to make writing this possible — and my children are the ones who made it necessary. I can't thank them enough.

PART

One

[*Where Are We?*]

ONE

·

Getting Out the Boats:
a Primer on Hard Times

The first rule of holes: when you're in one, stop digging.
— MOLLY IVINS

Anything more than the truth would have seemed too weak.
— ROBERT FROST

Time to Get Out Our Boats

IN 2005, ABOUT SIX MONTHS BEFORE HURRICANE KATRINA DEVASTATED New Orleans, killed thousands of people, cost us billions of dollars and reshaped the American South, there was a television movie on Fox, called *Oil Storm*. This rather mediocre docudrama predicted what would happen when New Orleans and the Gulf Coast experienced a category 4 hurricane that destroyed the region, broke the levies and destroyed much of the region's oil refining and transporting infrastructure. The film created this scenario based on readily available analyses, including large quantities of government material describing the possible effects of a large storm in the Gulf. The focus of the movie was on what would happen to the nation after such a hurricane precipitated an energy crisis, but the film touched on the human costs of the destruction of New Orleans, showing citizens unable to evacuate being moved into sports stadiums.

All of which means that not only could the American leadership have known what could happen in New Orleans because they'd had briefings by the National Weather Service and the Army Corps of Engineers, but the information about what could happen was available to anyone who watched Fox.

3

This point matters a great deal, because if you were to ask most of our leaders whether we are on the brink of a crisis that will change our world utterly, make you and your family poorer and more vulnerable, and transform the lives of ordinary people into something currently unrecognizable, I doubt the answer would be yes. And here I come telling you that we are, in fact, on the brink of such a crisis and that we desperately need to prepare for it. Why on earth would you believe me and not our leaders?

The only answer I can give you is this — the government and the media aren't paying any more attention than they were before Katrina and, either by negligence or intent, do not understand what we face, even when the evidence is right in front of them. On the other hand, I'm paying attention because I don't have a choice. I'm watching the price of food go up because I have kids who have to eat. I'm watching data on oil depletion and price rises because I realize how much the whole society depends on cheap energy. I track data about the impact of Climate Change because my children and grandchildren are going to live in this new world we're creating. I have no choice but to know — and neither do you.

Naomi Klein, in her remarkable book *The Shock Doctrine: The Rise of Disaster Capitalism,* makes a compelling case that the disaster in New Orleans was permitted to happen by our government, and it is hard to believe otherwise. We must recognize that Hurricane Katrina was not an isolated incident, and that we cannot trust that distant leaders will protect us and act in our best interests. Whether by negligence or intent (and I am persuaded that some, at least, is by intent), the US is already falling apart — literally in some cases as we saw in the summer of 2007 with the Minnesota bridge collapse and the largest-ever oil leak coming out of underground Brooklyn oil lines — and we are not being protected. Klein quotes attorney Bill Quigley as saying,

> *What is happening in New Orleans is just a more concentrated, more graphic version of what is going on all over our country. Every city in our country has some serious similarities to New Orleans. Every city has some abandoned neighborhoods. Every city in our country has abandoned some public education, public housing, public healthcare and criminal justice. Those who do not support public education, healthcare and housing will continue to turn all of our country into the Lower Ninth Ward unless we stop them. (Klein, 221)*

Actually, it is worse than that. Quigley and Klein are reckoning without Peak Oil and Climate Change and the effects that will occur throughout the system. Unless we get to work both protecting our families and building existing mitigating structures, most of us may face lives that will make those of Katrina victims look rich and pleasant.

If we can take one message from Hurricane Katrina, it is that our government is probably not going to lead. And if our government does enact policy changes, it certainly isn't going to do it in time to protect your kids, or the rest of the world's kids. The sad truth is that governments mostly don't lead — they follow. And who do they follow? One way or another, most governments follow the will and anger of their people. That is, they are waiting for us to lead them, to tell them what we really care about. It is time — and past time — that we do. And it is past time that we protect ourselves and our communities, even if the government can't or won't.

> • • •
>
> Talk to people about Peak Oil and Climate Change, and encourage them to prepare.
>
> • • •

It wasn't the federal government that was first on the scene in Hurricane Katrina. It was regular people with boats, or at least courage, who got out there and rescued their neighbors and people they'd never seen and would never see again. It was ordinary people who tended one another's hurts. It was ordinary people who sought solutions. It was ordinary people who led the way, and the government eventually followed. And now it is time for ordinary people like us to get out our boats again and lead the way — to save our kids and our neighbors' kids and the kids of people we've never met and never will. That's what this book is for — getting out the boats.

Facing Up to the Future

When my oldest son, Eli, was born, I was struck by how small and helpless he was. Of course, I'd expected that. What I hadn't expected was how small and helpless I would feel as a mother. I suspect anyone who has been a parent knows that queasy feeling of realizing that here's a tiny human being who needs your protection. But our children's future depends on a host of things that many of us have little control over.

Most of all, I want to provide stability, security, peace and comfort for my family, to give them the best possible future, but the world keeps growing in the other direction. Economic inequities mean it is harder for me and billions of other people to meet basic needs. Food, energy, medical and housing costs are rising far faster than most family incomes. I want to give my children security, but the harsh reality of Climate Change makes food and water security increasingly unlikely in many places. The UN estimates that up to 1.5 billion people may be without clean, reliable sources of water in the future — and some of them will certainly be living near me. I want peace, but my country is on a quest for oil that seems likely to be endless. I want my family to have the comfort of a simple, clean, healthy life, but everywhere I turn there are more toxic chemicals in the air and food. Recent studies have shown that things as basic as plastic baby bottles and bath toys may contain endocrine disruptors and carcinogens.

And because I love my children so, I want other people who care equally for their families to have peace and security and health and sufficient food and water too. But the choices we're making simply don't seem to be taking us in that direction. Even more frightening, no matter how we protest and how we vote, we seem to be getting less secure each year.

The chances are you want the same things for the people you care about, and are experiencing similar struggles. I needed to know the truth about the future for my kids, and so do you. As difficult as it sometimes is to hear the bad news, you and I and all the working families in this country and other countries have to know this, because the consequences of ignorance are simply too terrible to bear.

> • • •
>
> There is no need for children to know all the bad news. Make adaptation fun — talk about how nice the new way of doing things is, or discuss living like people did long ago. Older children need more truth than younger ones, but don't rush it — or overprotect them.
>
> • • •

If we wait for someone else to fix things, we may find that we are like the people in New Orleans, drowning because no one took the time to prepare. We must begin to prepare, both at the personal level in our own homes and communities and by advocating for larger solutions. But all of us have limited time and energy; so being able to narrow our focus and decide what we must do is as important as knowing that we must prepare. As I researched these issues for myself and my family, I encountered a lot of information that didn't seem entirely relevant — either it argued for the same old kinds of activism or it was survivalist, assuming that all was already lost and we were going to turn on each other. Neither of these perspectives interested me much.

Other writers focused on science and the economics of Peak Oil — fascinating and important, but not always applicable for an ordinary person who has already seen that we can't simply go on trusting that important people will fix things for us. Though much of what I read was valuable, comparatively few analysts addressed the real questions, which are, Where do we go from here? How will this affect me and my family?

A lot of what I found described things that didn't seem very relevant to my life and the lives of the people I knew. Yes, news about funky electric cars was cool. But let's be honest — there's no way I could pay outright for a new, cutting-edge vehicle, and isn't part of the problem our national indebtedness? Yes, it was interesting to talk about putting solar power on my roof — but the $20,000 or so it would take to power my house was out of the question. And it occurred to me that I am not the only person who must feel this way. As I began to write about this, I found that there are thousands of people who are worried about how to care for their families and communities, and whose basic priorities haven't changed — they want healthy kids, a decent future for their children, to be able to feed themselves and their families and meet basic medical needs. They want something to be hopeful for, but also an honest dose of the truth and a direction to go forward in.

For me, the central issue is protecting my family and other families — the ones who live next door and the ones who live around the world. At the root of our problem is the fact that we are simply not thinking about the future. We talk a good game about wanting better for the next generation, but we aren't living our lives as though we love our own kids, much less anyone else's. It seems to me that the only way to give the next generation a decent shot at life is for those of us who care most about them to take things into our own hands and prepare for the changes ahead. That's why I wrote this book — because I suspect that if enough of us can focus our eyes on the future, we can at least mediate some of the worst coming harm for our own families and for others, and perhaps, just perhaps, make our voices heard in a world where that seems increasingly difficult.

And how should we focus our resources? There are many possibilities, many of them high tech. Do we look to electric cars or high-speed rail? Do we put solar panels on every roof or heat our houses with biofuels? What is perhaps radical about this book is that my answer is no, none of the above. So far the message most of us have received about Climate Change and Peak Oil and our financial situation is "We can go on exactly as we have been, with just a few little changes to renewable energies." Unfortunately, that's a fairy tale.

What I want to tell you is this: we are past the time at which we could hope to go on more or less as we have. For good or ill — and probably some of both — we have to make real changes in our lives. Most of us living in rich nations are going to have to learn to live simpler lives, using much less energy. We will build some windmills and we will do some things with renewable power. But a life that can go on for generations, a life that is truly sustainable, is going to be very, very different from the one we live now, and much more like the way our grandparents and great-grandparents lived. Few people will say this, because it isn't an easy thing to get your mind around. But it is true, as I will show you.

For this sacrifice, for this enormous change, if we can make it, we get some things in return. With good luck, we get healthier lives, more time with our families, a better, tastier diet, a stronger connection with nature, hopefully peace and more justice, a fairer economic system. Most of all, for those of us who care about our children and grandchildren more than we care about ourselves, we get to stop betraying the future and live our lives as though we really and truly love our families. We get to do what parents and grandparents are supposed to do for their kids — save and sacrifice to give their children a more hopeful future.

So where do we put our energies and resources? First, we take care of ourselves. We make sure we have food and shelter and a way of meeting our family's needs. Second, we move outward to our community, organizing groups that help our neighbors get along — remember none of us can be secure in isolation. And then we use our political and social powers to focus on the things that matter most. And it turns out that things we have to care most about in response to the present crisis are the same things we cared about all along — health care, education and security for the poor, the vulnerable, children, the elderly and the disabled. It really is as simple as that. If we've got time later on, great, let's build a network of electrified rail lines. But in the meantime, make sure your mom can get her heart medication, that the kids are learning to be real, engaged citizens, and that there's food in the pantry for all your neighbors. It turns out that this crisis hasn't really changed us at all — the simple stuff is still what matters most.

Speaking of fairy tales, I think sometimes of the story of Sleeping Beauty. The trouble starts because of what we forgot to do, because we left the bad fairy off the invitation lists. She's the representative of all the things we have left undone, of our failures and limitations, and she curses us because of our mistake. Now, that may not seem fair, and it is certainly an over-reaction, but that's how life is sometimes — we have to deal with the real consequences of our actions.

After the bad news of the curse, we can't spend time wishing it weren't so — we all start from the place we are now. It isn't always an easy place to begin, and there's a temptation to just hope that the bad things go away. But we can't. Each of us has power, the same power of the last of the fairy godmothers, the power of mitigation. She couldn't break the curse on Sleeping Beauty, but she could protect her a little and soften the curse. That's us — if we're courageous enough and willing to face the truth, we can soften the curse, and perhaps come out with a happy ending instead of a tragedy.

Hurry Up, Please; It's Time

Most books about Climate Change, Peak Oil, or economic crisis focus on the future. Their goal is to motivate you to action by describing what may happen. I will do some of that here, but as I began to put this book together, more and more I found myself replacing the future tense with the present, describing not what might happen, but what is. Unfortunately, the hard times I'm talking about do not lie in the conveniently distant future but have begun already. The only question is whether you or I have felt them yet.

By this I mean to say that though we do not know the exact shape of the long-term crisis we

• • •

Attend zoning meetings and consider running for zoning board. Work to amend local zoning laws to encourage green building, composting toilets, clotheslines, small livestock, mixed-use housing, front lawn gardens and other future essentials.

• • •

face from energy depletion or environmental degradation, we miss the point if we focus only on models and hypotheses. Right now we are in the midst of an environmental disaster, at present experiencing the high personal costs of energy depletion, at present losing economic ground to policies designed to increase inequity. I know that many of the people who read this book won't necessarily see the makings of a crisis — yet. Others will already be caught up in the early stages of the problem, experiencing job losses, foreclosures or the struggle to keep afloat economically as prices rise. So while we will speak of the future, my case that the world is about to change, irrevocably and deeply, rests primarily on the painful fact that it already has begun to do so.

And is there really any doubt that this is true? Is it possible to imagine any other time in American history when we would have consented to see an entire major city laid waste, without ever rebuilding even its most basic infrastructure? Is it possible to imagine another time when we would have shrugged and accepted the knowledge that our basic infrastructure, things like highways, sewers and subways, were simply falling apart and that we had no intention of fixing them? Is it possible to imagine another time when we knew we were in danger of handing our children a future of hunger, poverty and drought, and sat around debating whether congress might want to consider raising fuel efficiency standards? Has there ever been a time in history when citizens felt so powerless to stop the forces that were driving them to disaster?

If, in the face of all the evidence in front of our own eyes, we find that things really are falling apart, we might listen to the respected voices issuing the same opinions. There are some out there — despite the overwhelming lack of responsiveness of our government. For example, in the summer of 2007, David Walker, comptroller general of the US General Accounting Office, warned the nation that the US was increasingly looking like Rome at the point of its collapse. A few months later Walker resigned in frustration at America's failure to respond to the collection of crises facing the nation.

Few of us have put all the pieces together, but when we failed to rebuild New Orleans, when we accepted that we can't afford the tax base to keep bridges from falling on motorists and sewers from backing up, when we accepted that electric grid failure will kill people in the inevitable heat waves, we implicitly acknowledged what we have not yet faced up to consciously — that things have changed, and many of our problems are going to continue getting worse because we lack either the will or the money or the energy or the time to fix them

• • •

If your community doesn't have a food co-op, start one, focusing on local foods.

• • •

When I realized that everything was going to change, I was at first afraid. Because I thought, if my government or public policy or other choices weren't going to fix everything, what could I possibly do? What hope was there, if I had to take care of myself, if my community had to take care of itself?

But when I began looking for solutions that could be applied on the level of ordinary human lives, that involved changes in perspectives and pulling together, the reclamation of abandoned ideas and the restoration of strong communities, I began to feel hopeful, even excited. Because I realized that when large institutions cease to be powerful, sometimes that means that people start being powerful again.

Defining Our Terms

I'm not going to devote a lot of space to explaining what Peak Oil and Climate Change is, or why the nation is in the shaky financial shape it is.

You'll find a lengthy bibliography in the back with lots of resources written by the same authors that I learned so much from. I will, however, define my terms here, so that we're all clear on what we're talking about.

Peak Energy (sometimes called *Peak Oil* because oil is the first major fossil resource likely to reach the halfway point) refers to the point at which we've used up half of the accessible fossil fuels in the world, and what's left begins getting ever-more expensive and harder to get hold of. There is no controversy about whether Peak Oil or gas or coal will happen — whenever there is a finite amount of something, at some point, you use up half — that's just common sense.

Figuring out when this will happen is difficult, but there's a growing consensus that "when" is either very soon or has already happened. The General Accounting Office, for example, states that a majority of petroleum geologists believe we are at or very near Peak Oil. The US Army is preparing for Peak Oil. The US Department of Energy has commissioned studies on the subject. The International Energy Agency recently released a report expecting "supply constraints" for decades to come. A number of equally credible sources believe that natural gas and coal will peak fairly shortly after oil and that all the world's major fossil energy sources will be in decline soon. This is a huge matter — kind of like learning that soon the entire world's oxygen will be gone. Because, just as oxygen keeps us going, fossil fuels keep our economy and society running in a whole host of ways.

Fossil fuels are the most concentrated and accessible sources of energy out there. For example, it takes about one barrel of oil to get between 30 and 100 barrels of oil out of the ground. On the other hand, for solar panels, one barrel of oil equivalent gets you three barrels of oil equivalents, and for ethanol, at best you get 1.34 barrels for every barrel you invest. This is called EROEI, energy returned over energy invested, and it helps us measure just how expensive it will be to produce energy and how much we'll need to replace, say, a barrel of oil or a truckload of coal. Detailed analyses can be performed, but it is enough here to know that the answer to how much of our energy infrastructure we can afford to replace is "not much, not quickly." Shell's CEO recently announced that despite heavy investment by his own company, it would take "decades" for renewables to make a dent in fossil fuel consumption. If other technologies were cheap, easy replacements for oil and gas, we'd have replaced them already.

In 2005, the US Department of Energy commissioned a report, known as The Hirsch Report, which said that to address Peak Oil and keep our basic way of life going, the US would require "unprecedented" effort *20 years in advance of* the world's oil peak — a giant, World War II style national project of switching over, but vastly larger than World War II. Otherwise, we could expect real hardships, even disaster. Even the most optimistic estimates, such as the US Geological Survey's, suggest that our oil will peak in about 15 years — which means that, in a sense, it doesn't really matter when Peak Oil happens — we simply don't have enough time to make an easy transition.

Public figures on every part of the political spectrum agree. It isn't an issue of left or right — people from Bill Clinton to Dick Cheney, from film-maker Michael Moore to George Bush's former energy czar Matthew Simmons, from Al Gore to the CEOs of many major energy companies and the US Army believe the peak is here or coming.

An army report on energy trends and security said,

> *Peak oil is at hand with low availability growth for the next 5 to 10 years. Once worldwide petroleum production peaks, geopolitics and market economics will result in even more significant price increases and security risks.*
> *(US Army Report: Energy Trends and their implications for US Army Installations. energybulletin.net/docs/EnergyTrendsUSArmy Summary.pdf)*

We have already begun to experience supply constraints, and just about everything that is made or transported with oil has begun to rise in cost. Virtually every purchase we make involves oil at some stage (often at every stage) — from the shoes on our feet to the houses we live in. Our food is grown with oil, packaged in oil, and transported to our grocery stores with oil. Many of us have an instinctive assumption that Peak Oil is mostly about gasoline, because that's how we think about oil. But in fact, oil is every-where, and our whole economy floats on a sea of oil and other sources of fossil energy that are nearing their peaks.

Rising energy prices mean rising prices for everything else — and in fact, we're seeing that right now indirectly. Rising oil prices have driven us to try and replace oil with ethanol, which is making food prices spiral out of control, as agriculture copes with higher grain prices, higher fertilizer prices, higher equipment prices and higher shipping costs.

Food represents a special problem in Peak Oil, perhaps the most urgent of all problems. Those of us who have never known hunger may find it hard to believe how close we are to a world food crisis. In 2007 world grain stocks fell to the lowest levels in modern history because of drought, Peak Oil-related biofuel production and other environmental consequences. As world population rises, we face being unable to feed ourselves. Lester Brown, director of the Worldwatch Institute has argued,

> *The first big test of the international community's capacity to manage scarcity may come with oil or it could come with grain. If the latter is the case, this could occur when China — whose grain harvest fell by 34 million tons or 9 percent between 1998 and 2005 — turns to the world market for massive imports of 30 million, 50 million or possibly even 100 million tons of grain per year. Demand on this scale could quickly overwhelm world grain markets. When this happens, China will have to look to the United States, which controls [over 40 percent of] the world's grain exports ... some 200 million tons.*
>
> *This will pose a fascinating geopolitical situation. More than 1.3 billion Chinese consumers, who had an estimated $160-billion trade surplus with the United States in 2004 — enough to buy the entire US grain harvest twice — will be competing with Americans for US grain, driving up US food prices. In such a situation 30 years ago, the United States simply restricted exports. But China is now banker to the United States, underwriting much of the massive US fiscal deficit.... (Brown, Plan B 2.0 14)*

Since Brown wrote this passage in 2006, China has become a net importer of food for the first time; and the boom in biofuels to replace scarce energy has used up one-quarter of the US corn crop, making the oil/food link even more fragile. Hunger rates are rising, and American food pantries and world hunger relief agencies are failing to keep up. Recently, an analysis by *Oil Drum* editor Stuart Staniford argued that under current food and energy policies, several billion people could starve to death in the next decade. The collision course the US and China are on bodes badly for nearly everyone. The 35 million Americans who now suffer from food insecurity and hunger do so not because of any shortage of food nationally, but because they cannot afford to eat. There is no reason to believe that as more of us struggle to feed ourselves, and as we confront real food shortages, we will not see hunger rise to affect some or even most of us.

• • •

Grow an extra row of your garden for the local food pantry or soup kitchen. Encourage neighbors to do the same.

• • •

Along with rising prices, we may also experience shortages. For example, as China and India require more imported oil, the US may sometimes experience shortfalls. War and terrorism caused by oil conflicts may also lead to shortages. There has been much discussion of what might happen if the US bombs Iran and Iran elects to close the Strait of Hormuz, through which a significant percentage of oil tankers pass, or if Venezuela cuts off oil exports to the US. This could result in a sudden, catastrophic reduction in available oil. Nor is it terribly unlikely that hurricanes will take more of the refining capacity in the Gulf of Mexico offline. The truth is that we may find someday that there's no gas at the pumps or no food in the stores because it cannot be transported.

Peak Energy will appear as an economic problem; that is, the way we are likely to experience Peak Oil is not in the sudden disappearance of oil

• • •

Encourage your kids to get involved with political and social issues they care about. Help them raise money or awareness, and help them understand the role of citizens in hard times.

• • •

from our lives, but in the steady rise of gas prices, food and goods prices, and job losses, along with shortages and disruptions. It is likely to steadily make us poorer, less able to afford the lifestyle we've been living. But peak alone is far less serious than the disastrous one-two punch of Peak Oil in combination with Climate Change.

Unless you've been living in a cave, you know about Climate Change. You probably know there is no longer any real controversy about whether Climate Change is anthropogenic, that is, caused by human beings. And you know that the things that cause Climate Change are the energy emissions of burning fossil fuels. What you probably haven't heard is just how dire the situation is. While individual scientists have been sounding the alarm, governments and institutions have gone out of their way to make Climate Change sound like a problem we've got a long time to worry about — and that isn't true.

The one absolute truth about Climate Change is that it is happening much faster and harder than anyone expected. In the spring of 2007, the Intergovernmental Panel on Climate Change (IPCC) report came out, detailing the state of the climate. Within a few months, parts of the report were completely out of date — which we know from observed data that demonstrated that the Arctic ice was melting 75 years ahead of what they'd expected a few months before.

Climate Change is caused by human emissions; it moves faster or slower partly in response to our rate of emissions, but also because of natural "tipping points" that make the planet take things in its own hands. So, for example, during one of the last great climactic shifts, the planet may have gone from being fairly warm to an ice age in less than ten years; and then the ice age may have ended in a single season! These things are very hard to model, but projections for the future that imagine Climate Change will occur in a gradual and orderly fashion are probably wrong.

Chief climate scientist of NASA James Hansen has argued that we have

> about 10 years to put into effect the draconian measures needed to curb CO_2 emissions quickly enough to avert a dangerous rise in global temperature. Otherwise, the extra heat could trigger the rapid melting of polar ice sheets, made far worse by the "albedo flip" — when the sunlight reflected by white ice is suddenly absorbed as ice melts to become the dark surface of open water. (independent.co.uk/environment/climate-change/the-earth-today-stands-in-imminent-peril-453708.html)

The idea that we have very little time to stop burning fossil fuels is one that more and more scientists are endorsing. Though conversations still emphasize high-tech solutions, simple mathematics seems to indicate that the vast majority of our carbon cuts are going to have to be simply by ceasing to use fossil fuels. Even if we had the resources to perform a large-scale buildout, it would take decades — far longer than we actually have. So we must prioritize cutting back our energy usage. That means bigger changes than most of us have been expecting — not buying energy star appliances, but getting rid of the appliances altogether.

What could happen if we don't fix this? More than half of the US population lives near a coastline. A one-meter sea rise would inundate many major American cities and coastal areas. Such a sea rise could come quite rapidly if a tipping point, such as an ice-free Arctic, is reached as early as predicted (predictions suggest it could happen as early as 2013). Seawater rise is already eroding coastlines off California and North Carolina, contaminating drinking water in Miami and bringing water into basements in Boston.

Catastrophic drought is already occurring all over the world. Australia is paying its farmers to walk off their land because there's no evidence there will ever be enough water to grow food. The drought in the American Southwest is expected to last another 100 years. Grain harvests in Africa are expected to halve by 2020.

That means less food and water to go around, not just in poor places, but in rich ones as well. It means people leaving places that are too dry or that are repeatedly destroyed by storms. It means millions or billions of people made refugees, and people with houses they can't sell because no one wants to live there. It means food prices rising higher and higher, and hunger stalking our families. It means more deaths during more heat waves every summer. That is, it means getting poorer and having less stability and security; it means migration and people leaving their homes and having less. It means, in fact, the same things as Peak Oil — and we're facing both of them together. James Howard Kunstler has called this confluence "the long emergency," and that's a good term for it — because what we are facing is one endless, grinding crisis.

Financial collapse now seems to be a near inevitability. We've borrowed so much money from our inflated housing and on credit cards that the average American has a negative savings rate and borrows 5 percent more than they earn. Foreclosures are rising, and more and more of us are paying mortgages on houses that could never be worth what we paid for. Some analysts have suggested that our homes may lose up to 50 percent of their peak value. At this writing housing has already lost nearly 25 percent of its value over 2007, and home sales are down by nearly 40 percent in some regions. The dollar is falling and is increasingly not the currency of choice. This is a far larger subject than I could ever hope to take on, but it is enough to say that we have dug ourselves into a massive hole that there seems to be little way out of.

In the spring of 2008, currency and economic crises were springing up all over the world, from Iceland, experiencing massive inflation, to China, struggling to avoid the impact of the world economic crisis in its rapidly growing economy. Food prices worldwide have risen dramatically, with rice prices rising 30 percent in a single day in March 2008, increasing both economic and political instability.

Secretary of the Treasury Henry Paulson announced in 2007 that "the nature of the problem will be significantly bigger next year." Nearly everyone is warning of severe recession, or even a depression. Among those who foresaw this situation is New York University Professor Nouriel Roubini, who said, shortly before the Thanksgiving 2007 stock market meltdown,

> It is increasingly clear by now that a severe US recession is inevitable in next few months.... I now see the risk of a severe and worsening liquidity and credit crunch leading to a generalized meltdown of the financial system of a severity and magnitude like we have never observed before. (rgemonitor.com/blog/roubini/228234/)

With What Will We Fix It, Dear Liza, Dear Liza?

Now, is all of this inevitable? Do I know for certain that some magic technology won't come along and fix everything up so that we can all have unlimited clean energy? Nope, I don't. My crystal ball isn't any better than yours. The odds are against it, as we're already in the crisis and it hasn't appeared. But the logic behind preparing for hard times and getting my family and my community ready is very simple. It is simply a matter of asking myself "What happens if I do?" and "What happens if I don't?"

Well, if I do get ready and protect my family, I'll have to devote some of my money and a lot of my time to things like gardening, cooking from scratch and insulating my house. I'll also probably eat better food, save money, get more exercise and spend more time with my family. I will have to pay a price and make some sacrifices, but I'll still have the things that matter most to me.

If I don't prepare for these times, the worst case scenario is that we could die. If you think I'm exaggerating, you aren't paying attention — poor people in the US die much younger and faster and harder than rich people right now. So if I get very poor, if my family can't pay for medications and I can't take time off work to treat basic illnesses, if I can't afford healthy food and I'm away from my kids all the time trying to make ends meet — I could die, or my kids could. If we have wildfires or hurricanes because of Climate Change we could die. If we can't heat our houses because of the rising prices of oil, we could die. If diseases to which we have minimal immunity have moved north in a warming climate, we could die. Actuaries are already saying that nearly a million people died in 2007 from Climate Change. If any of us are imagining that we aren't vulnerable to the worst price of Climate Change and environmental degradation, we're deluding ourselves.

• • •

Now is the time to prepare for illness. Keep a stock of remedies at hand, including useful antibiotics, painkillers and tools for handling injury and illnesses itself.

• • •

As Samuel Johnson said, "When a man knows he is to be hanged in a fortnight, it concentrates his mind wonderfully." That is, there's nothing more likely to change our lives than knowing that our kids and grandkids might go hungry, that we might die in middle age because we can't afford basic medication, that people we love — or even total strangers — might suffer horribly because of our actions. We need to concentrate our minds and our lives on this — it is the greatest challenge in history.

So this book's most significant suggestion is that we simply get over the notion that we're all entitled to use a lot of energy and have a lot of stuff, and that we start living within our real means (within our incomes, not on credit cards) and with a fair share of the world's resources.

Our terrible affluence is at the root of our current crisis. Somehow most people in the rich world have gotten the impression that we're here not to care about others or do good work but to get "ahead" and accumulate stuff. Most of our energy use goes to make us a little bit more comfortable, not to meet essential needs. Perhaps the most important work we can do is to distinguish between wants and needs, and to find something besides consumption to value and put at the center of our lives. My suggestion is that we put our hope for the future there, and begin to live our lives as though we hold the world — and our particular piece of it — in trust for future generations.

Actions as Activism: The New Home Front and the Riot for Austerity

> There is no such thing as the State
> And no one exists alone;
> Hunger allows no choice
> To the citizen or the police;
> We must love one another or die.
> — W.H. AUDEN ("SEPTEMBER 1, 1939")

> The most alarming sign of the state of our society now is that our leaders
> have the courage to sacrifice the lives of young people in war but
> have not the courage to tell us that we must be less greedy and less wasteful.
> — WENDELL BERRY

The Riot for Austerity

IN THE SPRING OF 2007, MY FRIEND MIRANDA EDEL AND I WERE DISCUSSING
the fact that although scientists and activists all over the world were saying
that the rich world had to reduce its total emissions by 90 percent or more,
no politician had proposed such a thing. In fact, every time I mentioned it to
anyone, the reaction I got was, "That's not going to happen!" How could we
make people believe this was possible? we wondered. Was such reduction
even possible, not in some hypothetical future of nuclear fusion and billions
of wind turbines, but in the world we actually live in? Well, we said, someone
has to find out whether it can be done, and not just by hermits living in caves,
but by ordinary families. Why not us?

Now, this project would have been a lot easier with help — if the leadership
in our states and nation were building public transportation, subsidizing small-

scale agriculture and investing in renewable resources. But more than a year after Climate Change first flooded onto the national stage, exactly nothing of note had happened to reduce emissions. In fact, they were climbing steadily.

Even for Miranda and I, who had been cutting back for some time, the challenge seemed overwhelming. And yet it also seemed utterly necessary. All the political targets for emissions reduction were just that — political. Instead of the 10 years to cut emissions by 90–95 percent that scientists mostly agreed on, governments were talking about 50 percent in 40 years, or at most 80 percent in 40 years. And governments all over the world were failing to meet even the most conservative targets. Information was coming that most of the Kyoto signatories would fail to hit their mark — and the US hadn't even signed. We couldn't wait for our government any more.

So, half jokingly, I asked Miranda, "Want to do it with me?" And she, being an enormously intrepid woman, said yes. We both wrote about it, and suddenly, without our ever intending it, dozens and then more than a hundred readers asked if they could do it too. And then, as word spread, there were hundreds of people. News stories started to pop up on radio and in newspapers. Now there are nearly a thousand participants all over the world, and the movement is still growing. It is, of course, a drop in the environmental bucket. But if there are a thousand people willing to make a 90 percent reduction in their energy use, even though it is hard, simply because it is right, perhaps there are tens of thousands or hundreds of thousands who might do so if they knew it was possible.

> Use spring holidays and the subject of rebirth and freedom to bring up the subjects of Climate Change, Peak Oil and the future with family and friends.

We called it "The Riot for Austerity," because in his compelling book *Heat: How to Stop the Planet from Burning,* George Monbiot argues that what is required to save us all from the worst consequences of Climate Change is something that has never been seen before — a mass demand for less. Monbiot, an acute observer of our deepest psyches argues,

> *As people in the rich countries — even the professional classes — begin to wake up to what science is saying, climate change denial will look as stupid as Holocaust denial or the insistence that AIDS can be cured by beetroot. But our response will be to demand that the government acts while hoping it doesn't. We will wish our governments to pretend to act. We get the moral satisfaction of saying what we know to be right, without the discomfort of doing it.*

> *My fear is that the political parties in most rich nations have
> already recognized this. They know we want tough targets, but
> that we also want those targets to be missed. They know that we
> will grumble about their failure to curb climate change, but that
> we will not take to the streets. They know that nobody ever riot-
> ed for austerity."* (Monbiot, 41–42)

I believe Monbiot has put his finger on the nature of our inner dilemma.
Again, we are putting off the burden to the future rather than facing up to
it ourselves. We're too scared to really commit to what we must do. This is
wrong. But perhaps we can change — in fact, we must change.

So Miranda and I decided we would be the first people to Riot for
Austerity. Instead of waiting for the government to tell us what to do (in case
they never do), instead of waiting for someone to find the perfect wind tur-
bine, we set to work, hundreds of us sharing ideas and solutions, comparing
our numbers in seven categories (electricity, heating fuel, gasoline, consumer
goods, food, water and garbage) to the national average and shooting for a
90 percent reduction.

We started the project on June 1, 2007, planning to take a year to get
down to 90 percent (after which the goal is to stay there for the rest of our
lives). I like to joke that three days after we started, my friend Larry was
done. That's not quite true, but when Larry announced that his total electricity usage for October 2007 was 34 kwh (national average is about 900 a
month) people asked "Do you actually live in your house?" Not only does
he live there, Larry and his wife, Gail, both work out of their home.

Miranda started traveling around her city almost entirely on bike
and public transport. One woman took up the challenge, starting from
more than twice the national average in most categories, and made enormous personal reductions. People shared tips on finding local food in inner
cities and how to keep warm in cold weather. People made their
own beer, built passive solar heaters and developed a bicycle-powered washing machine.

Overwhelmingly, the focus of the solutions was on low technology, low
cost and human power. The solutions were creative, imaginative things that
almost anyone could do. That is, most of us made our cuts not by buying
high-tech things but by cutting back to the bone. And most of us found that
we could do it, or come very close to a 90 percent reduction in most categories, while still living in the same places and with the same dubious,
imperfect family members we're dragging along on the journey. We have

members from 15 nations, living in every kind of city, town and country location you could imagine.

All of us believe that the kinds of things we are doing are the kinds of things that most people will have to do — either from necessity or desire — to protect the planet and live in a lower-energy, lower-money world. So we set about trying to figure them out, to offer some kind of guidelines for what saves us energy. It has been a fascinating project. A year into the project, our family is down at least 80 percent in all categories, and has achieved our goals in four categories. We've had a blast, too — the community, the creativity, the energy have been exciting, engaging and inspiring. Instead of a sense of loss, we've found joy.

This started out as two women wanting to find a way to show people that something could be done. It turned into something more — a movement, in part, a community, certainly, but also a way of thinking about change, a philosophy about the intersection of the personal and the political, and a design strategy, using what we have to make a future for ourselves.

On the New Home Front

The coming hard times will not be a war against anything, and we must remember that. There is no enemy, or rather, as Walt Kelly's Pogo once said, "We have met the enemy and he is us." That is, there is no bad guy "out there" — the problem lies in our relentless consumption of resources, our living like there is no tomorrow, the society's rejection of the values of thrift and continuity with the past. We may use war as an analogy, but we should remember it is only that; this is not about fighting but about regeneration.

But it is also true that for most of the rich world, the last time we were asked to make sacrifices for the greater good, to work together to face a common crisis, was during war. For most of us, that is not so much a memory as the subject of our parents' or grandparents' stories and movies and books. We know that once Americans and the British and our Allies were joined in a great endeavor. It was difficult, tragic and harrowing — but it also made the people who endured it great and gave us a future we could not have had under fascism. It was terribly hard because it demanded that ordinary people become heroes to save themselves and future generations. And if we are to go forward from where we are, we must believe that we are their honorable descendents who, like our parents and grandparents and great-grandparents, have the courage and love for the future to make heroic sacrifices and unite to quite literally save the world.

To do this will require enormous unity of purpose. During the 1940s, the US and Britain spent 50 percent or more of their total GDP on the war. Besides the conscription of young men into service, virtually everyone in the nation worked doing war work on the "Home Front." Women and older men flooded factories, manufacturing planes, ships and munitions. In Britain, young women were conscripted into the "Land Army," planting and harvesting in the place of the men gone to war. Rationing and national behavior-change campaigns regulated everything from the undergarments that were available to what people ate, from how many pairs of shoes they owned to what they did in their free time. Virtually every facet of life, public and private, operated in service to the war effort.

But despite this unity of *purpose*, World War II represented enormous fragmentation of *people*. That is, young men were separated from their families and sent off to war. Some young women went too as nurses and military support workers. Most women stayed behind and had to take over the entire management of households, and the vast amount of war work left behind. Children were increasingly left to their own devices (if they were old enough) or put in the hands of other relatives or newly created childcare facilities. Large chunks of the population migrated, moving, for example, much of the African American population of the rural south to the industrial north to serve the war effort.

. . .

Pay attention to your marriage/ partnership. Stress is a probable for many marriages and is likely to increase in hard times. Make sure you have healthy, enjoyable ways of dealing with each other, and that your partner knows that you love him or her and are committed, even when things are hard.

. . .

The physical separation of families led to emotional separations as well — the divorce rate rose dramatically during World War II and never entirely returned to pre-war levels, rising steadily through the 1950s. Families were undermined by prolonged separations, communities broken apart, and people left to put the pieces back together as best they could.

I believe it is fair to say that what we had during World War II was national unity of purpose but fragmentation of families and communities. In that sense, World War II's divided fronts represent an extremely poor model for addressing Peak Oil, which requires not just unity of purpose but, even more, human unity and community. We cannot afford a two-front war, where some are off warming the planet and involved in oil wars while others at home frantically try to compensate for the loss of desperately needed resources, both human and economic. We must have a single front, a New

Home Front, in which families and communities, towns, and ideally states and nations work together with a single purpose, focusing our resources together.

In wartime, the Home Front is where civilian action supports the larger national goal, where every part of domestic, social, political and economic life is unified in a single purpose. In time of war, governments acknowledge what they otherwise generally deny in market economies — that our ordinary human actions have a powerful political and social context. In time of war, we are told that how we eat, what we wear, where we live, what work we choose to do, how we save and spend our money are vital issues of national security and personal survival. The rest of the time such actions are put away in a box called "personal," and we're told our individual actions don't matter. But in time of great crisis the truth comes out, and we're asked to think hard before we spend, to eat carefully and choose wisely, and to accept the obvious truth — that those actions are matters of life and death, and that we should live and work with a heightened awareness of our impact on others.

We should ask ourselves why it is that if those everyday actions are a matter of fundamental national security during a time of crisis, why does that change when the crisis is over? Presumably our choices still have a powerful impact — so why are we told in a host of ways that they do not?

• • •

Draw attention to your local watershed and your vulnerabilities in that regard.

• • •

Thus World War II advertising, public policy measures and rationing intervened into every aspect of Home Front life. From whether you cleaned your plate (wasting food meant less food for soldiers and starving allies) to what you did with your worn out tires and scrap metal (give them to the war effort), the integration of every element of daily life into policy matters reminded us that these "private" things were, in fact, powerful public acts. And in fact, they are powerful acts. It is not the times that make them matter, they always matter.

Reconsidering Public and Private

I want to bring our attention back to the political nature of our Home Front activities. There is a tendency among environmentalists and activists to disdain "private" solutions — that is, to claim that individual action has comparatively little power to solve our present crisis. For example, Richard Heinberg, one of the environmental writers I most admire, has an extended analysis of this issue in his book *Powerdown: Options and Actions for a Post-Carbon World* that I think deserves some consideration here. Heinberg writes,

One brief trend in the sustainability literature was the suggestion that individual, small-scale initiatives would be sufficient to turn the tide .... The point being made (by the critics of this idea) was that the unsustainability of industrial society is due not just to individuals' decisions about product choice and personal behavior but to fundamental socioeconomic structures, institutions and processes. Some writers went even further: as Garrett Hardin pointed out in his widely discussed essay "The Tragedy of the Commons," efforts towards self-limitation on the part of a few, undertaken in a competitive environment, are predictably futile and will result simply in the marginalization of self-limiters and the exhaustion of commonly available resources.

It would be reassuring to think that we could save the Earth if only each of us were to make one small contribution each day. But the challenging reality is that making human society sustainable will require a large-scale reform of governments and economic systems and the use of mechanisms of authority to apply penalties and offer incentives. (Heinberg, Powerdown, 95–100)

I both agree and disagree with Heinberg here. I agree that mechanisms of enforcement and reform will absolutely be required and that larger forms of social organization, such as nations and governments, will have to be involved. Where we differ is on the question of the power individual actions can have in bringing about such changes — to move governments, enforce corporate behavior and offer incentives to others. I believe Heinberg makes a common and entirely understandable error here in that he has accepted the artificial division of "public" and "private" as natural. This division has a long intellectual history, but it is a cultural assumption, not a material truth.

Historically, the division between public and private is bound up with gender. Any common sense analysis will recognize this — women historically inhabited the space of private life. Food, clothing, cooking and child-rearing were the work of women, in their houses. Public life — the world of economics and politics and other "big, important things" — was associated with men in Western society. The classic Victorian ideal argued that a woman's name should appear in print only three times in her life — at birth, marriage and death. That is, women were supposed to live entirely "private" lives.

The old Victorian divisions between public and private still have a hold on our thinking. We retain the assumption that private acts don't "count" in the public sphere. We often believe that work done for money in the "public" world is more valuable than work done to avoid needing money in the "private" realm. This is one of the reasons that we tend to devalue homemaking and other domestic labor. And such devaluation is deeply bound up in industrial capitalism.

Women's Work and Political Power

In *Ancient Futures: Learning from Ladakh*, Helena Norberg-Hodge observes how the change to an industrial economic model in a previously undeveloped area harmed women and also men who did subsistence labor, whose work was now deemed "private" and irrelevant to the society at large. She writes,

> *Women, for their part, become invisible shadows. They do not earn money for their work, so they are no longer seen as "productive." Their work is not recognized as part of the gross national product. In government statistics, the 10 percent or so of Ladakhis who work in the modern sector are listed according to their occupations; and the other 90 percent — housewives and traditional farmers — are lumped together as "nonworkers." This influences people's attitudes towards themselves and others, and the lack of recognition clearly has a deep psychological impact. (Norberg-Hodge, 126)*

This is an enormously important point. When we decide something lacks value and power, we demean it. For a long time private labor was demeaned in part because women were considered secondary and inferior, and much private subsistence labor was done by women in the home. When women began to work more often in the public realm, they, for the most part, accepted industrial capitalism's diminution of the importance and meaning of home-based labor, deciding that working "out" was a way to achieve political and social power. Women came to see abandoning "women's work" as means to power. So some of it we stopped doing (gardening, canning, much cooking and sewing); other parts (childcare, housecleaning, food preparation) we contracted out to low-paid, often non-white workers of low status. So while women's status in society rose, domestic, private work fell even further in cultural value, and so did the status of "private life" and its practices.

We have spent the past 100 years gradually devaluing subsistence and domestic work, and placing all value on "public" labor, "public" political acts and industrial life. Thus, we're deeply invested in the notion that private actions have minimal public consequences. This is no accident. I can't emphasize this strongly enough. The version of the women's movement that succeeded, demeaned private life and private actions and denied them importance because doing so enabled us to "privatize" (to give over to corporations) the practice of what was once private life. It has been enormously profitable — McDonalds, Wal-Mart and Monsanto are just a few of the thousands of corporations that got rich providing services people used to do for their loved ones at home for free. My claim here is not that women should have continued to do this labor themselves, but that the industrial economy did a vastly worse job of this work than any human being, male or female, would have. And the movement of 60 percent of all women into the labor force gave us enormously more disposable income to spend on just about everything. Whether this was good for society as a whole or for families is another question, but the destruction of the domestic economy was undoubtedly good for the industrial economy.

Is there any truth to the notion that private acts — by these I mean the actions we choose in our daily lives — are not as powerful as political acts? Well, it depends on the situation. It is easy to second guess ourselves, to ask, for example whether those of us who tried to prevent the current Iraq war might have been successful had we spent less time protesting and instead held the US economy hostage by declining to shop or buy gas until plans for invasion were stopped. It probably wouldn't have worked — but it is manifestly the case that driving our cars to the protest didn't work.

. . .

Start a local gleaning program! Gleaners harvest food missed by mechanical harvesters. Some programs donate the results to food pantries; others provide food for the pickers and their families.

. . .

If we are to consider the potential impact of private choices alongside public ones, we might use food as a case study. Over the past 40 years, an enormous movement has grown up in opposition to the depredations of industrial agriculture, and a host of environmental groups have had mixed success at getting certain pesticides banned and some practices regulated. Overwhelmingly their gains have been overshadowed, however, by the sheer power of industrial agriculture's lobby, and they've lost more battles than they won.

On the other hand, at the same time, growing numbers of ordinary people who simply didn't want to eat pesticides began buying organic food and seeking out new sources, creating a burgeoning organic movement and transferring several hundred thousand acres out of chemical agriculture and into organic production. "Whole Foods Moms" refused to buy chemically grown produce, and this move toward organic food had an enormous impact on our agriculture. It wasn't a perfect victory, but it was a victory.

And it went further than that. Because organic wasn't enough — organic food was still grown with pesticides and migrant labor, and farmers were still not supported adequately — the local food movement began to grow. It started in Europe as devoted eaters and farmers in the "Slow Food" movement sought to protect local foodways, and in Japan where the community-supported agriculture (CSA) movement was created and called "food with a farmer's face on it." It then spread to North America, where Gary Nabhan ate for a year within 250 miles of his southwestern US home and where Alisa Smith and J.B. MacKinnon, of Vancouver, BC, founded the "100 Mile Diet," encouraging tens of thousands of people to try to develop their own local diets and enabling small-scale, local agriculture.

*   *   *

Get to know local farmers, and ask them to grow things that you'd like to get locally. A farmer might consider adding wheat or dried beans or an unusualy vegetable to their crops if enough people ask them.

*   *   *

The public power of these private acts not only was greater than the public power of the more formal public activism of agricultural activists, but it enabled environmental change — tens of thousands of people now much more concerned about their food could see the connections with activism, and writers like Michael Pollan were successful in getting Whole Foods Moms and Locavores to weigh in on their farm bill.

As I noted, the move of the whole society into the public realm was extremely good for growth capitalism — instead of a large chunk of the economy being done for free (or perhaps more accurately, from love), now there were all these new women working 9–5 and spending their disposable income, and we had all these new, low-paying jobs taking care of their kids, mowing their lawns, cooking their dinners and cleaning their houses. Chunks of the economy grew by leaps and bounds — half our food budget now went to restaurants, up from less than 4 percent in 1950. Daycare became a $60-billion-a-year industry. Housekeeping services like Merry Maids paid their employees a barely living wage to clean customers' toilets but made record profits.

Meanwhile our private acts were rendered invisible. We were told it didn't matter whether you stopped at McDonalds four days a week or if you drove your kids around most of the time. And that invisibility was no accident either — as long as "private" acts were divorced from their public consequences, as long as the old association with women could be used to implicitly suggest that nothing you did at home mattered very much, we could go on burning as much fuel as we wanted. More than 70 percent of our emissions are tied directly or indirectly to home life and purchasing, but we pretended they didn't count. This was part of a larger project, the "housewifization" of anything that was "private." Writer Maria Mies argues that capitalism makes women's labor at home and everyone's subsistence labor invisible, because what you can't see, you can exploit limitlessly. The same could be said of our home-based emissions — what we imagine has no consequences we can use without limit.

Now let me be clear, women cannot be held responsible for going out to work. Men could have picked up the slack; government could have stepped in to enable people to find other solutions. My claim is not that women are responsible for the rise in our personal energy use. The problem is all of us, and the society and economy that enable us. But when we took one additional person in each family out of the home and sent them to work we doubled the size of our economy, and thus our resource usage. In 1950, slightly over 30 percent of all women worked outside the home. In 2000, that number had doubled. Tellingly, per capita household energy use also doubled in the same period. Not all of that can be attributed to both adults in a household working outside the home, but a great deal of it can. Two incomes created a need for new services, all very energy intensive, and a new level of affluence that fueled our consumption.

These "private" actions had effects that can hardly be overstated — they transformed our diet, our agriculture, our educational system, our transportation system. The political impact of our private choices has been inestimable, and the corporatization of our society has, to large degree, been funded by our private actions.

So when Heinberg observes that purely private action, taking place in absolute isolation, cannot transform society, he is right — but that's not the whole story. The tremendous power of corporations, for example, to pollute without restriction comes in large part because of their power over the political process, a power that they get by selling us things, taking our money and using it to buy politicians. The attempts of activists to regulate corporations have mostly met with failure, despite enormous opposition from ordinary people who believe that corporations and industry have too much power. Why have we failed? In large part because while we were complaining about it or demonstrating, we were also out buying stuff from the same corporations and giving them huge wads of cash to fund their lobbying efforts. And many of us, including most of the protestors, were also working for those corporations or for other businesses that support them. That is, by our actions we were simultaneously undermining every principle we said we had.

The Political Is Also the Personal

It is no accident that we disdain the private — we have been doing it for centuries, after all. But in our acceptance of the public/private distinction, we have done two wrong things. First, we have taken an old, historical disdain for women and women's work and naturalized it. This taints our relationship to domestic life, prevents many of us from taking on new projects that would save us energy and improve our lives because we imagine such work to be pointless drudgery. And by demeaning the people who do this work, we demean all women and all men who cook and clean and garden. And as long as we reinforce this idea, implicitly and explicitly, most people will fear the coming changes that will bring them home and back to a low-energy domestic life.

Second, and perhaps more seriously, we allowed the claim of the women's movement, that "the personal is political," to conceal the fact that the reverse is also true. That is, we missed the fact that the political cannot be separated from our personal choices in most cases. The women's movement noted that acts that had been deemed purely personal had a political dimension — and we

· · ·

Apprentice yourself to a local senior citizen to learn some useful skill — gardening, preserving, quilting, knitting or crocheting.

· · ·

learned this lesson, while missing the urgent "personal" dimension of our politics — and the need to conjoin our political and personal lives.

One only has to look at the enormous emphasis placed on domestic life and the Home Front in times of crisis to recognize what we all should know, that the only possible way to address the crises facing us in the next few years is to practice integrity — real integrity, in the root sense of the word, which derives from the same origin as "integrate." That is, we need to integrate our "private" acts and our "public" life to an extent seen before only in times of war. We need a New Home Front, and a new way of understanding its role.

The Power Lines

The distinction between personal and private also prevents us from seeing some of the ways we have power. That is, we have often been willing to boycott one store or one product, but we end up simply spending our money somewhere else, for another company whose impact is just as negative, replacing a Wal-Mart with a Kmart is not a real and radical change. Because we have demeaned the private, we have thus failed to see that the solution has to go deeper — fewer clothes, bought from free trade or local producers, mended until they can't be worn anymore and perhaps some made ourselves. The solution to cutting Wal-Mart's power on our society and economy is to undermine that power by taking responsibility for clothing ourselves from radically different sources.

It is true that one person, making isolated changes, won't change the world. But power and information travel in many ways. If someone were to ask you how power is transmitted in your town, you might look up and point at the overhead electric lines. But when you began to think more carefully about it, you would also think of other sources of power — the underground gas lines, the trucks that bring in propane and heating oil and gas for the gas stations, for example. There are many ways to transmit power. And that's true of people power as well.

It is easy to dismiss power networks such as neighbor-to-neighbor interactions, churches, the PTA and book clubs as less powerful, less important than governments and municipal power structures. The big shiny edifice of our government stands overhead, showing itself like the power lines. But history suggests that there is enormous power in social networks, much of it the territory of women. Women don't stand for office as often as men in the US; they are less likely to be represented in the municipal, state or federal equivalent of the overhead power lines. But underneath everything, women's networks and communities transfer enormous quantities of information and make large-scale social change.

In fact, in World War I, it was women's garden clubs that created the "Victory Gardens," a system that produced a growing percentage of America's diet during both world wars. Later the US government would take up the idea, but ordinary people used social networks to ensure food security. Rationing during World War II was based on a model set up by women's groups in World War I. And when the US government began to implement rationing, they did it not at the municipal level, but at the neighborhood level, commissioning women to go door to door, passing out recipes.

When the Soviet Union collapsed in the early 1990s, Cuba experienced a massive drop in oil imports almost overnight. With Cuba embargoed by the US and unable to import food, people began to go hungry. Cuban agriculture was highly industrialized and highly oil dependent, so internal food production also collapsed. The average Cuban lost 20 pounds in short order. But they also almost immediately began to garden and practice organic agriculture. Eventually the Cuban government got with the program and began to aid those who had taken initiative on their own, but the survival of the average Cuban was not primarily due to government intervention but to the actions of private citizens in their "private" lives. Private acts rarely exist in isolation; they have larger impacts, some quite a bit more profound than our current language allows for.

The truth is that we have been sold a bill of goods by our society when we buy into the notion that we can choose between private and public solutions, rather than doing both. As long as loud voices cried out, "You go do the important work of manufacturing Business to Business Widget Distribution software, and leave the dull, unimportant stuff about dinner to ConAg and McDonalds" we did not look, we did not see, and we let a great deal of wealth and time and security be destroyed in the service of building corporate wealth. It is not now sufficient to say "We have to get our Widget distributors on board with cutting emissions and fuel use" — and still stop at McDonalds. We do have to do work on the corporate, government and municipal levels — but that work can't succeed if we are only aware of the overhead power lines, and if we don't use the tremendous power of "underground" networks and communities.

The other truth about the merits of "private" domestic solutions is that their very simplicity requires social networks to exist. That is, in isolation, buying local doesn't make much of a difference. But the reality is that finding local food requires talking to growers and changing shopping patterns, and it means collaborating and building relationships with other people who want local food. It means learning a little bit about how food is grown, and that usually means telling your friends and neighbors what you've been doing. It means joining Internet groups and sharing solutions. Whenever people take on a new project, it takes on a social dimension — something that is sadly lacking in most western lives.

What is remarkable is that the social dimension of not buying stuff or changing one's habits becomes as powerful in some cases as the old rituals of buying and spending. American Revolutionary War historian Timothy Breen has dubbed these social acts of constraint "rituals of non-consumption." That is, people bond in their shared restriction. During World War II, for instance, people got pleasure sharing meatless recipes and teaching one another to make homespun cloth to replace imported cotton. People got pleasure from exchanging meatless recipes and seeds for Victory Gardens — and those bonds came to replace something of what was lost.

The fact is that some things will be lost in our new way of life. It is useless to pretend that the transformation to a lower-energy, lower-consumption society will always be painless and easy. Thus, the only possible way we can bring it about is to replace some of the pleasures we are losing with new ones — with rituals of non-consumption that offer us something to replace what is lost. It is easy to underestimate these homely virtues, to imagine that the pleasure of exchanging recipes couldn't possibly match up with the pleasure of taking a vacation to a tropical island. In fact, however, the opposite is true — studies of World War II Britain suggest that people derive more satisfaction from national unity and the sense that they are doing impor-tant work, from social ties and ordinary exchanges, than they do from expensive treats like trips.

. . .

Throw a "work bee" and get neighbors together on a community project. This could be anything from a barn raising to a charitable cooking project.

. . .

The reason my work focuses so much on domestic life isn't that I don't think you should march, demonstrate, vote or write to your political lead-ers. It is that we have 50 years of evidence to show that when we do these things without truly integrating our daily lives with our values, the result is disaster and a world increasingly out of line with our basic values. There are places in all our lives for public action — both in the realm of what we've traditionally called "the public" and in the realm of the private that has equally profound public implications. The truth is that the future calls for a degree of unity we have not seen in a long time — unity between peoples and unity within ourselves. There is no other way to do this. If the govern-ment will not bring home our troops and help us form a New Home Front, we can do it ourselves. We can create neighborhood groups to do so. We can unify our purpose and our communities to do this.

Coming Together On the Home Front

So far, much of Peak Oil and Climate Change activism has focused on the overhead power lines — on getting governments and companies to change their policy. And so far, we are failing miserably. Richard Heinberg and Colin Campbell proposed "The Oil Depletion Protocol," which encourages nations to balance their oil imports with the available supply. But they have thus far failed at getting even nations who are effectively reducing their imports in order to comply with the protocol to actually endorse the program. Recent evidence suggests that nearly every rich nation that did ratify the Kyoto Treaty will fail to meet its targets, while the US and Australia failed even to ratify. Worldwide, emissions rates rose far faster after Kyoto than before it. I do not observe this to demean the hard work of those who have tried to move through traditional power lines, but they are failing. They are failing not for lack of will, or passion, or brilliant solutions — they are failing simply because things are falling apart too fast and they are too few.

We need another way — or an additional way. We need to start looking not just to the overhead power lines but to the ways that power is being transmitted quietly, beneath our feet. We need to think about all the energies we can muster, all the human power we have yet to engage. That means bringing together people who have not, as yet, understood the absolute urgency of this crisis, people who care very much about the future, but who have not yet realized they are being spoken to.

That means we need to speak more explicitly to women — both because women will be disproportionately affected and because women have a disproportionate power. For example, studies suggest that women control or influence 90 percent of all purchases in private homes, including items that we often don't associate with women, such as cars and power tools. It is women who decide whether the kids get Wii sets or gardening tools for their birthdays. It is women who decide how fuel efficient the next car will be. It is women who will decide whether to invest in insulation and sweaters or turn up the thermostat.

• • •

Domestic violence gets worse in times of stress. Support your local shelter for battered women, and keep an eye out for women in danger.

• • •

Women, especially women over 40, are the ones who manage a large part of the world. Oh, they may not be the mayors, the principals or the presidents (although nearly as often they are), but when the decisions are made and the work is getting done, it is often women's dedication and commitment that makes things happen. The next time you vote, observe who staffs the polls. Next time a fundraiser occurs, see who does the work. I am not demeaning the work of men, but if we do not engage the organizational and political power of women in this cause we have no hope of success.

A UN study recently established that women will suffer more from Climate Change than men. Women are generally poorer than men, and the poorest people in the US are single mothers and elderly women. An economic crisis will strike them harder than the rest of us. Women live longer than men, and millions of baby boomers now reaching retirement face a dark future unless we prepare now. A generation of young children will suffer hunger and malnutrition if their mothers cannot support them.

And obviously, women bear the children and make a majority of reproductive decisions. Nothing else will so shape our future as issues of population, reproduction and women's health care. Nor will our economy be the same in a low-energy future — most of us simply do not realize how dependent we are on cheap energy to pressure women back into the workforce after childbearing. Without infant formulas, electric breast pumps and refrigeration, most women would have no choice but to spend their childbearing years at home. Women have yet to fully realize how transformative our coming environmental crisis will be in their lives.

But it isn't just women we need to engage — we have also failed to engage minority communities. Low-income African Americans, Latinos, Native Americans and Asian populations will also be disproportionately affected. They are already suffering the consequences of reduced economic security, greater food insecurity, fewer jobs and poor access to health care. But many proposals for triaging our system and responding to lower-energy conditions effectively abandon urban, poor, non-white people, naturalizing the idea that if we haven't fixed their problems already, they cannot be fixed. This is, of course, nonsense, as for the most part we haven't tried. We plan to abandon urban dwellers as we did Katrina's victims, saying that there won't be enough to go around. Hurricane Katrina's message was "If you don't own a private car, we'll let you die." The sheer tragedy of that — the idea that people who are doing precisely what they should be doing should pay with their lives for living quietly and using public transport gives us a powerful vision of what our central message has been.

In fact, many poor people in the US are now living lower-energy lives that can offer models for those of us trying to adapt. When we ask "How will poor people live with minimal energy in the city?" perhaps we should look to our cities and ask how poor urbanites have dealt with power company shutoffs and intermittent resources for decades now.

The greatest victims of Climate Change will be the already poor people all over the world — that is, women, children, the elderly, and the disabled and non-white people. We should care about that because it is right and also because we are them. Every one of us is either female or has a woman we love — a mother, daughter, sister, friend. Every one of us will be old. Any of us could become poor. Most of us are not white and do not live in the

US. Any of us could become disabled. For a very long time, some percentage of Americans were able to pretend that "we" were not like "them" — the people most victimized by our society. Those days are over. Economic inequity is rising so fast and our world is changing so rapidly that most of us have every reason to believe that someday we will be poor, elderly, disabled or "minority" in some way.

Peak Oil is a women's issue. Climate Change is a racial issue. Justice is everyone's issue. And so is the Home Front. It would be lovely if our governments would step forward and lead us to work together. In the absence of that leadership, we need to create a national movement ourselves. The Riot for Austerity, conceived more or less by accident, might provide one such model — the support group as activist community.

The Church Model of Community Building

There are other groups now attempting to do this, such as the Post-Carbon Institute's "Relocalization" groups, and many of them have had some success in some regions. In Britain, the Transition Towns movement has been perhaps the most remarkable success on the municipal level, and has managed to avoid many of the pitfalls I discuss in relation to other adaptation groups. But the scale of such groups has been too large so far; they have focused on Peak Oil and Climate Change-aware people, who often travel long distances to spend time with one another. Right now, in the early stages of the crisis, there are simply too few people who have put all the pieces together. Compare this to churches or synagogues or mosques, who invite everyone in a given community, opening their doors as widely as they can.

If we are to have success we are going to have to use a different model, one that I call "the church model." I say this not to be alienating to those who are not religious, but in recognition that religious communities have been far more successful at building community structures than any secular organization, and that if we are to create overarching community organizations that sustain us in hard times and enable us to manage our communities in the face of crisis, we're going to have to use a successful model.

The "church model" has three factors that are very different from groups like the Relocalization groups I'm familiar with. They are:

1. low barriers to entry

2. something to offer immediately

3. a plan and a routine for dealing with crises

The first factor is enormously important if we are to move beyond regional groups to the local level. Right now environmental groups tend to have a fairly high entry barrier. That is, you have to be aware enough of Climate Change or Peak Oil to consider work on these issues a high priority. Given that the majority of the country still considers these problems secondary, that level of awareness is fairly unusual. Which is why these groups are still regional. The nearest one to me is a 45 minute drive away. It is unlikely that in a crisis involving energy shortages, we'll have the gas to drive that distance. This means that we need to engage not a few aware people half an hour from us, but our neighbors.

How do we do that? We lower the barriers to entry. Instead of having groups for the Peak Oil or Climate Change aware, we have neighborhood co-ops or community preparedness groups. Robert Waldrop, founder of the Oklahoma City Food Co-op, observes that he doesn't talk much about Peak Oil with the people he works with. Instead he talks about how good local food tastes and about how hard it is to make ends meet. The terminology doesn't matter — the common ground does.

• • •

Encourage your religious community to reconnect with the agrarian roots of your faith. Every religion has special harvest and planting rituals, and traditions about generosity and sharing, spring and rebirth. Plant a garden for your food pantry, or plant special festival foods and invite the community to share them.

• • •

The second and perhaps most important thing that such groups have to do is offer members an immediate reason to work together. Some of us will do thankless work for long periods with no reward, but most of us join groups for selfish reasons — we want to find community, we want support, friendship, a platform for our ideas. We may also care about the larger world, but we get some gratification from being together and doing the work. Churches do this well. When people join a church, eventually they are asked to do their share of the work, to donate money and volunteer, but initially they are offered something — friendship, a pleasurable worship experience, a meal, religious education for their kids. We need our groups to provide something now, not just hypothetical help in the future.

This is even truer because we are now in the early stages of a crisis, and many of the people who join with us may be undergoing personal difficulties. It is not feasible to have a Climate Change group that has no support or solutions for the victims of Climate Change now, for example. That doesn't mean we have to be able to fix everything or have immediate funds for major investments, but we do have to be able to offer emotional support, a lift for someone out of gas, a casserole for a neighbor dealing with illness. We need to start where we are, start small, with the ordinary work of human exchange.

Finally, such groups need to begin creating a plan for the longer term. How will people in your neighborhood get water? Who has yard space to grow food? How will you check on the elderly and disabled? Where will the kids go to school if the buses stop running? Your first steps should take you toward your next ones — today a carpool to get neighbors to the grocery store, tomorrow a bulk buying club and a Victory Garden group to make fewer shopping trips necessary. That's the Home Front talking.

THREE

Time to Pick Up Your Hat

*Engineers like to solve problems. If there are no problems
handily available, they will create their own problems.*
— SCOTT ADAMS

*Lord, feels like I'm dyin'
from that old used-to-be*
— LYLE LOVETT

Pick Up Your Hat

YEARS AGO I READ A SHORT STORY BY ROBERT HEINLEIN THAT HAS STUCK WITH
me. In it, the main character, a bartender, overhears two customers, both nuclear
scientists, discussing the imminent likelihood of nuclear war. The bartender
is frightened, and he says they can't possibly really believe what they are saying, because if they did, they'd get away from the large city they live in. The
two scientists insist they do believe but have various reasons for staying. The
bartender argues what they were saying, if they really believed, they'd pick
up their hats and leave now. The bartender himself becomes convinced,
picks up his hat, leaves his bar and walks out of the city, only to turn around
and see a fictionally convenient mushroom cloud going up behind him.

Now, life very rarely justifies our assumptions so rapidly, but I find this
story interesting because it illustrates just how hard it is to live life as though
you believe hard times are coming — even if you do believe it. The scientists
argued with the bartender, saying they still had jobs to do and a life to live,
that even though what they said was true, they couldn't afford to live their
lives based on the truth. Even when we know what is most likely coming our
way, it is awfully hard to pick up our hats and set aside one set of options to
pursue another.

My husband's grandmother, Inge, was a girl during the rise of Nazi Germany. As the situation became dire, her mother sent Inge and her cousin out of Germany on the kindertransport, during a brief period in which Hitler permitted Jewish children to be sent to Britain. I try to imagine her mother's decision to send her only child, a thirteen-year-old girl, to a strange country, away from her family, knowing she might never see her again. Inge escaped and her mother survived (her father did not), and they eventually reunited in the US. But among the pictures she saved was one of a young cousin, about the same age, whose parents thought that she would be better off staying with her family. That cousin died in the concentration camps. Her parents made the wrong choice, but how could they know for certain? How do you know what to do and when?

The answer, of course, difficult as it is, is that you don't. You can't know with certainty. The victims of Hurricane Katrina sat tight, using a strategy that had served them in prior hurricanes. They could not know for sure whether they were better off dragging medically fragile elderly people out of town to a shelter, abandoning their pets, risking being stuck on the road during a storm. Some had no choice, of course, but some did, and they made the best decisions they knew how. Sometimes even our best decisions are wrong. None of us can predict the exact outcomes of actions. What we can do is use some basic tools of logic and reason to figure out the potential costs of each option.

One of the most basic ways of deciding what to do is to make use of the precautionary principle. This is simply a logical tool that explains that, given a reasonable likelihood of several particular outcomes, you need to figure out the worst possible *likely* outcome of each eventuality. You can reduce risk by figuring out the worst possible outcomes and assessing whether you are prepared to bear the consequences of the worst outcome if your decision is wrong.

• • •

Can't afford health insurance? Many community colleges and state universities have low-cost, subsidized health insurance available to anyone who pays for a class.

• • •

For example, let's say I'm trying to decide whether I should get life insurance. The outcome of my getting insurance is that I will spend a little more than I'd like and I'd have to cut back somewhere else, and I might not enjoy that. The possible outcome of my not getting insurance would be that my husband might struggle to take care of our kids if I died young. In this case, the negative outcome of one is so much worse than the negative outcome of the other that even though I'm not nearly as likely to die as I am to live, it is worth the minor consequences.

The same line of reasoning applies to preparing for the long emergency; only in this case, the likelihood is that you and your family *will* experience dramatic changes in circumstance because of global warming, Peak Oil and economic instability. It is far more likely that we will struggle because of Climate Change and Peak Oil, say, than that most healthy forty-year-olds will drop dead. And yet, many healthy forty-year-olds have life insurance. We carry fire insurance, car insurance, health insurance. And it turns out that preparing for hard times is really far more like having health insurance — eventually almost everyone gets sick. In the same sense, everyone is likely to be affected by the confluence of crises we face.

The simple truth is that I want people who read this book to think seriously about whether they have a viable backup plan for a crisis in the near future. Why? Not because I think the whole world is likely to collapse at once, but because I think any crisis will come in stages and segments.

For me it might be tomorrow; my husband could lose his job because of rising energy costs, for example. For you, it might wait a while — or it might not. We don't know; we're playing the odds. And if, like me, you have loved ones you don't want to risk by playing the odds, the choice becomes clear. Begin now. Begin thinking and preparing for a difficult future today.

The other reason to do this now is that the majority of the actions I'm suggesting are good for you in other ways. They will help you and your family enjoy better food, lower your energy costs, get more exercise, spend more time together. It has helped my family live more happily, save money, have stronger community relationships. Almost everything I recommend in this book is not just good practice for reasons of environmental and personal security, but also because it will make sense in a whole host of ways, from the moral to the practical.

It also makes sense because advance preparation ensures that your family has access to what you need. James Hansen and the other NASA scientists who argue that we don't have much time say we only have a decade to fix this — a decade to make the "draconian" changes that would stop the worst sea rises. Let's say we do make good on all those measures, that our government does begin to act — what will that be like? What will it be like when 300 million people have to slash their personal emissions to the bone? I'd tend to bet on competition for resources, and lots of price rises for useful tools and goods at the time that most of us can least afford them.

During the Y2K scare woodstoves, grain grinders, garden seeds, ultra-efficient appliances and solar panels, among other useful equipment, were bought in huge numbers by panicky people. Backorders on those items ran several years, and many suppliers simply couldn't meet demand. Now, Y2K was not a real crisis — but it offered a small-scale model of what demand might look like in a nation facing a real and serious problem.

When policy changes are made, when we all finally begin to realize what is going on, we can expect it to be very hard to get the right tools. Right now the market for things like grain grinders and solar lighting is small. Ramping up production takes time, so there are usually shortages when demand rises. As those markets expand, and prices rise because of energy costs and demand, many people are going to struggle to get what they need. Being ahead of the masses makes it more likely that you will have what you need when you need it.

I understand how difficult it is for this to feel real — things seem okay on many levels as I write this. We may believe that these are crises, but life is still going on, so it is hard to imagine that so much change could happen so fast. We're still caught between the life we live now and the life we will live in the coming years, and it can be damned hard to navigate that distinction. All of us have to figure out what we believe and hedge our bets as best we can. Do we pick up our hats and give up the present for the hypothetical future? How do we know that something won't pull off a miracle?

We all know people who had nuclear bunkers during the Cold War, went back to the land because the end was at hand in the 1970s, were prepared for Y2K or have been expecting the rapture for decades. And it is tempting, because the disasters others have predicted have never happened, to think that the system is strong enough to endure any crisis. And who knows, it may be. I'm not a prophet.

But look back a little. Ask yourself if your grandparents and great-grandparents ever endured a time of crisis? Again, we're not talking about movie disasters here — we're talking about poverty, war, economic disruption, having to leave a beloved place for a new one, epidemic, hunger, want. Now, maybe none of your family has ever had those things, but looking back at my grandparents' and great-grandparents' generation, I see two world wars and a host of smaller ones that affected my ancestors' lives. They endured hunger and poverty during the Great Depression, and rationing and short-ages during the world wars. Their families were made refugees and they migrated to other countries. They struggled to learn the language and to

make a living. And those were the lucky ones, who survived to have k
grandkids. Other family members were lost altogether.

The generations of rich-world folks born after World War II are among
the first in human history to live their whole lives in peace, wealth and good
fortune. Should we bet that we too will be so fortunate, that this comparatively brief period of luxury and wealth for people in the rich world will go
on without end, despite all the evidence to the contrary? And what is the
price if we choose to believe this?

That last question is a real bugger, isn't it? That is, sometimes the price is
light — putting up the rain barrels or growing a garden is easy and pleasurable.
But sometimes the choices are hard. Do we stay
in Arizona, in a place getting dryer every year?
How will we take care of our aging parents
when they live across the country and air travel
is getting more and more expensive? What do I
study in college, and do I go at all? Do I invest
for retirement or put my money in land? Those
are hard questions. Living life in two worlds,
looking toward the future and also maintaining
an existence in the present isn't always easy. But
I believe passionately that for most of us, the difficulty of doing both is smaller than the price we risk paying if we do not begin to prepare for the future.

. . .

Do a "preparedness" dry run
in the middle of winter. Turn out
the power, turn off the water and the
heat, and see how things go
for a few days. Use what you learn
to improve your preparedness.

. . .

I want everyone who reads this to make your own choices based on your
own experience, your own reading of the data available, your own needs and
circumstances, and your own ability to change. My bet is that change will
come soon to some of us, later to others, but the changes I'm worried about
are now essentially already in motion. Whatever happens, we're probably
never going to be quite as comfortable or privileged or ready as we are today.

That is a hard and sad realization to come to. Like everyone, I want just
a little more time. But unfortunately, we must confront reality, and live our
lives based on what is, rather than what we wish were true. If you see the evidence much the same way I do, if you read this book and others and believe
what the data show you, then it really is time to pick up your hat, or at least
memorize the train schedule heading wherever you want to be.

Feels Like I'm Dyin' From that Old Used-to-Be

I tend to be an optimist, at least by the standards of Peak Oil and Climate
Change activists (which isn't very hard). By that I mean that I believe in the

power of our actions and I believe we could change the system we live in and make better choices. But I also think that while we work to bring a better world about, we should be working under the assumption that we might not succeed — or that success might not quite look like what we'd hoped for. Because to transform our society, we'd have to change deep habits of thought, and that may be harder, in many ways, than changing our practices.

Many Americans have gotten into habits of thought so destructive and so automatic that we don't even recognize their basic limitations. And if we don't recognize the failures in our own heads and overturn them, we're in big trouble. One of those problems is that we can't stop looking for a quick fix, even when we have ample evidence that such solutions are part of the problem.

A lot of the calls we hear for "solutions" actually translate to finding "ways to keep things mostly the way they are." And that's not only not possible, it's a lousy idea. That is, we all know if we think about it, that the world can't afford 9 billion people who try to live like Americans — to do so would require the environmental resources of five planet earths. And we also can't afford a world in which some people are desperately poor, starving to death and suffering while other people are terrifically rich. That's wrong (which should be enough of a reason), and it's a recipe for violence, terrorism, war and disaster. So the only ethical and practical solution is to create a world in which most people live in a fairly ordinary way, taking only a fair share of their resources. If we stop to think about it, the only choice we have is to try to divide resources fairly.

The quest for ever more magical technologies is part of the problem — the idea that we can solve environmental destruction by just finding a more efficient kind of environmental destruction is properly demolished by Thomas Princen in his book *The Logic of Sufficiency*, in which he argues,

> *Efficiency will provide little guidance because it so readily translates into continuing material throughput. A little intensification here, some specialization there will not make things better. A feedlot is still a feedlot, a conveyor belt still a conveyor belt. (Princen, 360)*

That is, we cannot look to the structures that got us into this mess to get us out. Fundamentally, the trouble of depletion of resources is not an accidental byproduct of industrial society and growth capitalism — it is a necessary prerequisite. You cannot have large-scale globalized economic growth, high-technology societies and lots of affluence without enormous ecological destruction.

How do we know this? As anthropologist Jared Diamond points out, we know this because we can look at the history of technological solutions to environmental problems. He says,

> ...*actual experience is the opposite of this assumed track record. Some dreamed-of new technologies succeed, while others don't. Those that do succeed typically take a few decades to develop and phase in widely: think of gas heating, electric lighting, cars and airplanes, computers and so on. New technologies, whether or not they succeed in solving the problem that they were designed to solve, regularly create unanticipated new problems. Technological solutions to environmental problems are routinely far more expensive than preventative measures to avoid creating the problem in the first place.... Most of all, advances in technology just increase our ability to do things that may be either for the better or for the worse. All of our current problems are unintended negative consequences of our existing technology. The rapid advances in technology in the 20th century have been creating difficult new problems faster than they have been solving old problems; that's why we're in the situation in which we now find ourselves. What makes you think that, as of January 2006, for the first time in human history, technology will miraculously stop causing new unanticipated problems while it just solves the problems that it previously produced? (Diamond, 504–5)*

Diamond's articulation of this issue is very clear. The idea that we can solve our problems with more of the same is the idea that most drives us to ruin right now. As we struggle for just the right techno-fix, we find ourselves unable to contemplate real solutions — self-restraint, greater simplicity, a lower-energy lifestyle. As long as we keep imagining that we just have to find the one right technology, we will miss what is in front of our own eyes — that the correct technologies already exist, indeed, many have existed for centuries.

The Long-Term Problem of Technological Solutions

Not only is it unlikely that we can find a technological solution, even if we did, such a solution may well amount to simply dumping the problem on future generations. Ethanol, biodiesel, solar panels are all tremendously fossil fuel intensive. We can't make a solar panel without using a lot of silicone and metals that are mined, smelted, crafted, assembled, sold and transported using fossil fuels. The day we can create a solar panel made from cradle to grave with renewable energies, I'll buy the notion that we're all going to be running around in electric cars fed by solar panels.

Now, when I say that, people start arguing that it is hypothetically possible that someday we'll use bioplastics and mine metals using electrically powered machinery powered by the sun. I say, show me a case of having done it, having made even five solar panels that way, and I'll buy it. Heck, I'll write a free ad. If we can't do it right now, when we're comparatively economically stable and when we're pumping as much oil as we ever will, why do we think we'll be able to do so in the future, when we will have fewer fossil-fueled backups and when we may be poorer than we are today?

Most people don't grasp that solar panels or wind generators or ethanol aren't a magic bullet unless they represent a self-perpetuating system. Oil was nicely self perpetuating, at least for a good long time — you used oil-based equipment to get oil out of the ground in a nice ratio of energy returned over energy invested (EROEI) of 100:1. That is, it took one barrel of oil to get out about 100 barrels. That's a pretty big return on your investment. But we don't have the infrastructure, the grid system, the renewables, the tools or in some cases the technology to make things like solar panels or wind generators entirely out of renewables. They take fossil fuels at 20–50 spots along the ride. When you add up all the fossil fuels involved, the EROEI of most renewables is somewhere between 1:1 and 10:1, probably on the low side for most of them. That means that even to match our current energy needs, we'd need four times as much power generated from wind as coal and 50 times as much generated from solar as natural gas. Do you begin to grasp the scale of the problem? We're not just talking about replacing the oil and gas and coal infrastructure with an equivalent number of renewable energy sources — we're talking about producing many, many, many times more energy generators than our highly industrial society has now — and making all of them out of fossil fuels. This is technically feasible — and deeply unlikely.

• • •

If you have a diesel vehicle, consider locating a source of waste vegetable oil to power your car.

• • •

These alternative energies aren't a permanent solution. It is true that a solar panel might last 20 to 30 years. It is also true that it might not — and the batteries certainly won't. But even if the solar panels or windmills do last 20 or 30 years, unless we build a self-perpetuating system, in which there is so much renewable power that we can use it to make more renewable energies in addition to all of our other usages, then we are effectively just sticking the problem to our children.

Let's say we do a massive build of windmills and solar panels, enough to keep our whole society going. (Never mind that we will find it enormously difficult to fund or engineer this.) Imagine that we use up a huge amount of our remaining fossil reserves to keep everyone comfy and in their cars, and we go into massive debt to do it. Well, five years from now, all the solar panels need new batteries. But the enormous investment of energy we put into keeping our society running didn't include enough energy to run all the factories to self-perpetuate — doing that requires double or triple the already huge number of solar panels and windmills. Remember, we have to run all the mining equipment, the trucks that ship the aluminum around, the chemical refining equipment used to create the acids, all the shipping, manufacturing and installation equipment and to manufacture everything we made from plastics and oil with something else. Again, this isn't impossible, merely unlikely — and unlikely to be done rapidly enough to meet our growing energy needs.

And then a decade after that we have to do it on an even bigger scale — to replace all the worn out windmills and solar panels. And as we go along supply constraints are increasing and prices of fossil energies (which we are still using during the transition) are rising. Capital costs go up, investment costs go up, and remember, because energy costs are way up, there may not be as much money to invest. Twenty-five years from now, when a barrel of oil costs $300, how much will a replacement windmill, which requires fossil fuels at several stages, cost? Will it even be available 20 or 30 years after oil has peaked, when nations are struggling to meet basic needs with limited oil supplies?

Whenever I bring this up with people looking for techno-solutions, they tell me that eventually we'll be able to make things from renewables, of course. But that response is betting our kids' lives on the hope that at some point renewables will become self-perpetuating, even though we have no idea how that will happen. In some cases, that would require major, multiple, large-scale technical breakthroughs, and we're not willing to do it now, when we have energy to burn, lots of money and no crisis. Instead, we're going to stick the next generation with the problem, and hope it isn't too serious.

Does anyone else see a problem here? This is an utterly immoral reversal of what parents and grandparents are supposed to do — we're supposed to be willing to work our behinds off and make sacrifices for the wellbeing of future generations. Instead, we expect them to bear the burden of the coming crisis. That is wrong, and I have no idea how we came to the point of even considering this as a reasonable solution.

I would suggest that the "find-a-short-term-solution" solution, even if it were feasible, is morally bankrupt, ugly, inelegant and in part responsible for the trend that each generation seems to want less to do with their parents than the previous one. Even if we could continue the way we are, should we? Would we truly want to be the people who were so selfish that we refused to inconvenience ourselves so that others, our own children and other people's children, could live?

The thing is, there is a solution, and like most good solutions it is really, really simple and equally elegant. The vast majority of the technologies we need to live already exist: the bicycle, the solar oven and wood cook stove, the solar-powered pump. All that is needed is for us to look in the right direction, to actually live our lives as though we care more about future generations than our own comfort and to live simpler lives with less. That means we do things with our hands and our heads, and with fewer fossil-fuel-powered appliances. It means we accept that we're headed toward a lower-energy lifestyle and that we embrace it and go forward from there.

It isn't the end of the world to go back to living more simply, more gently. Our great-grandparents lived those lives, and so do billions of people all over the world. And contrary to our belief, their lives weren't unvarnished hell — some things were little harder; other things were actually easier. Eric's grandparents used to live with us. One day his grandmother was watching me load cloth diapers into the washing machine, and she said, "Oh, I can't believe I used to boil the diapers in a pot on the stove to get them clean." I waited a minute and asked, "Was it awful?" She said, "Well, no, not really ... but it seems so strange now." We've been taught that the past must have been awful because it was strange. But what if we were to recognize that strange is not the same as bad?

Not the End of the World

If the ideas of Peak Oil and Climate Change are new to you, or even if they aren't, you may be in a bit of panic right now, thinking that we're on the brink of absolute destruction. The truth is, both Peak Oil and Climate Change are big deals. The likely economic restructuring that will accompany both of them is a big deal. But it is important to remember that this is not the end of the world, that things will go on, even if they change.

Author Maria Mies recounts the story of attending a symposium on the future. The scholars prognosticated bleakly on an environmentally devastated future in which nuclear violence, Climate Change and overpopulation end the world as we know it. And then Mies spoke, saying,

> *Please, remember where we are in Trier, in the midst of the ruins of what was one of the capitals of the Roman Empire. An empire whose collapse people then thought would mean the end of the world. But the world did not come to end with the end of Rome. The plough of my father, a peasant in the Eifel, used to hit the stones of the Roman road that connected Trier with Cologne. On this road where the Roman legions had marched grass had grown, and now we grew our potatoes on that road. (Mies and Bennholdt-Thomsen, 25)*

Empires end. Eras end. Ways of life end. But people mostly go on. And much of what is required to keep going on, to prevent the worst outcomes is simply to come to terms with the notion that a radical change in your way of life is not the same thing as the end of the world. We have always been wealthy and comfortable and lucky here in the west, and the loss of some or all of those things seems like a disaster of unimaginable proportions. But it doesn't have to be — that's a way of thinking we can choose to discard, recognizing that those who live less comfortable lives often value them equally.

• • •

Throw a barbecue or open house and get to know your neighbors.

• • •

The truth is that we need to find a way to find pleasure and hope and joy in a much simpler, less consumptive lifestyle. That means sacrificing some things we care about. It also means getting back some things that truly matter.

The Theory of Anyway

So what, exactly, do we do? How do we preserve our values and find out what is essential? Which changes should we make? If we're not going to have all the energy and tools and toys we once had, how do we know what we can and should have? How do we know where to go from here?

My friend Pat Meadows, a very smart woman, has a wonderful idea she calls "The Theory of Anyway." She argues that 95 percent of what is needed to resolve the coming crisis is what we should do anyway, and when in doubt about how to change, we should change our lives to reflect what we should be doing "anyway." Living more simply, more frugally, leaving reserves for others, reconnecting with our food and our community — these are things we should be doing because they are the right thing to do on many levels.

That they also have the potential to save our lives is merely a side benefit (a big one, though).

This is, I think, a deeply powerful way of thinking because it is a deeply moral way of thinking. We like to think of ourselves as moral people, but we tend to think of moral questions as the obvious ones: Should I steal or pay? Should I fight or talk? But the most essential moral questions are the ones we rarely ask of the things we do every day: Should I eat this? Where should I live? What should I wear? How should I keep warm/cool? We think of these questions as foregone conclusions — I should keep warm a particular way because that's the kind of furnace I have, or I should eat this because that's what's in the grocery store. Pat's Theory of Anyway turns this around, and points out that the way we live must pass ethical muster first. We must always ask the question, Is this choice contributing to the repair of the world or its destruction?

• • •

Talk to your kids about your values. Begin explaining early on that "local food is better because it doesn't use so much energy, so let's go ask where these carrots are from." As they get older, you can offer more information. "The reason we don't want you to have those clothes is that they come from a company that forces kids like you to do work for them. Would you like to help me write a letter to the company and do some Internet research about labor practices?"

• • •

So if you told me tomorrow that Peak Energy had been resolved, I'd still keep gardening, hanging my laundry and trying to find a way to make do with less. Because even if we found enough oil to power our society for a thousand years, there would still be Climate Change, and it would be wrong of me to choose my own convenience over the security of my children and other people's children.

And if you told me tomorrow that we'd fixed Climate Change, I would still keep gardening and living frugally. Because our agriculture is premised on depleted soil and aquifers, and we're facing a future in which many people don't have enough food and water if we keep eating this way; and to allow that to happen would be a betrayal of what I believe is right.

And if you told me that we'd fixed that problem too, that we were no longer depleting our aquifers and expanding the dead zone in the Gulf of Mexico, I'd still keep gardening and telling others to do the same, because our economy and our reliance on food from other nations impoverishes and starves billions of poor people and creates massive economic inequities that do tremendous harm.

And if you told me that globalization was over, and that we were going to create a just economic system, and we'd fixed all the other problems, and that I didn't have to worry anymore, would I then stop gardening?

No. Nurturing and preserving my small slice of the planet would still be the right thing to do. Doing things with no more waste than is absolutely necessary would still be the right thing to do. The creation of a fertile, sustainable, lasting place of beauty would still be my right work in the world. I would still be a Jew, obligated by my faith, to "the repair of the world." I would still be obligated to live in a way that prevented wildlife from being run to extinction and poisons contaminating the earth. I would still be obligated to reduce my needs so they represent a fair share of what the earth has to offer. I would still be obligated to treat poor people as my brothers and sisters, and you do not live comfortably when your siblings suffer. I am obligated to live rightly, in part because of what living rightly gives me — integrity, honor, joy, a better relationship with my deity of choice, peace.

There are people who are prepared to step forward and give up their cars, start growing their own food, stop consuming so much and stop burning fossil fuels — just as soon as Peak Oil or Climate Change or government rationing or some external force makes them do so. But that, I believe, is the wrong way to think. We can't wait for others to tell us or the disaster to befall us. We have to do now, do today, do with all our hearts, the things we should have been doing "anyway" all along.

PART

Two

[*Money Changes Everything*]

FOUR

·

Meet the Real Economy

*Rats and roaches live by competition under the
laws of supply and demand. It is the privilege of human
beings to live under the laws of justice and mercy.*
— WENDELL BERRY

*Give me neither riches nor poverty,
but enough for my sustenance.*
— THE BOOK OF ISAIAH

Confronting the Real Economy

IF WHAT I'VE BEEN SAYING IS TRUE, IF WE'RE ABOUT TO GET POORER AND
have less, what can you do about it? What should you be doing to protect
yourself and your family; to reduce the impact of an economic crisis, rising
energy and food prices, a housing market meltdown, rising taxes; to help
deal with the problems of Climate Change?

One way to answer these questions is to talk a little about economics.
In doing so, it is essential that we make a distinction that rarely appears in
popular discussions of the economic issues, the distinction between the "formal" economy and the economy as a whole, which includes both the formal
sectors and informal ones. Most of us, if pressed to explain economics,
would speak mostly or entirely about the official economy, the one in which
most people in the rich world live. This is the world of taxes and forms, official
business, job growth and GDP statements.

Our culture trains us from birth to see this official economy as the
whole, or at least the only one that matters. No one's mother suggests that
when they grow up they should live in the under-the-table economy, or

hopes that they will barter for economic security. We are trained for a job (if you are among the privileged, for a career) and told that our lives depend entirely on making a go of things in the official economy, the only one we really know anything of. Because of that, because we have a hard time envisioning anything we can't describe mathematically, we believe that is all there is.

But anyone who thinks carefully about what is essential to human needs recognizes that an enormous amount of economic exchange, work and benefit occurs under the table and outside the purview of the official economy. Estimates vary, but we know that the informal economy (what I am here calling the "real" economy because it is the primary economic structure of our lives) is far larger than the formal one. For example, the real economy includes all the work done free by volunteers. How much would that be worth if you had to put a dollar amount to it? Just because it isn't paid doesn't mean it doesn't have value. In fact, the official economy couldn't run without it. Think about how many libraries, museums, universities and political movements depend on volunteer support. Go to a local festival, to a church rummage sale, to a protest, to your food pantry or shelter, or look at who sits at the tables for your local election.

Or perhaps we should consider household labor. Economies cannot proceed without someone doing the work of raising the next generation of laborers and professionals — and yet that enormous, essential labor is largely unpaid. Housework (which is in large part about creating a healthy, pleasant environment and reducing the need for medical intervention), cooking (keeping workers fed), and other ordinary household work is done outside the market economy, but the market economy couldn't function without it. Feminists have at times attempted to calculate the value of women's work outside the real economy, and the numbers have always been staggering. Occasionally, those who do the housework go on "strike," and the results are always fearsome. The official economy operates with the quiet consent of the unofficial economy.

Then there is the criminal economy to consider. What is the highest value plant product in the US? Corn? Soybeans? Nope, pot. In 2004 marijuana was our biggest cash crop; we grow $35.8 billion worth per year. World wide, drugs represent between 2 and 5 percent of the world's GDP. That's a lot of money, supporting a lot of households, and feeding a lot of people. A pound of opium grown in Afghanistan may indirectly support the lives of up to ten people. Because, of course, the money from pot or opium growing doesn't stay in the pockets of local growers. Money raised by growing and selling pot enables people to shop at Wal-Mart, buy groceries, redecorate their homes, and do all those ordinary things that official economy money does, although without the tax burden. I am hardly proposing that anyone enter the criminal economy, but this information helps give a sense of the scope of the unofficial economy.

Then there is the "under-the-table" economy. Perhaps you have participated in it yourself — you paid the neighbor kid to mow your lawn or hired a babysitter without filing a form with the IRS. Maybe you got your mortgage down payment from Grandma and didn't pay taxes on it, or you lived rent free with your parents and didn't claim the value of that on your taxes (yes, you are supposed to). Perhaps you traded some work on your kitchen cabinets for helping repair someone's car or mending some clothes. You occasionally play guitar at a bar or drive for your brother-in-law's taxi service or do a little tutoring, and you don't declare your earnings. This may or may not be unethical, depending on your relationship to your government, but it is certainly normal.

The founder of *Peasant Economics,* Teodor Shanin, points out that "the modern formal economy needs only about a quarter of the global workforce. The other three-quarters are engaged in survival through the informal economy. As Shanin describes,

> The concept emerged in Africa 25 years ago. Researchers began to notice that there was no economic explanation for how the majority of the population survived. They didn't own land. They didn't seem to have any assets. According to conventional economics they should have died of hunger long ago, but they survived. To understand this, researchers looked at how these people actually lived, rather than at economic models. They found that their way of life was completely the opposite of how a human being in an industrial society survives. They didn't have a job, pension, steady place to work or regular flow of income. Families held a range of occupations from farming and selling in the market to doing odd jobs or handicrafts. Their aim was survival rather than the maximisation of profit. Rather than earn wages, labour was used within family. (archive.newscientist. com/secure/article/article.jsp?rp=1&id=mg1).

Shanin's own research, which focused primarily on Russia, has been duplicated all over the world. As in Africa, after the collapse of communism in Russia, economists couldn't understand why Russians weren't starving to

h. It turns out that collapse of the official economy was compensated for part by the rise of an expanded unofficial economy. Under-the-table economics took over and kept the population fed. People began doing things like running unlicensed businesses or growing vegetables for sale.

Shanin documents how the 1998 collapse of the Russian ruble actually benefited parts of the peasant economy even as it destroyed Western investment. When imports ceased to enter the country, Russian farmers and small manufacturers made up the difference — stores filled with Russian-grown produce and locally made goods. It was bad for the official economy, but it actually improved the lives of many ordinary people. Most of us can think of some changes that might be bad for the official economy under current orthodoxy but good for us — for example, the "onshoring" of a new manufacturing industry, where Americans could be employed making things again.

. . .

Hire a neighborhood teenager to work with you on your garden, a building project, an energy-saving program. Listen to them talk about their lives and treat them with respect.

. . .

In my own rural area, there are still people who live largely in the informal economy. They grow some vegetables, fish and hunt, sell a little firewood or do odd jobs or seasonal work, most of it under the table. Their income is small and their needs are few; they often live with family or in housing they've inherited. How many people live outside the official economy is not known, partly because most of them don't want it to be. But a surprising number of people are deriving some or all of their income from patching together work, trading and economizing.

The subsistence economy is central to the real economy, although attempts to calculate it are inadequate at best. The value of money you don't need and things you don't buy is something deemed irrelevant, or at best, too difficult to calculate. So the seeds we save, the clothes we sew or remake, the food we grow, the toys we build from scraps, the things we reuse, the children we homeschool, the work we do that enables us to live and prosper is to a large degree not part of any economic calculation.

Self-sufficiency as the Opposite of Poverty

The subsistence economy is powerful. Because self-sufficiency is, as Jeremy Seabrook puts it, "the opposite of poverty," it makes it very hard for us to tell what constitutes real poverty. For example a family that grows virtually all its food and barters for much of what it needs but makes a cash income of only $2 per day and a family that owns no land, lives in shack on a garbage dump and gets all its food from selling things scavenged from that dump (a way millions of people live) and makes about $2 per day are lumped together among the desperately poor, as though their situations were equivalent. It is possible to be poor in money and yet have enough for your needs — the subsistence economy is what makes that possible, and it represents a possibility for most of us.

Similarly, although we tend to assume that the subsistence economy is subsidizing the formal economy, it often works the other way around. Agricultural writer Peter Rosset documents that millions of poor subsistence farmers whose livelihoods have been damaged by globalization actually subsidize their subsistence lifestyle by sending family members to work in cities. It can be hard to understand how radical that is because we're used to assuming that subsistence (say, growing some food) is at best a way of allowing you to function better in the official economy. But for millions of people in the world, the subsistence economy is the primary economy, and their goal is not the maximization of profit, but simply to make enough money to keep the subsistence way of life afloat for families. We meet many of these people in the US, because tens of thousands of Mexican immigrants fall into this category — healthy men sent to the US to work so that their families can keep growing corn and feeding themselves. Generally speaking, the market economy has failed farmers; cheap corn dumped on markets has undercut local farming. But the value of subsistence life doesn't rest just in how much you can sell a bushel of corn for but in the way of life itself.

The resilience and power of the subsistence economy, then, must be central to our understanding of how to protect ourselves in hard times. If we can get much or most of what we need outside the monetary economy, and improve the resilience of the larger economy, we can make ourselves more secure. Gene Logsdon, in his book *The Contrary Farmer's Invitation to Gardening*, titles one of his chapters "Gardening to Save us From 'The Economy'" and says what he means is this:

> *It seems to me that the part of "the economy" that depends on biological processes, not industrial processes — especially food, but also renewable resources such as cotton and wool and other natural fibers for clothing, and wood for construction, furniture and fuel — is particularly vulnerable to the volatile and chaotic conditions of the industrial manufacturing marketplace. An ear of corn grows at its own sweet pace, no matter how the interest*

rates are manipulated. Much more biological production than is
now the case should be protected from this market vulnerability,
and the most practical way of doing so is by having more gar-
dens. A garden economy would provide society with a much safer
"social security" than pension money sunk into volatile stock and
bond markets that can collapse overnight. (Logsdon, 32)

Logsdon's call is to stabilize the whole economy by expanding the unofficial economy, and by removing some of the most delicate and essential elements of our security from the vulnerable space of growth capitalism. Now, this is quite the opposite of what we have been trained to believe. Our culture has pressed us to believe that security is monetary, rather than communal or biological, and that a stable economy is created by prioritizing the smaller formal economy over the larger informal one. But in fact, both Logsdon and Shanin argue, it is the unofficial economy that offers us stability, that keeps us alive and meets many of our basic needs, and the expansion of the informal economy ought to be our priority.

This is both important and radical for several reasons. The first is that it can relieve some of our fears about the future. That is, the end of our conventional jobs and the life we've been living need not be the end of the world. I don't want to romanticize what an economic or energy crisis will look like. But it is possible to live partly or even wholly within the unofficial economy, and to function well there. If we begin now to reinforce our own connections to the informal economy, to reduce our reliance on our jobs and our investments, and to strengthen our investment in our gardens and our neighbors, we can soften economic blows. The real economy is by its very nature, more robust than the formal economy, less vulnerable to short-term change. That is not to say that one can get rich in the informal economy — in fact, you almost certainly can't do much more than meet most basic needs there. But within the subsistence economy, most of us could have enough.

The other thing that this means is that our economic choices do not come down merely to capitalism vs. communism, as so many conventional economists would have it. A subsistence economy can contain meaningful elements of both and things that are neither. As Shanin puts it,

The conventional view is that every country operates somewhere
on a continuum between the state-run economy and the pure
capitalist economy; between left and right. Countries can move
along this line, of course: if capitalism isn't working, the state can
intervene and vice versa. After the fall of communism, eastern

Europe inevitably tried to embrace capitalism. But the truth is that most of mankind lives outside this model. So we find in the former Soviet economies that while officials are trying to privatise the economy, most people are living in the informal economy that is neither communist nor capitalist. (http://archive.new scientist.com/home).

This is important in part because again we find that we have not been offered, or even made aware of, the full range of economic choices. Shanin's scholarship tells us that whole chunks of our economic story — the largest chunks — were left out. Most of us are to a degree participants in the real economy. And, as Shanin points out, most of the world lives a subsistence lifestyle, mostly apart from the larger economy.

As in Russia, an economic crisis in the US might actually serve to improve some lives, recreating local jobs and local economies. We are, however, much more deeply implicated in the public economy than your average Russian. Still, it is not hard to imagine a revitalization of things like agriculture, clothing manufacture and small-scale production of goods if the dollar falls or an energy crisis drives the costs of imported goods too high. Indeed, this seems to be hapening already — the cost of shipping goods has risen with the cost of oil, and American-made goods are becoming newly competitive.

Peasant Economics for Everyone

The term "peasant" is a loaded one — very few people in the rich world think the word has anything to do with them. We're not peasants, in the sense of having a strong relationship with land and place (although more on this later), but we need to think about how peasant economics, in which people manage to have "enough" outside the formal economy, might transform our lives.

What does all of this mean in practical terms for ordinary families? First and foremost it means that it would be wise to hedge your bets economically, to slowly and steadily move more and more of your economy away from the formal to the informal sector. I'm not suggesting that you take up growing pot, but growing a garden and selling some surplus produce might be wise. If you have skills at building, repairing or sewing things, plan ahead for how you might set up a cottage industry.

Now, I am not suggesting that you go entirely to a subsistence economy unless you feel comfortable there. Most of us are still too tied into mortgages and the need for health insurance (more about that in a later chapter) to step entirely out of the formal economy. But I do propose that most of us begin to stand with one foot in the informal economy and the other in the formal one, and that we try and recognize and encourage the resilience, value and stability of the informal economy. By this I mean that we are taught to believe that our security derives from our formal wealth — our job that provides us with health insurance, our retirement fund, the kids' college fund. But these things are vulnerable to market crisis and collapse. As I write this it seems we may be on the verge of such a crisis, as the housing bubble bursts, the credit crisis worsens and the dollar is losing value. What happens if your pension fund evaporates, the kids' college fund is needed to pay the taxes and your employer stops offering insurance, as thousands of businesses already have?

We turn then to the security that can be found in other structures than the formal economy — to the informal economy and household economics. We turn to family to provide a loan or to work together to subsidize a new business. We turn to neighbors to apprentice a child, to a community scholarship fund to help her go to college, or to co-operative "uncolleges" to provide an equivalent education at much lower cost. We turn to our community emergency fund for urgent medical care and to a loved one to tend us at the end of our lives, while also developing a healthier way of life to minimize our reliance on the medical system. What are now solutions of last resort — community and mutual need — become the sources of security and certainty. Thus we can know that whether social security pays out or not, we will be there for our parents, and our children for us.

. . .

Consider working with your neighbors to create a local currency that keeps money in town.

. . .

And even to the extent that we must all pay our taxes and do our jobs and live, in part, in the formal sector, we can begin to view our household economy, our jobs, our homes, our plans through the primacy of the informal economy. What does that mean? Mostly it means moving to a subsistence and "family property" way of thinking. In practical terms, that would mean making choices in service of the subsistence economy. That is, instead of abandoning a house whose gardens can help support us because we can make more money in the formal sector by moving, we might choose to stay where we are because staying put enables us to need less. We might choose to see the formal economy as a supplement to the subsistence economy, requiring us to work out of our homes only enough to meet needs we truly can't meet on our own. Perhaps one partner might stay at home, or a cottage business might support the whole family with only a part-time supplemental income.

And we might begin to think in terms of the long view, rather than the short view. In peasant economics, "family property" is expected to be passed down from one generation to the next, and its primary purpose is to meet the basic needs of the whole family over many generations. Thus the "owner" of a farm or home in any generation has a responsibility to others. He can't simply choose to think in the very short term — sell the land and keep the profits — because others have a future investment in that land. This kind of ownership is best described as "stewardship" — the care and nurturance of something lasting. If we were to treat our land and our possessions this way, we would need fewer things, see greater productivity, and most of all, begin looking into the future more carefully, because our entire culture would be based upon the real, long-term value of what we have.

Now, I imagine most people who followed me this far are saying that it isn't possible for most of us to move into the informal economy. We're so pressed for time in the formal economy that we couldn't possibly begin to grow our own food, start a cottage business and get out of debt — we work, you know? And trust me, I know. In all the years I've been working on doing these things, the wall I run up against far more often than money is time. This is one of the hardest nuts for us to crack.

And yet, we have to figure this out. We have to find the time to do these things, both for ethical reasons and because otherwise we're simply going to be unprepared when the tidal wave of the long emergency starts washing over us. So how do we do that?

When we begin to live a subsistence lifestyle, at first, we have to find the time by cutting back in other areas — growing food and gardening start taking up the time we used to spend shopping (six hours weekly for the average American), watching TV, driving our kids to activities. But we find later that as our work begins to pay off we actually get time back. The things we don't need to buy any more cut our need for income. Finding good, satisfying work at home cuts back on our need for formal "entertainment." Practicing thrift, making and repairing things, for example, becomes a family activity, which obviates the need for some of the lessons and clubs that used to cost us money.

Digging for Dollars

The industrial economy devours our time. For the most part, Americans trade time for money and express extreme dissatisfaction at the trade off. Many of us would like to earn less and have more time. And life in the informal economy can enable that. For example, many working families might be able to cut down on working hours if they could save the 5.9 percent of their household budget that they spend on restaurant meals by growing and cooking food at home. They could cut their budgets significantly if one parent were to stay home and homeschool, reducing the cost of the parent's commute, school lunches, peer pressure wardrobes, dress clothes for the employed parent and a second car. And though you do have to live on less to do this, you get time in return.

You also get better work. Let's be honest, many of us do jobs that, at best, are of marginal utility — we build or sell things that other people don't need or do work that fuels the growth economy and work that leads to industrial destruction. But work within the home economy, most of us would agree, puts our resources where they are most valuable — into our children and the food that keeps our bodies healthy, into providing a business that serves your neighbors and your community, rather than people you have no relationship with. Thrift, repair, making things, growing things, and nurturing things — this is good and honorable work, and we need to do more of it.

John Maynard Keynes, the famed economist, once argued that having enough work to do was so important to morale (and morale to the economy) that one potential way that government could stabilize the economy was to bury money in the ground and pay people to dig it up. That is, Keynes said that what was important was that we have some work to do, not that it be useful or valuable. Productivity and utility had their places, but mostly, we need some busy work to keep the economy and our lives running.

To a large degree, our current economy is Keynesian — that is, the whole goal is simply to put people to work, regardless of whether they do good and meaningful work, regardless of whether the work they do is ultimately destructive to our larger goals, regardless of whether time spent on that work enables us to be happy, or comfortable, or to do the things we most want — care for our kids, spend time with our families, make the world a better place. That is, our economy does not, at present, serve us — it serves itself. And to a large degree, our current economy is based upon war and environmental destruction.

The term "military Keynesianism" was first used by a Polish economist to describe Nazi Germany, but it describes much of our economy since World War II quite well. That is, our current economy, to a large degree, owes its success to military expansionism and imperialism. People are put to work not at rebuilding the domestic infrastructure, but at war. The military industry and its offshoots (of which the Internet is one), account for an enormous portion of our economy and our GDP and millions of jobs, particularly among lower-income people. The war in Iraq alone is estimated by economists Joseph Stieglitz and Linda Bilmes to cost about $3 *trillion* or more — dollars that get paid out to soldiers and Halliburton consultants, folks in the aerospace industry and janitors in the Pentagon, to government administrators and construction companies that build military facilities. And in turn, those dollars get paid out to Wal-Mart and fast food restaurants, bookstores and movie theaters, and trickle down to the rest of us.

Chalmers Johnson, in *Nemesis: The Last Days of the American Republic,* documents that 60 percent of GDP growth in just 2003 was attributable to defense spending and that defense spending represents 50 percent of the government's discretionary spending. The American defense budget annually exceeds the combined defense budget of every other nation in the world. And, we should note, we are still losing the war in Iraq and precious human lives to people who build three-hundred-dollar roadside bombs. Perhaps this should tell us something about the utility of all this spending. But what it has been very good at is running up the economy for a while when things show signs of a slowdown.

Both the US and the Nazis came out of economic crisis in the 1930s by turning their economies into industrial war machines. Instead of burying cash in the ground and digging it up, we built bombs and planes and aircraft carriers. And much of our subsequent industrialization extended from this military run up — now that we had all the factories and farm folks moved to cities, we might as well keep going.

In World War II, we actually had something to fight against, but generally speaking in order to justify the next massive build up, we have had to have a major threat of violence, preferably a long-standing, endless danger like "the war on terrorism." Because, after all, one of the largest economies on earth is spending half its money — half the tax dollars of 300 million citizens like you and me — on war. We must be able to explain this away with some argument other than "It is good for Halliburton."

The part that we tend to forget about Keynesianism, military and otherwise, is that it is based on debt. This war and military Keynesianism in general are not making us richer. Quite the contrary — we're doing it on debt, and sooner or later we'll pay the price for that. At this writing, it looks as though payback time might be soon. Much of our economy is being fueled by investment from China and Japan, and China has recently bluntly told us that it will not keep buying our treasury bonds forever.

Now, Chalmers Johnson argues that an economic crisis may be good for our country in the long term — good rather in the way that a high fever is good, because it fights the root infection. Johnson rightly argues that we've lost much of what was good about American democracy over the past few years. If you read down the Bill of Rights, you'll find that just about the only rights that haven't been infringed are the right to bear arms and not to have Hessian troops quartered in your bedroom. We've paid a high price for military Keynesianism — and not just an economic price. Johnson argues that an economic crash might cause us to back off of our imperial aims and go back to democracy. He may be right, but I think we'll have to do more than get rid of military Keynesianism.

It isn't enough simply to deplore military Keynesianism. If we're ever to have an alternative economy that doesn't depend on finding people to make war against, that doesn't depend on exploitation and murder and that can actually help us face the crises that are headed our way, we're going to have to get rid of the make work and do useful things. And we're also going to have to value those useful things appropriately.

That sounds obvious, but it isn't at all under the auspices of modern capitalism. Many economists and politicians have for a long time been dedicated to the notion that it is best to pack poor young men and women off to be soldiers, to invest tens of thousands of dollars in their equipment, their training and their bodies, send them off around the world, and let them discover that a million-dollar helicopter is often no match for a thousand-dollar rocket launcher and that a six-hundred-thousand-dollar tank can be blown up by a hundred-and-twenty-dollar improvised explosive device (IED). We do this rather than give them useful work and demand that labor markets pay them fairly for it.

The poor young man (or woman) who goes into the military usually does so mostly not from a longing to blow up other people, but to be able to buy food and pay a mortgage or to be of service to her nation. We've managed to convince ourselves that it is economically more productive and of greater benefit to the nastion as a whole to give a person a tank and body armor, training and a ticket to some foreign country than to invest the same amount in a decent education, some job training, a piece of land and help learning how to build a house on it and grow food. The fact that we think the former is perfectly normal but would be outraged at the latter — and see it as "welfare" — is, of course, utterly insane.

The reason for this is that sending a person off to war creates jobs. The military base commander, the drill sergeant, the people who build military housing, body armor and tanks, the fast food place where the soldier eats, the government administrator who helps the soldier's family get food stamps because the military pays so poorly, the VA doctors that provide rehabilitation, the Halliburton employees that supply food and transport, the people who manufacture the body bags — all of them get a little piece of this, multiplied hundreds of thousands of times. Remind yourself that the US military budget is more than double the military budget of all other nations together.

On the other hand, if we spent that same money setting the same person up as a small-scale subsistence farmer, how many people would get money out of that? Certainly the manufacturers of hoes, nails and boots, maybe even small horse-drawn or efficient tractor equipment. The sawmill owner who cut the boards to build a barn, the logger who cut the trees for house and barn, some seed growers and a feed store. Probably the waitress at the local diner would get a tip when the farmer went in for a meal once in a while. But you can't run a global economy on that, can you? Where's the R and D money for high technol-

• • •

Encourage your children to start their own small home businesses, perhaps managing animals or growing food and selling it.

• • •

ogy so we can shoot people out of space with lasers? Where's the money for the people who will treat a soldier's drug problem and locate an apartment when he ends up homeless because of PTSD? You can't pay for global spy satellites off of the income of a small-scale subsistence farmer — such a farmer barely pays any taxes and doesn't need McDonalds because he grows his own food. He doesn't need a drug company to treat obesity-induced hypertension, because he doesn't sit on his ass all day, or trauma-induced depression, because he doesn't have any. In fact he doesn't need anything much more technical than a few good tools and a way of getting his crops to market. Heck, if he could have an acre within a few miles of city, he could do it with a bicycle cart.

There is simply no rational reason on earth why we wouldn't rather our young men and women have farms (or be teachers or artists or builders or any useful work) than that they go to the Middle East to die. Nor is there any rational reason why we should pay them enough to get along and allow them a college education for shooting people rather than for growing food. The only "explanation" is the magical thinking of "market forces." By magical thinking I mean that the idea that markets will magically produce better solutions than democratic people controlling their own lives and making good choices has not been proven to be true. In fact, there are few if any examples of even relatively unfettered markets being left to themselves. We know this because the people who manage the economy are quite explicit on this point. For example, in an interview with Jon Stewart, Alan Greenspan answered the question of whether the US had a free market.

> *Jon Stewart: Many people are free-market capitalists, and they always talk about free-market capitalism, and that is our econom-ic theory. So why do we have a Fed? Is the free market — wouldn't the market take care of interest rates and all that? Why do we have someone adjusting the rates if we are a free-market society?*
>
> *Alan Greenspan: You're raising a very fundamental question.... You didn't need central bank when we were on the gold standard, which was back in the nineteenth century. And all of the automatic things occurred because people would buy and sell gold, and the market would do what the Fed does now. But: most everybody in the world by the 1930s decided that the gold standard was strangling the economy. And universally this gold standard was abandoned. But: you need somebody to determine — or some mechanism — how much money is out there, because remember, the amount of money relates to the amount of inflation in the economy.... In any event the more money you have, relative to the amount of goods, the more inflation you have, and that's not good. So:*
>
> *Stewart: So we're not a free market then.*
>
> *Greenspan: No. No.*
>
> *(Transcription by Lawrence H. White, posted on divisionof labor.com)*

The simple fact is that where there is no rational reason for a policy, and where it does us no good, there is no empirical reason we cannot change it.

Or rather there is a reason, but it isn't a particularly noble one. The reason is that the economy is based on blowing things up and that the people who regulate it generally profit. There is little incentive to change. If we encouraged young people to do things that were useful, and paid them fairly for it, we wouldn't be rich and we couldn't afford to invade other countries. If we mostly did for ourselves and met most of our own needs in self-sufficient com-munities and regions (that is, if we were to be the kind of country that, say, Thomas Jefferson envisioned), we would have enough money for true defense spending, to protect the country from invasion, but not enough to go around invading other countries to protect them for oil ... er ... democracy.

So getting back to the painful but necessary question of how it is that we can find the time to start growing our own food and making things at home and getting along with less, we find that our jobs are probably mostly make-work, supporting something that most of us don't believe in anyway. Now, that doesn't help us all that much in many cases — we can't just quit our jobs. But it does mean that to the extent that we can cut our incomes to the bone, and replace the money we've needed with subsistence or local economies, we can also begin to stabilize the economy itself.

Maybe it would be morally acceptable for us to do make work, regardless of its collateral damage, if there was nothing else important to do. But we know that isn't true. Our make work is causing us to take shortcuts. Our jobs are causing us to buy fast food because we don't have time to cook, and thus they are hurting our health. Our jobs encourage us to dump chemicals on our gardens and lawns rather than build soil, because building soil takes time. Our make work is cutting into the time we could spend playing with our kids or educating them, taking care of elderly people we love or volunteering with others. It cuts into our time for community building, chopping wood, growing gardens, cleaning up messes, avoiding pollutants, being frugal, cooking dinner, making love, stopping the war.

It is a circular problem — how do we find time? We take it out of the things that prop up the formal economy. We stop watching TV, so we stop paying attention to the ads and to the story that we need to be in fashion, that we constantly need an infusion of "new" into our lives. We take the time out of our jobs, which have demanded more and more of us in recent decades, and cut back on our overtime or find jobs with more flexibility. At the same time, we find more time to live more frugally, to meet more of our own needs. And we find that our personal economies are more stable; we need less money; and we have more options. It is not an easy thing. But it is achievable.

It is also worth noting that it is the industrial economy that steals our time. In *1066: The Year of the Conquest,* historian David Howarth describes what it was like for pre-conquest medieval laborers to work on a typical estate in Britain.

> Slaves therefore had no place in the lives or thoughts of the people of Horstede: they were all free men. The humblest among them were the six cottagers. Some of these may only have been labourers, but among them were probably part-time craftsmen — the miller, a blacksmith, a tinker, foresters, sawyers, or hurdle-makers, perhaps a beekeeper or potter.... Their cottages were provided by the thane, with up to five acres of the village land and their tools and equipment; and in return they had to work

> *for him one day a week, and three days a week as reapers at har-*
> *vest time.... They paid no rent, but it was a symbol of their free-*
> *dom that they paid their dues to the church. (Howarth, 1066:*
> The Year of the Conquest, *18)*

One of the most remarkable things about this description is that it includes the factual observation that most poor medieval people worked about one day a week to support their homes, their land, tools and equipment. Try and parallel that to your own life. Do you know anyone who owns even a simple house and five acres of land who can pay the mortgage on that land with a single day's work each week, and three days' overtime a year? I don't. It is absolutely true that the cottages were small, food was cooked over an open fire, and life was vulnerable in ways ours is not. It is also true that generally speaking, 11th-century serfs had a good bit more leisure than we do. Think twice about that — about the idea that you work harder than your average medieval serf.

Why is this important? Because if we will have to give up some of our conveniences, we need to know what our lives will look like. Will we return to a life of endless drudgery, intolerable misery? That is the conventional wisdom, that our lives were vastly harder before all the gadgets that make them easy right now. Fortunately for those of us cutting back on our energy, it isn't true. As Juliet Schor points out in her exhaustively researched volume, *The Overworked American,*

> *One of capitalism's most durable myths is that it has reduced*
> *human toil. This myth is typically defended by a comparison of the*
> *modern forty-hour week with its seventy- or eighty-hour counter-*
> *part in the nineteenth century. The implicit — but rarely articu-*
> *lated — assumption is that the eighty-hour standard has prevailed*
> *for centuries. The comparison conjures up the dreary life of medieval*
> *peasants, toiling steadily from dawn to dusk. We are asked to*
> *imagine the journeyman artisan in a cold, damp garret rising*
> *even before the sun, laboring by candlelight late into the night.*
>
> *These images are backwards projections of modern work pat-*
> *terns. And they are false. Before capitalism, most people did not*
> *work very long hours at all. The tempo of life was slow, even*
> *leisurely; the pace of work relaxed. Our ancestors may not have*
> *been rich, but they had an abundance of leisure. When capital-*
> *ism raised their incomes, it also took away their time. Indeed,*
> *there is good reason to believe that working hours in the mid-*
> *nineteenth century constitute the most prodigious work effort in*
> *the entire history of humankind....*

Consider a typical working day in the medieval period. It stretched from dawn to dusk (sixteen hours in summer and eight in winter) but, as the Bishop Pilkington has noted, work was intermittent — called to a halt for breakfast, lunch, the customary afternoon nap and dinner. Depending on time and place, there were also midmorning and midafternoon refreshment breaks. These rest periods were the traditional rights of laborers, which they enjoyed even during peak harvest times. During slack periods, which accounted for a large part of the year, adherence to regular working hours was not usual.... The pace of work was also far below modern standards — in part because the general pace of life in medieval society was leisurely. (Schor, The Overworked American, *47)*

I quote Schor here at some length because I think her argument points up a truth that we've missed in all our glorification of the modern labor movement — we're working harder than our ancestors, and mostly not to our own benefit. I've talked in previous chapters about how we must find time to do these things for ethical and practical reasons. Now I want to suggest that our loss of time is, as Schor points out, not an inevitability, but a price we pay for living unsustainably. It is absolutely true that without our dishwashers, cars and electric tools we will find ourselves doing more work in some ways. It is also true that without the need to support an economy of these things, we may find our time again.

• • •

Have a gardeners' potluck. Invite friends and neighbors to bring produce and enjoy a meal together.

• • •

It isn't only medieval Europe that stands as a useful contrary example. Anthropologists found that the !Kung people generally are able to meet their needs in about two to four hours a day, and that most hunter-gatherer societies work less than a full day. Helena Norberg-Hodge, in isolated Ladakh, found that Ladakhis do most of their labor in fairly busy eight- to ten-hour days during the summer and spend their winters celebrating. A recent New York Times article suggests that 18th-century French folk spent their winters more or less hibernating, working only during the growing season.

Exploring this question of labor working among the Amish, writer Eric Brende found that even at peak labor time during threshing, the workload wasn't much more than an eight-hour day — and contained regular breaks and rest periods. He argued that running a small, low-technology farm was less strenuous than many jobs.

Brende's observation suggests that it is not just in the past that a lower-energy lifestyle with lower costs can save us time. We work as hard as we do to because of the high cost of keeping our lives going. Think about how much time and energy you put into paying for your vehicle. Professor Thomas Princen estimates in his book, *The Logic of Sufficiency,* that most of us spend two working months simply to pay for our transportation. If you were to calculate how much car ownership costs you, how much time driving saves you and add in the time you work to support your car, would it really be so much slower to ride a bicycle most of the time and rent a car for the occasional long trip? It is hard for us to grasp that industrial society steals our time from us, and that we could take it back.

The bad news is that if enough of us did this, it would seriously hurt some segments of the formal economy. But economists are fine with this sort of thing when, for example, we are trashing our manufacturing sector and throwing people out of work — then it is called "creative destruction." I suspect they'll be less happy about trashing the growth economy so that we can get rid of the war machine, get ourselves better food, a healthier lifestyle, better hope for the future and more long-term personal security.

I said earlier that this book is going to emphasize moral arguments, because I believe powerfully that economic arguments must eventually cede to moral ones. This was one of the great arguments about slavery and about the end of the British Empire — the naysayers said, "It will hurt us financially to do this." And yes, that was true. Not stealing money from other people, not enslaving them makes the people who had been stealing and slaving less rich. But some things you do because they are right, not because they are expedient. Ceasing to fund the war machine will, in the long term, be good for us. But that's not the primary reason for changing our lives. We should reduce our participation in the formal economy because it is the right thing to do.

The good news is that as we have seen, the informal economy, based on networks of family and community, is remarkably robust, vital and alive — it supports more than three quarters of the human population. That is, most people in the world get their eating money and the things they need not from a company that is traded on a stock market but from Jaime down the road, who repairs shoes and raises chickens, and from Mama, who loaned us enough money to buy the house without interest. And we could live far more in the informal economy than we do now. It need not mean poverty or insecurity but can provide stability. So one of the projects we all have to address is how to be less rich, but still have security, stability, pleasure, comfort.

·

FIVE

Making Ends Meet

The Problem of Consumption

OKAY, WHO REALLY DOESN'T LIKE SHOPPING? I'VE ALWAYS CLAIMED I WAS ONE
of those women who didn't like to shop, by which I mean that I don't like the
way I look in most clothes well enough to want to spend time trying them on.
But if you look a little deeper, I really enjoy buying some things. I like to buy
books most of all, but I can be enticed into shopping for yarn and cute baby
stuff and into yard saling, in part from the sheer pleasure of acquisition. The
thing about shopping for stuff is that it makes you feel so good. With this

thing, we imagine, we'll be better, or prettier, or happier or ready for the world. This, we think for just a moment, will be the thing that quiets our anxieties and makes us feel secure enough.

I've shopped for comfort. My husband's grandmother died suddenly after a bad fall. I was the person elected to attend her in the hospital. After several days of being there for 12 to 15 hours at a stretch and watching her suffer and die, I was so tired and overwhelmed I just wanted to escape for a little while. I remember wandering into a knitting shop and coming out with an armload of yarn I didn't need, but it felt so good to simply wrap my head around the easy questions — mohair or wool? would I wear that shade of purple? I came out of the store feeling better — because I'd pushed grief and exhaustion away and served only my own interests and needs for a moment.

So let us just say that I understand the urge to buy. And yet, for the past couple of years, I've done virtually none. For most of 2006 and part of 2007, we decided not to buy anything but food, gas and other necessities. We cheated a few times — we ate out a couple of times; I bought a Reeses peanut butter egg (a weakness of mine) and a pair of shoes; and we bought the kids a few treats. I also made an exception for buying children's clothes at yard sales. Oh, and my attempt to make all my Chanukah gifts meant that a whole bunch of people got IOUs last year. But mostly, we didn't buy anything. And mostly, we didn't mind that much.

And that in itself was revelatory. There were moments, of course, when we really wanted stuff. But we loved not having to go to stores or to the mall all the time. We loved that our budget stretched better to the end of the month. And we enjoyed making things and making do. We loved that the holidays weren't so hectic.

At the end of the year, we started another project, the Riot for Austerity, and had only a thousand dollars to spend on non-food and energy consumer goods for the whole year. That felt like incredible luxury. And that may be the best part of reducing our consumption. If we shop all the time, the magic of consumption to take us out of ourselves goes away — we have to buy more and more and spend more time at it, and the power diminishes anyway. But if we restrain ourselves for a while, the smallest, simplest luxury is a pleasure untold.

Use-What-You-Have Adaptation

What we all have to avoid is the notion that we can buy our way out of our problems. Instead, the goal is to reduce our costs by extreme frugality. This is psychologically difficult because if there is one great certain confidence in

American society it is this: you can buy your way out of almost anything. Other than a few things that will land you in jail even if you are rich, we tend to look for solutions that involve buying things. Having trouble with your marriage? Take a vacation. Pay a counselor. Don't want to eat pesticides? Buy organic food! Indebted? Buy a book about how to get out. Worried about Peak Oil? Look around at all the things there are to buy. Got a crosscut saw and a year's supply of dry milk yet? Don't want to give up driving and flying? We'll sell you some nice carbon offsets!

To every problem there is a purchasable solution, for those who can afford it. And some of it is true — living a low-technology life, for example, requires some new tools, and those tools cost money. I own some of them, and I covet others. I have shelves of books about the problem and the solutions, and I haven't missed the irony that those books take out trees and use energy in printing. I am writing a book that will take out some more trees. I certainly have profited in the past from people buying the organic vegetables I grew. So I'm not innocent here. I don't think anyone is. But though we will always need to buy some things, the notion that we can purchase our way out of the problem keeps us from perceiving the real, root trouble we are in.

Because it turns out that all those solutions come with problems of their own. More global warming gasses are produced by shipping stuff around the world than by flying. Some of what's killing us comes just from getting those clothes you like from overseas. And that doesn't even count all the climate-changing and oil-depleting gasses produced in making the doohickey, whether an SUV, a stuffed polar bear (so that kids can see what one looks like after they are extinct) or a six pack. All of them warm up the planet when they are made, when they are transported, when you go shopping to get them, when you bring them home and dispose of the wrapper, and when eventually the thing ends up in the landfill emitting methane gasses. Shopping is itself the root problem. Even if you buy better, more sustainable products, ultimately at the root, we have to buy less of them — a lot less.

That means not having the right product all the time. During the buy-nothing year, I did something rather embarrassing. I violated my no-buying-new policy to purchase some waterproof garden shoes (on sale, of course — is there anything that motivates us more than "on sale?"). I justified this by noting that I wreck a pair of sneakers every year, and with these shoes I could cut down on sneaker purchases. But, the basic assumption that I must always have the specialized item, the perfect tool or I won't be able to manage is nonsense. I could take off my shoes or wear my sneakers with more holes.

You know it. I know it. I cooked fabulous meals when I owned four pots, two knives and a whisk that my mom and stepmom picked up at yard sales. I cook fabulous meals now in a kitchen stuffed with pots. Do my cast iron Dutch ovens do a better job than a big old tomato can would? Almost certainly. Could I cook a good dinner for my children in an old tomato can? Yup — that's what billions of poor people all over the world cook in.

Of course I would like the right tool for the job, and sometimes the right tool is worth it, but we absolutely must get over the notion that the process of preparing for the long emergency is the process of purchasing a totally different infrastructure.

We cannot purchase our way out of our present troubles. But perhaps, just perhaps, we can not purchase our way out of it — save ourselves and our future by not buying things, and taking much greater care we do shop.

We have to make enormous changes, and some of those changes will take new things. But for the most part, we need to change our thinking. I'm told there is a book called *Use What You Have Decorating* — a design theory that says you don't have to go out and buy all new stuff; you can make life beautiful with what's already in your home. What a great idea that is. In fact, it is so great that I'm officially stealing it now and suggesting that all of us begin use-what-you-have adaptation.

. . .

Don't go on vacation. Stay home and transform your house into a paradise instead.

. . .

You see, we have a lot of stuff — I do, you probably do, most people do. We usually have more than we need, more than is required for our happiness. We all know that. What if we used that stuff — the houses we live in now, the tools in our workshops and garden sheds, the warm clothes we own — and set our creativity and artistry to work, transforming our lives mostly with what we already have?

What would the result be? I don't know, but I suspect it would require less energy than most of the proposed solutions out there, that it would bring out our creativity and strengths, be accessible to most people, save us money and help us find uniquely personal solutions to the personal problems created by our collective crisis.

Get Out of Debt

If we're to make basic personal preparations, those of us who are not rich are going to have to reduce or eliminate some of our regular expenses so that we can do things like reinsulate our houses or put up rainwater catchment.

Nobody I know is handing out cash for these things, so we're going to have to cut our budgets for food and clothing to find the money to get them. How do we find that money? The first thing we do is to get out of debt.

Debt makes you poorer. I bet you've heard this message over and over again. And if you are like most Americans, you listen, you may even give lip service, but on some level, you don't believe it. Because, after all, in a lot of cases, debt seems to make you richer. Because you have credit, you can have a nice house and a nice car and a lot of nice stuff. People tell you debt is bad, but a lot of the things you want and need to do can only be done with debt; most of us can't buy a house or go to college or get a car without some debt. So although nearly every financial book says "no debt!" you probably are pretty accustomed to ignoring them. After all, the average American savings rate is negative, and our consumer debt has boomed. And it has, in many cases, *worked* for us to be in debt — not in every respect, but we've gotten things we wanted from debt with comparatively small consequences.

That, however, is about to change. Nationally, interest rates are going up and lending standards are tightening. The 2005 changes in bankruptcy laws now mean that bankruptcy can equal debt slavery. We're pissing away more and more of our income in debt payments and interest fees, and we can't afford that. We need the money to do too many things — to put insulation and new windows on the house, to buy that truckload of compost or those fruit trees. I hate to be the one to say it, but now we actually have to pay attention to the "no debt" idea.

Which is easy to say, of course, and harder to do. It means finding places in your discretionary income to make additional payments on your debt — getting rid of cable TV, losing the second car, eating more beans and rice. There are books about this that can offer more strategies than I could here, but remember, no one is going to be kind and forgiving about your debt in the future. We're simply going to have to live more frugally. That's hard for those of us who weren't raised in frugality or who associate living cheaply with poverty, ugliness and other negative connotations. So perhaps we need to start by changing some of the associations.

Use It Up, Wear It Out, Make It Do or Do Without

The famous quote about frugality, "Use it up, wear it out, make it do or do without," applies very well to reducing one's emissions and dependence on fossil fuels. Everything we buy has an embodied energy cost — that is, the energy to make it contributes to global warming. Everything also has personal energy costs — spending more of our hard-earned dollars means more time working or more stress over our credit card bills. Frugality and environmentalism don't have a 100 percent overlap, but often, doing the frugal thing is also doing the environmentally sound thing. Every time we buy new, we say to that manufacturer, "Make one more." One more is often too many.

So how do we do this? First, we use things up — extract every single last drop out of something. That means we scrape the pan thoroughly, so that we don't end up throwing away food. It means we use our thumbs to get the last bit of egg out of the shell. Take those ratty old T-shirts and make a quilt or make handkerchiefs to substitute for tissues. Take the time to really get all the use we can out of things. That includes pleasure, time and love — that is, if we get all the pleasure we can from our simple lives, we won't always need more. If we make good use of all our time — rest and work — we won't be running all the time. If we make full use of the love and support of others, we might look up one day and have a community to rely on.

Wear it out. That means making things last as long as possible. That means darning our socks, mending our jeans, having our shoes reheeled. The longer we extend the lifespan of things, the less we'll need to buy. With that in mind, it is often wisest to buy things that really last and that have potential for long-term reuse or repair. Whenever possible that means wood furniture, not plastic, metal tools, good quality clothing. It isn't always frugal just because it is cheap. We need to start thinking about the whole lifespan of an object from where and how it was made to what we will do when it breaks or is worn out. A wooden toy that your grandchildren will use is a better investment than a plastic one that will be broken by the week after Christmas.

Make it do. This requires living life artfully and imaginatively, much more so than saying "Oh, I need a new dish drainer — off to the store." What substitutes can we find? How can we use something we have, instead of something new? We ask children to make do all the time, or at least we used to. Don't have a train set? Use your imagination. Carve one? Make one out of a cardboard box? Pretend? We need to take the advice we used to give children and start finding ways to make do with what we have. Most of us have houses full of stuff. Our sense that we need just one more object to make it complete is probably wrong. Oh, there are exceptions — particularly if you've been living a fossil-fueled life and now need to power down, there probably are a few things you really need in order to do so. But most of the time, if we just imagined, we could make do with what we have.

Do without. I live in a 3500+-square-foot farmhouse filled with books, tools, kids, toys, etc. I've met people who live in 200-square-foot huts filled with family and a few tools and pots. Many of those people considered themselves happy, fortunate and blessed — so if one can be blessed with 200 square feet, what is the rest doing for me? If you and I can't do without, who can? After all, we have more than most people in the world. Before you buy something, ask yourself — can everyone have one? That is, if everyone had one, would it be good for the world? Did my grandparents have one? Did they need one? If not, why do I need one? Sometimes you will need it. But surprisingly often you don't.

We all need food, water, shelter, love, education, joy, clothing, some simple tools, good work to do, comfort, support, peace, security, art, imagination. More than half of these you can't buy at any price; in fact, having too much can prevent you from enjoying things fully. The rest of our needs can be met 90 percent of the time in our present society by making things or finding things or reusing things. Doing without isn't impoverishment — it is life as art.

Hang On to Your House

In the last few months of 2007 we got the nasty economic news that the mess of foreclosures because of below-prime mortgages was penetrating into middle class families. The prediction is that the number of foreclosures will rise steadily for at least another year or two. Millions more Americans are finding that their houses are no longer worth what they paid for them. At this writing, nearly half of all Americans have negative equity on their homes.

What if you are one of the many people who stand to lose their homes? It could be rising interest rates, job loss, overbuying, or rising costs for everything else that push your family into a crisis. Even if you don't think this is your problem yet, it doesn't take much to tip a teetering economy into a real recession. Given the confluence of unpleasantnesses facing us, do you really want to bet your life that you'll keep your job? And how long could you keep up your mortgage payments without a salary? How long before the costs of meeting basic family needs would make it impossible to keep up with everything else?

Americans are very poorly prepared for the coming crisis — they are overwhelmingly in debt and have little or no savings. With the dollar falling, we can expect to see prices rising for a good long time, and inflation mixed with a tight housing market is the makings of a real mess. None of us should be too complacent about what we have.

First of all, you should think seriously about whether your house is worth saving, or savable at all. That is, before I offer any suggestions on how to avoid being foreclosed upon, take a clear-eyed look at your life and think about whether you want to even try. Some people are going to lose their houses anyhow, and others may be pouring good money after bad to keep something they don't need.

The questions you should ask yourself are these: Did I buy my house at the price peak? If you did, sorry to say, there's a good chance you'll never regain your equity. So you need to ask yourself, do I want to spend 30 years paying off a house that cost too much? Will I be able to do so? Can I really afford my house? Think seriously about this one. We are told that the logical thing to do is sit tight and keep paying until the market goes up again and we get our price back, but that may not happen. Yes, you may lose money getting out now, but you may also save yourself a lifetime of costs. Are you prepared to see equity drop even further, to stay in your house for a decade or more, or to take an even bigger loss? Sometimes it is better to cut and run.

Did you put much money down? Do you have an adjustable-rate mortgage set to reset, or an interest-only loan? How much of your income goes to this mortgage? If it is more than one third of your household income, and you absolutely need two of you working full-time jobs to pay your mortgage, you should seriously consider buying a smaller, cheaper home or sharing with family. Because the odds are good that sooner or later you'll lose your house — or be trapped in it forever, scrimping and struggling to own a property that will never be worth what you paid for it. It is always better to get out on your own terms than to have the bank foreclose on you. Even if you lose some money, it is better than losing everything you've paid into the house up until now.

Remember, banks don't really want to own houses. They don't like foreclosing (although they don't dislike it so much they won't do it). And they know that the longer they can keep you paying for something, the better off they come out in a foreclosure situation. So they are likely to be extremely "kind" for a good while, offering to lower payments or help you out with late ones. But only you know if this is a real kindness — there's nothing helpful to you about your paying the bank a lot of money that you'll never see again, only to lose the house later. Again, if you think you will have to get out, do it on your own terms.

Do you want to live in this house for the long term? If you bought this house in the hope of trading up, if it has no yard, or is in an area with restrictive covenants and high property taxes, if it is a house that shows off your old lifestyle more than it supports your future, perhaps getting out and buying a much cheaper property somewhere else is worth it.

Remember, there are areas of the country that are not overvalued. And even if that means changing jobs or careers, you might have a better, more secure life if you lived less on the financial edge. We tend to think that our jobs and careers are non-negotiable: "I have to live here — this is where the jobs are." But there's no need to fetishize your job. It is, presumably, mostly how you manage to keep body and soul together, not the whole reason for your existence. And if that is true, consider carefully whether you might not be able to live as well somewhere else, being paid a bit less or doing something somewhat different. Obviously, this won't work for everyone, and there are those for whom a job is a passion. But if your job isn't your life, think seriously about going somewhere cheaper. Salaries will be lower, but then, so will costs.

If you've thought all of this over seriously, and assuming that you do want to stay in your house, how do you do it? Of course, the first thing is to get out from under any other debt you have. If you can see this coming while you still have an income and things are mostly okay, then the first thing you do is cut back on everything. That means no more meals out, no more cable, no more keeping the heat and a/c at 70. It means getting rid of the car with the payments and replacing it with something cheaper or taking the bus. It means buying everything that you need used. Get rid of the dryer and line dry your clothes. Plant a garden and eat the food you grow.

If you are planning a move, now is the time to research markets and find that country property or the urban duplex with a big yard. Remember that an acre is quite a large space.

For some of us, this will be hard. You won't die from it, though. Divide the money you save (track it!) into two funds — one savings, one debt reduction. Pay off the highest interest rates first. Consider consolidating to a short-term, 0 percent interest credit card, and then paying it off diligently.

Are things more serious than that? Are you starting to feel the pinch already? Well cut back some more. Sell the computer, and give up the Internet — go to the library instead. Find a carpool and give up your car, or get on a bike. Dump the tae kwon do lessons for the kids, and teach them to cook from scratch and play pick up soccer with the neighbor kids instead. Go vegetarian, and eat more whole foods. Give up luxuries like coffee and beer. Make your fun at home — play games instead of going out. Turn the thermostat way down (or up, depending on whether we're talking about heating or cooling), cut the water bill by limiting showers to three minutes. Again, use the money to pay down debt and build some savings.

What if you are already in trouble and the utility people are threatening to shut you off, the mortgage people are threatening to foreclose, and the bill collectors are calling day and night? What then?

First of all, the bill collectors can't call you if you tell them not to. Tell them not to. And don't panic or go into denial. It is easy to feel that you "just can't deal" with all of this, or to be so ashamed that you can't focus on fixing it. Right now, people are getting poorer — real incomes are falling, inequities are rising. If you are one of them, you should not buy into the notion that you are a bad person, who is making bad choices in a vacuum — a whole lot of people are helping you make those choices.

And if you have made bad choices, remember, all of us have. So forgive yourself, resolve not to do it again, recognize that this isn't your fault (or wholly your fault), and get your butt in gear and concentrate on ensuring yourself a stable place to live. One of the most remarkable things about American culture is how much we blame poor people for being poor — we isolate them, tell them it is a moral failure and that they are scum. Don't accept that message! This is the beginning of a systemic failure. That's not to say you aren't responsible for your actions; you just didn't do it alone. Don't take all the blame.

* * *

Plant a garden and grow some of your own food. Even apartment dwellers can grow lettuce and dwarf cherry tomatoes in window boxes or participate in community gardens.

The rest of us can transform our yards into food-producing areas.

* * *

Second, if things are that dire, put your needs in order of priority. First is food. Get the cheapest healthy food you can. Don't live on ramen noodles — buy whole grains and beans, and live on bread and bean soup, along with the dandelions from your yard and produce you buy at the very end of the day for bargain prices at the farmer's market. Second, is needed medicine. Every state now has insurance programs for poor children — get your kids on them. Check out drug company programs if you are genuinely dependent on some medication. But also think about whether you really need what has been prescribed for you — we are the most overmedicated people on the planet. It may be that a little less medication would help. Or perhaps you could choose a cheaper, older drug. Talk to your doctor about this, and don't mess with it on my advice alone, of course.

The next thing should be your house — the reason you should keep your house (assuming it is worth keeping as we discussed) is that the land you are on allows you to grow food, the house is shelter, the garage is where you start your home business. You will probably be much less healthy, happy and secure without a home. So you need to keep your home and garden going. Make sure you are planting every inch of lawn with fruit trees, bushes and gardens. You'll want to eat that food.

If you aren't an experienced gardener, your best local resource will be your county agricultural extension agency. They will help you find sources and get to know locally trained master gardeners, who volunteer their knowledge for free. Call and ask if they can help you find sources for plant divisions and inexpensive seeds or hook you up with a garden mentor. Every dollar you don't spend on food is one you can put toward the mortgage. If you are older and can't do as much, call your local garden club or 4-H and explain your situation — tell them you need to garden but can't do all the hard work of putting one in; could some nice strong teenagers help you out?

Consider adding more people to your house — allow a friend, college student or relative to live with you for a small rent. Or perhaps you could take in a local elder who can't live independently, but can meet most of her own needs. Those giant houses we've been building all these years of the boom mostly suffer from not enough people in them.

If you have children, talk to them about what's going on and enlist their help. Any child over 10 can work to meet some of their own needs, or even give a little money to the family. I know you don't want to worry them; you don't want to ask your kids to help support the family. Well, I'm going to be blunt. First of all, they already know things are dire — they aren't stupid. What they may not know is exactly what's wrong, but unless you are very gifted at denial they've already felt your fear, seen your stress and heard you fighting. So talking to them (at an age appropriate level) can only make it better and help them work out their own anxieties.

Giving them something productive to do, while valuing their contribution, is actually good for them. I don't mean that your kids should quit school, but saying, "It would be a big help if you would mow lawns for your snack and activity money" or "If you could watch your sister so that Daddy could look for a job, we'd be grateful" is not only okay, it is a good idea. One of the real problems our society has is that children don't do enough work, and they don't feel valued. Let your kids help you out. You may worry it will scar them to have to give up activities and go to work. Once upon a time, we used to call this "building character." I suspect we will again.

Sell stuff. Don't just turn off your freezer, sell it. Get rid of the big appliances. Get rid of fancy, newer stuff and replace it with cheaper older stuff.

It may not seem like selling those new sofas would be worth it, but if you can get $250 on Craig's List and then get a replacement for $50, you are $200 ahead. To be blunt, the whole nation got into an economic mess by looking at pretty pictures and thinking "I want that. I should have that." Well, we need to go back to houses that reflect our real standard of living — poorer. That's no shame and we'll have to get used to it. And while you're at it, stop reading the catalogs and magazines and watching TV — don't look at the pretty pictures that create desire.

You may not like this, but there are other places to cut back. It is perfectly possible to continue living in your house without electricity or heat in many cases. It won't be easy. But if you consider your house worth it, think seriously about it. The average American could save more than a thousand dollars a year by giving up utilities. First you minimize, but if things get tough, turn it off. You can turn off the a/c and keep cool by sitting outside in the shade with your feet in a five-dollar kiddy pool. You can keep warm by bundling up, moving around a lot and drinking hot tea. There's no reason for anyone to die of heat stroke or cold in a house — I know it happens all the time, but it doesn't *have* to.

I'll talk much more in Chapter 9 about how to adapt your house to work without heat, electricity, even running water, so I won't repeat here. The one thing I would do is caution you to avoid letting people know that you have turned off your utilities. There are a few cases of over-zealous social workers taking children out of homes without power because this is deemed a necessity. A Mennonite family I know approached a social worker in my state about wanting to adopt disabled kids and were told that they could lose their own children for not having running water. Later they were told this was not true, but this isn't something you want to mess with.

On the other hand, feel free to make use of support programs and other resources if necessary. If your kids need school lunches or breakfasts, get them. If you can't buy clothes, check the free bin. If you need food, don't be ashamed to use the food pantry. Just remember — pay it back and then some when you can. Because the next time, it will be your neighbor.

Ultimately, the moment you know your house is in danger, you should go into triage mode — first, decide whether to keep it. If you are going to keep it, make that your focus, and recognize that everything else is secondary. Don't get trapped in the classic American problem of confusing "want" with "need."

PART

Three

[
Real Family Values —
Facing the Future Together
]

SIX

Talking Population With the Old Men

Somewhere on this globe, every ten seconds, there is a
woman giving birth to a child. She must be found and stopped.
— SAM LEVINSON

It is essential to bear in mind that the sexual
relationship must also be understood as an ecological one.
— VANDANA SHIVA AND MARIA MIES

Why Bring Up Population?

THIS IS PROBABLY THE HARDEST CHAPTER FOR ME TO WRITE BECAUSE IT involves my talking about my personal reproductive choices and about my family. But I believe passionately that we have to talk about this subject. Why? Because the impact we have as a society depends on two factors: how much we use and how many people use it.

Most of our environmental problems stem from large numbers of people consuming too much, especially in rich places like North America. If we calculated our population based on the total consumption of the world's population, with each "fair share" calculated as a single person, the world would contain 57 billion people, most of them in the rich world. The average American child will consume almost 30 times the resources the average child in India does. One of the most important choices we can make is to reduce the distinction between the child in India and our own children as much as possible — to use a fair share of the planet's resources. But what a fair share actually is depends on how many people there are in the world sharing.

Generally speaking, I am increasingly trying to live my life in a way that proves it is possible for us to close the gap between the world's poor and rich, with each receiving a full fair share. But I have four children, and if every person in the world had four children (the average world wide total fertility rate is now a bit under three children), we would be in even more disastrous circumstances than we are now. So I cannot say that my family is a model for other people or that my choice was an environmentally wise one. So where do I get off talking about this?

I get that question a lot, and my answer is always, "Well, where do I get off not talking about it?" We can't pretend that my kids don't exist or that population isn't an issue. Nor can I do anything about the fact that I have four children, even if I wanted to. Everyone who is here, is here.

Frankly, I think it is really important that I talk about population, that mothers and fathers not leave this discussion to the far ends of the spectrum. The debate will ultimately go on with or without us. Up to now, most of the loudest voices speaking and writing about the need to address the population issue have been men, often old men who have chosen to father few or no children for reasons of conscience — Albert Bartlett, Garrett Hardin, Paul Ehrlich, and, of course, the grand old man of the subject, Thomas Malthus (who actually had almost as many children as I do). I admire and respect these voices and think some of what they say is true. But those of us who speak from a different experience need to bring our voices to the table if we are ever to have a truthful discussion about human numbers.

So I talk about this and write about this issue as much as I can. I write about it from the perspective of a mother who believes her children are the greatest gifts she could ever receive and from the perspective of a woman who didn't always make conscious environmental choices. I write about it as a scholar whose doctoral work included serious study of demography and as an activist who believes strongly in the adage that we should tell the truth and shame the devil, that we should approach hard subjects head on, even when it hurts.

This all requires me to admit that I have a less than perfectly environmentally aware past. And unless you've lived your whole life in a one-room cabin lighted by your own hand-dipped beeswax candles, you've probably had one too. The truth is I flew long distances to take frivolous vacations. I bought industrial meat from the supermarket. I played with plastic Barbies, and I didn't always fully understand the implications of population. And so I start writing from a post-lapsarian, fallen position, in which I have consumed more than my share, done environmental harm and contributed to quite a few problems — including overpopulation. I admire those who have done better than I have, but I think most of us start from where we are. I'm starting here.

My position is suspect, my limitations visible, and I have the pitter patter of little ecological footprints running about me. But these truths are advantages in a sense, because our future is not one of the environmentally pure living perfect lives, but of ordinary people going forward from where they are.

Most of us have not much wanted to talk about population — it is hard and brings up loaded issues like gender, religious freedom and sexual practice. But we cannot face our present crisis without also talking about the future of population. So let's talk about it. Let's bring the hard subjects to the table along with the easy ones.

Trusting Women

At the root of my own perspective on population issues is the premise that we have to respect and trust women. Obviously, women aren't the only ones who create babies — but study after study has shown that population policy is linked to policies on women, and that population and women's status are inevitably tied together. We cannot talk about population without talking about women's lives and women's bodies.

I write from the perspective of someone who has lived in my body a significant part of the material reality of our childbearing, our medical system, and motherhood. Now, that's not all there is to say about population, but I flatter myself that that means that I've got something to say that the old men might not.

. . .

More children are born in the summer or early fall than at any other time of year which suggests that some of us are doing more than chopping wood to keep warm. If you don't want your family size to increase, now is a good time to update your birth control.

. . .

I can understand why even people who admit we have to talk about population struggle to speak about it. For women, this can be particularly difficult, because in the abstract conversations about bodies we bang hard into our real bodies, and our real fears about how policy and culture affect them. When people speak of abortion as a solution, I think about my own, about the physical pain and deep grief it caused me — but also about my gratitude that I had the right to have one. When we talk about one-child policies, I look at my autistic, disabled son and ask, If I had had only one child, what would be his hope of survival and success in a depleted world? Who would care for him when I am gone? Who would love him and ensure his survival? When we talk about birth control, I think about getting pregnant while breastfeeding, using condoms and the pill — and yes, I know that's statistically unlikely. But I'm here as the voice of the statistically unlikely — the real woman into whose body devices must be inserted. When we talk about abstinence, I wonder what the price of the failure of abstinence will be — will others pay a price I didn't?

I wonder whether pressure toward abstinence will also include a future where women's "no" is always powerful — because we certainly don't live in such a world now. If women have limited ability to choose whether to have sex, then abstinence can never be a credible choice. Right now millions of poor women trade sex for food and shelter, millions of children and women are trafficked sexually; millions of women are raped and sexually abused each year all over the world. The idea of "abstaining" means that both partners in any relationship must be powerful enough to say "no" and have that respected.

And of course, there's the blurring of personal history with theory. I once met a woman who told me that she worked for years for various environmental organizations, and never once spoke about her six children — children born before most of those organizations were founded. Ultimately, any movement that wants people to feel ashamed of the children they have is bound to fail. So too is one that forgets that population is not a subject that comes up in isolation — that people have children for complicated reasons, and that things like money and power and military policy and medical care are mixed into this mess — if we try to talk about population without talking about the world around it, we will fail to change anything.

The Limits of I=PAT

Demographers historically talk about population in terms of the I=PAT formulation, invented by Paul Ehrlich, famous for the book *The Population Bomb.* "I" means total impact here, and it is the product of Population times Affluence (consumption) and Technology (pollution). Feminist critics of the I=PAT formulation such as T. Patricia Hynes have pointed out, however, that the I=PAT formula leaves all actors out of the equation — everything happens in the passive voice, and thus, all the responsibility is spread out equally, even when that responsibility shouldn't be equally distributed.

The structure of I=PAT conceals power relationships. It obscures, for example, that western consumption influences patterns of reproduction in the poor world, that, as Vandana Shiva puts it, the Global South "carries" the Global North, providing workers and natural resources to feed our appetites for consumer goods and energy. Our common framing of the population question leaves out the reality that the concentration of wealth in the hands of Western people means that children are the one source of security available to the poor or that, worldwide, military uses drive both emissions and consumption as well as the need to have babies to become future soldiers.

Donnella Meadows, one of the authors of *The Limits to Growth*, writes about her own experiences of seeing Hynes and others complicate the I=PAT formula here:

> *Suppose we wrote the environmental impact equation a different way, said the annoying panel at the front of the auditorium. Suppose, for example, we put in a term for the military sector, which, though its Population is not high, commands a lot of Affluence and Technology. Military reactors generate 97 percent of the high-level nuclear waste of the US. Global military operations are estimated to cause 20 percent of all environmental degradation. The Worldwatch Institute says that "the world's armed forces are quite likely the single largest polluter on earth."*
>
> *Suppose we added another term for the 200 largest corporations, which employ only 0.5 percent of all workers but generate 25 percent of the Gross World Product — and something like 25 percent of the pollution. Perhaps, if we had the statistics, we would find that small businesses, where most of the jobs are, produce far less than their share of environmental impact....*
>
> *An equation was beginning to form in my head:*
>
> *Impact equals Military plus Large Business plus Small Business plus Government plus Luxury Consumption plus Subsistence Consumption*
>
> *Each of those terms has its own P and A and T. Very messy. Probably some double counting and some terms left out. But no more right or wrong, really, than I=PAT.*
>
> *Use a different lens and you see different things, you ask different questions, you find different answers. What you see through any lens is in fact there, though it is never all that is there. It's important to remember, whatever lens you use, that it lets you see some things, but it prevents you from seeing others. (sustainer. org/dhm_archive/index.php?display_article=vn575ipated)*

I agree here with Meadows — the way we elect to phrase the discussion now is going to shape whether we are able to talk about population, and how, and whether we actually ever get anywhere. What we include and what we exclude, how we think about religion, politics, war, justice, sex and everything else has to come with us to the table. That doesn't mean we can't narrow things down for the purpose of discussion — we'll have to. But the phrase, "talking about population" cannot be a code term for "Let's all agree that we shouldn't be having babies," nor can it mean "The Bible is the final arbiter of everything." I don't think either perspective applies to most people, but sometimes when I hear people lamenting that we can't talk about population, I wonder whether the reason we're not talking is that there have been so many voices from the fringes of the discussion and such a resounding silence from the vast middle of the discussion.

Here are some things I think we have to talk about. If we're talking about voluntary limitations, do we mean really voluntary or the kind of voluntary where you'll intimidate me if I don't comply? Can we offer financial and political incentives for people to choose fewer children without discriminating against minority groups like the Amish who would choose to pay the price and have more children? How do we deal with power disparities, such as women who are victims of violence and the poor who may have limited control of their own fertility? Will we be improving the medical system so that someone's one child gets to live to a reasonable old age?

> Talk to your kids about sex, birth control, responsibility, your values and what you expect of them. Have this conversation early and often, and combine it with a discussion of the future so that children understand what the implications of early sexual activity might be in a poorer world.

• • •

What will we do for the disabled? How about elderly parents? Will we form low-energy, low cost, human-powered and humane ways to care for the aging baby boomers if we reduce the size of our families? What about women in India, who have to have six children in order to be certain one will live long enough to care for their parents in their old age? How will we make sure that a woman in India who has only one or two children does not starve to death when she gets old? Is it better to put our resources into discouraging her from having kids, or ensuring that the ones who are born get to live?

What about war? Will the state be allowed to take away one's single child and sacrifice him or her on the altar of resource wars? If people voluntarily sacrifices their right to more children, must they also sacrifice those children's lives? Does the fact that military action world wide is responsible for 10 percent of all carbon emissions and half of all US discretionary spending matter at all? Might we not make a greater impact focusing on war than on reproduction?

What about accidental conception? If we had a population policy, how would you treat someone who becomes pregnant by accident, in an abusive marriage or by rape? What about abortion? How do we navigate the shoals of the abortion debate in this discussion? What about the costs of birth control and access to medical care? Will these things be free? Subsidized? Which ones? For who? By whom?

How will we bring religious communities respectfully into this discussion and listen to their voices? How will we bring poor women to the table to speak as equals with the old men? How will we deal with sex selection and the disabled?

What will we teach our sons and daughters about sex, love and family in a world with less energy and less access to birth control and medical care for many? What kind of family structures will substitute for the work and emotional needs now made up by aunts, uncles and cousins, nephew and nieces? How will the voluntarily childless get access to family life, ensure security in their old age?

I don't claim we have to have answers or that we must have perfect solutions in place before we have this conversation, but we cannot simply speak in isolation of the question, How do we get the population stabilized? As Meadows put it, the equation is imperfect, complicated, troubling — and that may be the only way we can talk about this. Nor do I expect to like the answers I get in many cases. And I think any solution will be at best an imperfect compromise. The real test of how committed we are to preventing disaster will be how we act when confronted with unpleasant truths that hurt us — whether, in the blur of our hurt, we can look past our personal feelings to the consequences of others, whether we can recognize that we don't want to know or acknowledge all truths, but that we have to begin in honesty, even if in pain.

Understanding the Demographic Transition

Though there are more questions than answers, there are some things we do know about population, and one of those things is that we are already in the midst of a dramatic, world-changing move toward a smaller population. The term "demographic transition" describes the movement of human populations into a roughly steady state. Generally speaking, there is a rough pattern in population trends all around the world. First populations rise, then they stabilize and begin to fall.

The classic argument of environmentalists has been that population has risen in conjunction with energy growth and the green revolution, and that the cause of the world's move from a world population of around a billion to 6.5 billion at present has been surpluses of food and energy. This is a compelling vision in many ways, and graphs showing the dovetailing of population growth and energy growth are commonplace. It also implies that our population changes have nothing to do with politics or choices, but simply happen in a biological vacuum — food comes, we eat, we have babies. Again, there are no actors here — I am suspicious of this model precisely because, like I=PAT, it conceals power relations.

And I wonder whether we have not mistaken correlation for causality if we assume that the quantity of available food is the defining factor in our population. In fact, population rises began before cheap energy and the green revolution made their way into many nations. For example, in the US, the demographic transition took place over a period of a century — in 1830, the average American woman had eight children, and European visitors to the new country reported amazement at the average family size. Agricultural production was growing and would continue more or less steadily. But by 1850, the average number of children had fallen to five, and by 1930 to 2.5. During periods of both food surpluses and limits, birth rates fell steadily. This was not caused by any of the things we assume to be the root of reproductive changes. It wasn't caused by birth control (which was largely unavailable); some of it was shaped by infanticide and abortion, but this was a comparatively small percentage. Nor was it caused by food shortages. During most of the period in question the US experienced booming harvests. By every measure based on a simplistic relationship between food and population, our birthrate should have been increasing, but it was not. Nor was this happening in isolation; other nations began their demographic transitions in the same period.

We don't usually talk about the US when we talk about population or the demographic transition because it doesn't fit our contemporary assumptions and models, but we should. We should also talk about India. Again, the conventional assumption is that India's population grew because of food surpluses and because of reduced mortality. But, as Vandana Shiva points out, the facts are otherwise.

> Population growth is not a cause of the environmental crisis but one aspect of it.... *Until 1600 India's population was between 100 and 125 million; in 1830 it remained stable. Then it began to rise: 130 million in 1845; 175 million in 1855; 194 million in 1867; 255 million in 1871. The beginning of the "population explosion" dovetailed neatly with the expansion of British rule in India, when the people's resources,*

rights and livelihoods were confiscated.... What is also ignored in this "carrying capacity" discourse is the history of colonial intervention in people's reproductive behavior. This intervention was initially motivated, as in Europe, by the need for more disposable labour, labour freed from subsistence activities and forced to work productively *on plantations, farms, roads, in mines and so on for the benefit of foreign capital. (Shiva and Mies, 284–85)*

I've emphasized part of this analysis in regular type, because I think it is so terrifically important. In India, in the US, in Europe, the demographic transition wasn't simply a mindless eating our way into large populations, but was in part a managed and created problem, a product of our industrial disaster. When we focus on population out of context, we miss the point, and we end up blaming women for their choices, choices that are generally made in response to conditions created around them. Shiva argues that population growth is less about consumption of resources than about top-down influences.

Right now, the same demographic shift that the US underwent in the 19th and early 20th centuries is occurring all over the world. Generally speaking, in the early stages of the demographic transition, birth rates were at some sort of equilibrium. Many population analysts claim that this was simply because mortality rates were so high, but study after study suggests this is not true. People were managing their fertility; women were able to make choices about how many children to have.

The demographic transition began in the 19th century in the rich world, but didn't happen in much of the poor world until the mid-20th century or later. Generally speaking, however, the poor world has undergone a much faster demographic transition — in many cases, radical change has come in less than 50 years, compared to 100 or more in Europe and North America. And because in many places in the poor world there has been considerable instability, the factors that lead to a transition haven't been consistently available — so the fact that the whole world's fertility rate has dropped dramatically is quite remarkable.

The fact that many poor nations have managed to reduce their fertility so dramatically is astonishing. We all know that rich-world nations such as Japan and Italy have a TFR well below replacement, but more than half of all poor nations are below replacement rate, and the rest are following. The highest reproductive rates are in sub-Saharan Africa, and those too are following the pattern of other poor nations but are 20 years behind. Sub-Saharan Africa now has a TFR of 5.0, down from 6.3 in 1990, an enormous reduction in less than 20 years. Latin America is now at 2.6 as a whole, and has nearly halved in the same short period. All over the world, population rates are generally falling much faster than even the most radical demographers expected.

What's most interesting about the demographic transition is that modern-style birth control is not the defining factor. Don't misunderstand me, I don't in any sense mean to imply that it is unimportant, but its impact is smaller than we often assume. We can see this by looking back at the United States, where disseminating any information about birth control was illegal during most of the time fertility rates were dropping. Despite a widespread increase in birth control availability after World War II, American birth rates rose to produce the baby boom — they rose above the level they were at during the age of the Comstock laws that prohibited the use of birth control. Medical birth control is estimated to affect about 15 percent of demographic decline — but that's a comparatively small percentage.

The reason women were able to limit their own fertility before medical contraception was available was that women had a greater degree of familiarity with their bodies. Even today natural family planning, a method of temperature-based birth control, has a fairly high rate of success, as does extended breastfeeding and traditional means of sexual limitation. Modern society has given us greater degrees of surety about contraception, but it has also put the power to control women's bodies in the hands of doctors and the medical establishment, and made access to fertility control, in many cases, a function of wealth. This too is something we will have to rethink as we grow less wealthy.

In their book *Understanding Reproductive Change: Kenya, Tamil Nadu, Punjab, Costa Rica,* editors Bertil Egero and Mikail Hammerskjold observe that fertility change seems largely unlinked to contraception access. That is, people tend to have about the number of children they want and need, regardless of access to birth control. So the question becomes, how do we make it desirable to have fewer children?

And the answer to that question is that, generally speaking, people make fairly rational choices, based on their personal economics, their personal situation, their desire to have a child of a particular sex, the family size they want, their need for someone to help them in old age. Time and time again, studies demonstrate that women worldwide mostly choose their family size by what is best for them and their family. When circumstances change and give them positive incentives to want fewer children, they make that choice.

One of the most misleading things we have done is to imagine that a decrease in TFR is primarily a product of wealth. The argument is often made because the demographic transition occurred first in rich-world nations. But the current, ongoing demographic transition is not, as it is commonly thought, primarily a feature of the rich world. Poor nations as diverse as Albania, Costa Rica, Cuba, Sri Lanka, Thailand and the Philippines have rapidly declining birth rates. And what factors do most of these nations have in common?

Generally speaking, basic commodities are widely available — that is, people get to eat. For example, a 1996 USAID report documents a direct link between subsidizing rice in Sri Lanka and a drop in TFR from 3.1 to 2.0 in less than a decade. Basic access to medical care is widely available. Women have high literacy rates and political power. Women are comparatively well protected from rape and can choose their husbands. A 1994 study by Yale Economist Paul Schultz found that female literacy was perhaps the most defining factor in TFR in poor nations. In India, the state of Kerala, with a near-100 percent female literacy rate, has a 1.7 TFR, compared to a 4.1 TFR in regions of the same country with a 30 percent literacy rate.

All those individual factors add up to what Jeremy Seabrook rightly observes is "security." If children are the only safety net you have access to, then you will have children as a form of security and wealth. If there are other options, you will turn to those. Education represents the possibility of work if a husband dies, knowledge of laws, access to information on medical care and hygiene — it is not in itself a reproductive constraint but an aid to security. What most people want when they have children are security, pleasure and comfort. If two children can do that as well or better than five, they will have two.

• • •

Consider having a midwife delivery or training as a midwife or childbirth assistant (doula) to serve families in your area.

• • •

So to stabilize and begin to reduce population all over the world, we need to improve women's security. But most of the things we need to do are neither expensive nor energy intensive. Education can be human powered and local or rely on school buses to get children over long distances. Support for the elderly can be as low input and simple as a neighbor checking up, providing food and assistance, or it can be as energy intensive and expensive as Social Security. Reproductive medical care can be local, inexpensive and woman-centered. Generally speaking, the demographic transition occurs as a result of a certain degree of wealth — that is, there's now money for infrastructure improvements such as water systems and sewers. But very poor nations can and sometimes do make these solutions a priority; as desperately poor Tanzania under Julius Miserere did.

Although all this information about the demographic transition is useful, we cannot ignore the fact that every American is the equivalent of 30 of the world's poor people in terms of consumption. Though population is a consequence of and a contributing factor to our environmental crisis, affluence, imperialism and consumption are the root causes. As long as we talk about population in comparative isolation, we will be dividing the world into the "good" Global North who are lowering their birthrates and the "bad" Global South who have too many children and whose children are immigrants to our nations. This division is both essentially false and has the effect that the people who have the least power and the fewest choices are penalized for decisions made by those with the most choices and the most wealth.

People in the rich world must get our consumption down. We have been phrasing the problem as though the poor of the world are the source of our difficulties — for example, economists have said that the Chinese are "eating the world" because they want cars and meat and we don't have enough to go around. But it is not the Chinese who are devouring the world. The average American uses eight times more energy and resources than the average Chinese person. It is we who have devoured our share, our children's share, our poor neighbors' share and are considering stabbing our fork at the Chinese man who has just come to the table.

• • •

Eat a little less over the holidays and donate the cost of what you are not eating to your local food pantry.

• • •

Our consumption must be in proportion to our population impact. There are some groups in the US who consider having children to be a religious imperative — the Amish for example. There are also always going to be people who have imperfect control over their fertility. If people like the Amish are going to have four or five children, if people like me are going to have imperfect control over our fertility, we absolutely must consume vastly less than people who choose to have one child or none at all. At this point, large families are still statistical outliers, and we can absorb some of them — if we reduce our consumption in relationship to our family size.

For example, Miranda Edel, my Riot for Austerity co-founder, and I both have large families. By reducing our energy use to one tenth of the average American's, my four kids will use half the energy one average American child will. That is not to endorse anyone's family size, but it should be observed that the larger your family, the more urgent it is that you live sustainably.

I have no wish to see people compelled reproductively — we don't want to go to a world of forcible abortions or sterilization, but I would be glad to see policy initiatives that tie energy rations to a family of four. Those who have large numbers of biological children would receive only as much energy as a family with two children was entitled to. I personally would rather have my kids than the energy, and I know that I and other people could reduce our impact correspondingly. I believe we should also cap the child tax credit at two children. Since cost is the overwhelming deciding factor for most families when having children, this would present a further incentive not to have kids, and allow those who wish for children to pay the price.

It may sound as though achieving a worldwide population stabilization is impossible — as though we must fix all human problems first. But that's not the case. In fact, it turns out that the total investment in reducing world fertility levels voluntarily is comparatively low, because most of the changes are human powered, low input, and comparatively cheap. That is, most of what would be required would simply be to prioritize these things. Fossil fuels, for example, are not required to have small local schools — the US had its highest literacy rate ever in New England in the colonial era, long before the discovery of most fossil fuels; and the tiny, impoverished state of Kerala has a higher literacy rate than the US. Small amounts of fossil and renewable energy are required for some basic medications, but as we can see from the timing of the European and North American examples, the demographic transition in the rich world was mostly not a product of fossil-fuel based medicine, but a result of improvements in nutrition, hygiene and access to food and water. Political power for women is not a product of fossil fuels either. States can far better afford price supports for local farmers and public cafeterias where prices are kept low than they can afford war, famine relief, etc.

Can we enable a population stabilization in the face of Peak Oil and Climate Change? Absolutely. We are going to need to make massive changes in our infrastructure. Thus far, much of the discussion of what to do about Peak Oil and Climate Change has been about trains and renewable energy, new economies and new extraction technologies. And as long as the conversation stays there, we'll be missing the point. The reality is that the most important projects we can invest in are education, health care and social welfare. But what would be required is that we reallocate wealth from rich nations to poor ones, something that would require, among other things, a real reduction in worldwide emphasis on short-term, national interests.

The Tragedy of the Bathroom

What would be a rational policy to take on childbearing? That is, what personal choices are better than mine? What should an environmentally responsible person do?

Well, one choice you can make is simply to have one child. Jim Merkel, author of *Radical Simplicity*, points out that if everyone on earth did this, we'd reduce the world's population to 1 billion people by the end of this century. Another possibility, with a similar impact, would be for everyone to have two children, but to wait until they are 33 years old to begin having them. Because the age at which you have children is as important as the number of children, it is possible have a two-child family with only a slightly greater impact than a one-child family.

Sound strange? Imagine for simplicity's sake that there are only two people in the world, and everyone has a lifespan of 80 years. In scenario one, the couple has their first child at 20, and their children continue the tradition. So at year one of this scenario, there are two people in the world. At year 20, the number rises to three. At 40, when the couple's first grandchild is born, the number goes up to four. At 60, it rises to five, with the first great-grandchild. At 80, another child is born, but the original couple dies, bringing the number back to four. At 100, the population stabilizes at four, as another child is born but one more adult dies. (No, I don't know who these people are marrying.).

If the same couple had had two children each time, here's what it would look like. Two people at year one, four at year 20, six at year 40, eight at year 60, and it would rise to 10 and immediately fall back to eight at year 80, and remain at eight, not too surprisingly double the number of people in scenario one. But let's look at it again with the age spacing changed.

Imagine the same scenario, only this time they have two children, starting in their early 30s. At year one there are two people. At year 20 there are two people. At year 33 there are three people, and at 36, four people. At year 66 we're up to five, and at 69 we go up to six. At year 80 we're back to four people, and at 99 back to six for a few years. The population will average at five, only one more than the original scenario.

Except that fertility rates fall steadily after age 35, one could get precisely the same result from everyone having one child at 20 as having everyone have two children at 40. But the latter isn't medically possible in many cases.

Still, delayed childbearing is as powerful a tool as the number of children we have. Ideally, what we'd do is a combination of these approaches — work to avoid teenage pregnancy, make education available and encourage young men and women to wait to have children until they are older, more economically stable and more mature, while also voluntarily reducing family size.

But the most powerful thing we can do to reduce our impact on the earth is to reduce our total consumption of resources. It takes generations, obviously, to make any change in the number of people on the earth. But it takes only a short time to change what we use and how we consume resources. And this, perhaps, is the thing that I think gets most lost in discussions of population — the simple truth that while every additional person may alter the nature of a "fair share," it doesn't mean it isn't possible for people to still take only a fair and just share.

• • •

Breastfeed your child. The World Health Organization recommends that women nurse until "at least" two and the worldwide average age of weaning is four.

• • •

Dr. Albert Bartlett, who produces a famous and excellent series of lectures on population, quotes Isaac Asimov in a metaphor I find particularly distasteful, despite my enormous respect for Dr. Bartlett. This quotation is reproduced in many places, including in Richard Heinberg's (who is not an old man) latest book on energy and the environment, *Peak Everything*.

Here's the quote as it is offered up by Dr. Bartlett:

> *I'd like to use what I call my bathroom metaphor. If two people live in an apartment, and they have two bathrooms then they both have freedom of the bathroom. You can go to the bathroom anytime you want, stay as long as you want, for whatever you need, and everyone believes in the freedom of the bathroom. It should be right there in the constitution. But if you have twenty people in the apartment and two bathrooms, then no matter how much every person believes in the freedom of the bathroom, there is no such thing. You have to set up times for each person; you have to bang on the door, "aren't you through yet?" and so on. He concluded with one of the most profound observations I've seen in years, he says, in the same way, "...democracy cannot survive overpopulation. Human dignity can not survive over population. Convenience and decency cannot survive over population. As you put more and more people into the world, the value of life not only declines it disappears. It doesn't matter if some one dies, the more people there are, the less one individual matters.*

And so, central to the things that we must do is to recognize that population growth is the immediate cause of all our resource and environmental crisis". (Heinberg, Peak Everything, *120)*

Now in the most basic terms, Drs. Bartlett and Asimov are correct. There are real, material limits on the world. If there were 100 billion people on the earth, none of us could have a large enough share of resources to survive. With 10 people on the earth, what we did could hardly matter — no 10 people could use enough resources to make a difference. With 6.5 billion people (and probably 8.5 or 9 billion by the end of this century) we are struggling to find a way to share resources justly. And at some point we will run up against real and material limits on our ability to share fairly. But this quotation implies that *any* degree of sharing or constraint on what you can do is an attack on dignity. It implies that we're already long past "a fair share" and that other people's mere desire to use some of "your" stuff is an assault on your rights and on democracy. That part is just plain wrong.

And I can say this because I've lived the tragedy of the bathroom. That is, I've lived in houses where five to ten of us shared a single bathroom. And despite the claim that doing so is inevitably destructive, it doesn't have to be. My memories of those households are very fond, and the bathroom simply wasn't that big a deal. And all of the people in those houses were able to comfortably accommodate one another with little or no difficulty. It did require that we acknowledge and respond to one another, that we place less priority on our modesty and recognize that the half-hour shower was not just. But it did none of us any harm. Billions of people in the world know how to share. In fact, that's one of the most basic things we teach our children — that sharing is an essential human behavior, one that creates dignity.

Now, it is true that eventually, if there are no limits on the number of people sharing it, the bathroom will get awfully crowded. Two bathrooms for 20 is one thing, two bathrooms for 1000 is another. I am not arguing that population is irrelevant. What troubles me about this, however, is something more subtle, because I don't think it's an accident that the comparison is between "I can always use the bathroom as much as I want" and "I would be slightly inconvenienced by having to share the bathroom." I think the implication of this argument is "dignity is equivalent to wealth, to my own private bathroom."

Not only can human dignity survive sharing your bathroom with a lot more people than we Western folk are accustomed to, but I actually believe the contrary — that real dignity begins at the point that we recognize that other people have rights to the bathroom too and we find a means of accommodating them.

Consider another version of "the tragedy of the bathroom" that Vandana Shiva and Maria Mies quote in their book *Ecofeminism*. They quote a local family-planning worker in Bangladesh as telling their clients,

> *You see, there are only 9 cabins on the steamer launch.... In the nine cabins only 18 people can travel. The ticket is expensive, so only rich people travel in the cabins. The rest of the common passengers travel on the deck. The latrine facility is only provided for the cabin passengers. But sometimes the cabin passengers allow them to use the latrine because they are afraid that if the poor deck passengers get angry, they might go down and make a hole in the launch. Then the launch will sink: they will die, no doubt, but the rich cabin passengers will not survive either. So, my dear sisters, do not give birth to more children as they cause a problem for the cabin passengers. (Mies and Shiva, 280)*

Try and imagine someone reading this story aloud in place of the story Asimov tells! Both, of course, relate the problem of basic biological necessity to population, but how absurd does the one make the other look? And yet, they are both the same story, and both of them arise from Garret Hardin's concept of "The Tragedy of the Commons" which argues that when resources are shared and managed collectively, no one has any incentive to care for them. In the simplest sense, this is false because it ignores examples of well-managed commons, including the public grazing commons of New England, which often were managed quite successfully. We can also observe that privatization of resources has given us enormous incentive to exploit resources. In *Peak Everything*, Richard Heinberg quotes analyst William Stanton offering a version of Hardin's argument about population and resources. Stanton is a classic Hardinist, saying,

> *Compassion is a luxury available to people enjoying peace and plenty, who are confident of their place in society.... They apply it to the hungry, needy or oppressed. It makes them feel virtuous, until the needy try to take advantage of them.... (Quoted in Heinberg,* Peak Everything, *117)*

Hardin himself is famous for the lifeboat metaphor, which argues that we should provide no aid to the poor of the world. While Heinberg is manifestly unready to support Bartlett and Stanton's hardest-edged solutions — and says specifically "I'm not ready to give up humanitarianism" — the very fact that Heinberg ignores any of the critics of these kinds of analysis suggests a broad sympathy with the larger narrative, that selfish breeders are annoying the cabin passengers.

As deeply as I admire Heinberg, I find that troubling because it plays into our deepest fears about hard times. When Heinberg uncritically quotes Stanton's claims about compassion, for example, he implies that compassion really is a product of wealth and privilege, and he ignores that most poor societies share more and donate more of their income to even poorer people than we do. He ignores the fact that religious doctrines of compassion and folk stories requiring generosity grew up not in suburban rich nations, but among desperately poor communities.

I have spent most of the past two years asking, Can the world feed and house nine billion people without burning fossil fuels? And I am increasingly convinced that the answer is a tentative yes, although not forever — we can feed the world, and enable ourselves to reduce our population gradually, without mass disaster. But it involves all of us accepting that we live in this world with all these other people and that that means that there is no place for rich people. We must share far more equally.

• • •

Up your charitable donations. Sometimes we get more by what we give away than what we do for money.

• • •

We must all accept that our own allotment of meat, fossil energy and other valuable, polluting resources is much smaller than it has been in the West. And I believe equally passionately that this is no tragedy, that we can indeed share the planet passably well if we so choose — not without limits, but allowing for voluntary changes. But "The Tragedy of the Bathroom" changes the terms of the debate from, "How can we share what we have?" to "It is too late to share, and others are taking mine."

The bathroom metaphor equates "freedom" with "no limits." It says that freedom and dignity are constructs of privilege and lack of constraint. That is, you have the perfect freedom of the bathroom when you never have to wait or accommodate anyone else, adapt to or respect anyone else's needs. But that is not what freedom is. And I think this is an important point for our society as a whole, because our consumer culture tells us over and over again that freedom is the ability to have whatever you want, whenever you want it.

Freedom is imagined as "freedom of choice" and thus is the equivalent of 63 choices of soda on the grocery store aisle. But in fact, we might better describe freedom from want, or freedom from repression — freedoms that work only when other people are aware of and attentive to the needs of others.

The bathroom example perpetuates the "freedom is choice" notion — that being free means never having to say, "Excuse me."

I think that's truly and deeply wrong, and if we think this way about the population issue, we are perpetuating our most foolish habits of thought. Freedom is the right to assert our wants and needs in a world where others exist, and the right to have them respected; but it is not the right to never have to accommodate others or to sacrifice any of our wants. That's not freedom, but greed. We all experience greed, but we need not valorize our worst and most foolish assumptions by calling them natural and inevitable.

Jim Merkel, author of *Radical Simplicity*, uses the ecological footprint to analyze what kind of population the world can support. He argues,

> When people would say, "Population is the problem, there are just too many of us," it raised my hackles. I'd respond, "Yes, but if we became as skilled at extracting life quality from less land as the people of Kerala, 60 percent of the global bioproductivity could be left wild (and still maintain the present population). Then population wouldn't be such a big deal. The high income countries need to consume less." (Merkel, 183)

Merkel goes on to say that we need to do both — reduce population and consumption. Merkel's point is important: we are not yet in the position of having to share our bathroom with so many people that it is impossible to accommodate one another — it is merely challenging to learn to do so. We can live (with careful and wise management) at the 20 person for two bathroom stage that Bartlett quotes. And that is not a tragedy or a serious constriction of human freedom, dignity and access to justice — it is merely a situation where we have to share.

Moreover, using biology and silly metaphors to imply that sharing is impossible naturalizes our resistance to giving up our own privileges — it makes our unwillingness to reallocate some of our wealth to others seem natural, because, after all, we are unfree and burdened, unable to provide others with dignity because of the tragic experience of overpopulation. That, of course, is errant nonsense. Human beings can choose the society we want to live in. We have the capacity to alter our way of being, and extend our hands and open our bathroom doors to others. There is nothing inevitable or biological about our refusal to share, nor anything tragic about our having to shit and get off the pot so someone else can use it.

We need to recognize that our own assumptions about population sometimes contain some not-very-productive underlying thoughts. I would argue that we need to replace those thoughts with their logical opposites: the idea that human dignity begins at the very moment that you recognize that other people are fully real, as real as you are, and at the moment you begin drawing your identity and sense of freedom not from the amount of time you get in the bathroom but from the society that you create and the way you manage your constraints.

The culture of our society is created by how we manage limited resources like bathrooms. Culture is cool — a thousand societies can come up with a thousand different rules. It turns out that many people like and value their cultures, even the parts of their culture that represent limitations. We like the rules that limit what we can do on a sports field or the rules that tell us how to behave at weddings or funerals — we are comforted by self-imposed limits.

What does impinge upon human dignity is the scale of management — global structures are less humane and wise than local structures. Though larger populations do mean a smaller share is available to each of us, we can manage our resources fairly if we have real and democratic control over them. Your dignity does depend on your being able to choose how you use your share and on being able to expect the culture to help you receive your own fair share. And that's easier when governments are smaller and people have more democratic power. As we saw above, population is absolutely about power — so is consumption.

That is, if we're all going to have to share the bathroom, we're better off having a lot of small bathrooms that are organized and maintained by small groups of users for everyone's benefit than to have one, centralized toilet in the middle of the earth and have everyone stand around and wait in line.

·

SEVEN

The Permaculture of Family

The truth is that man needs work even more than he needs a wage. Those who seek the welfare of the workers should be less anxious to obtain good pay, good holidays and good pensions for them than good work, which is the first of their goods. For the object of work is not so much to make objects as to make men. A man makes himself by making something useful.
— MAHATMA GANDHI

In expressing love we belong among the undeveloped countries.
— SAUL BELLOW

Home Economics and the "Mommy Wars"

NOMINALLY, AT LEAST, I'M AN AT-HOME MOTHER, WRITER AND SOMETIMES farmer. That is, I don't "go" to work; I don't wear pantyhose; and one of us is at home with the kids virtually all the time. What paid work I do, I do from home. We are fortunate that a combination of good luck, frugality and having bought our house with extended family has enabled my husband to do much of his work from home and not to work horribly long hours. Because Eric is paid by the class, we try hard to need as little money as possible. The less we need, the less he has to work, and the more time we have together.

Now, those of you who are not parents probably don't really know about the "Mommy Wars." That's the official name for a really stupid, cruel conflict, mostly played out among women who otherwise would be natural allies, over whether it is better to stay at home with your children or go to a job and work. Some working mothers level the charge that at-home mothers are dumb, or wasting themselves and their educations, or that they aren't contributing anything to society, and that their own time is more valuable than that of women who do not go to a job. Some stay-at-home mothers assert that women who go to jobs are selfish, that they don't care about their children, that most women don't "need" to work and only do so for luxuries, and that they don't raise their own children. People who rightly argue that children need their parents are set up against people who rightly argue that children need health insurance.

Everyone involved slings around statistics about daycare, the number of children who grow up to become axe murderers and the cost of living. As could be expected, no resolution is ever achieved. People who should work together find that they can't, and everyone gets their feelings hurt. I've been on both ends of this. The conflict is foolish and petty on both sides, fueled by people who are unhappy, and rightly so, with the choices available to them.

Of course, the whole discussion not only makes everyone miserable, it misses the point — or several points. One of them is that neither party really has what they need. All the working mothers I know agonize over leaving their children, often with people who do not love their children as much as they do. All of them struggle to find adequate childcare that deals with the realities of working life. Most of them are also deeply ambivalent about how much they like working — that is, many of them (including me) feel a deep-seated sense that they *should* want to be home with their kids every minute of the day, even though they like their jobs, and particularly like the community and connections they find there. Many of the women I know who work full time are exhausted and frustrated with the things they can't do, and they gain time by hiring out as many things as possible — they eat take out and have someone else clean their house and tend their yard. But they never feel that the things they pay others to do are done as well as they would do them. And often, to be blunt, they are right — the health of their children is sometimes compromised by the fast food and their family structure by their shortcuts.

That this isn't just Mom's responsibility, but Dad's and society's too, doesn't change the ugly truth. Women who work often don't spend much time with their spouses alone, and much of the time they spend with their children is spent driving places. Everyone reports a great deal of stress, a desire for more time together, and anger and frustration that this is not enabled by their jobs and their lives. For poor working women, there is often no choice, no job satisfaction and no ambivalence. Many of them believe that feminism sold them a bill of goods, claiming to give them something positive, and mostly doubled their workload. And they are not wholly wrong.

For stay-at-home mothers, there is a sense of isolation, the loss of the community they had at work. Because this is the less common choice, it is often difficult to find company. The economic pressure for a two-household economy is very high, and for many poorer women the choice to stay home means a loss of security — no insurance or poor insurance, no economic safety net if something happens to the working spouse, or in case of divorce. Many have little time with their husbands, because the husbands have to work long hours to compensate economically for having only one income. And being home is sometimes boring for women — they secretly admit that they sometimes wonder if the accusations that there is something wrong with them because they are willing to do this dull work are true. This is not conducive to self-esteem.

In short, both sets of mothers are often having a lousy time. I asked 40 women I knew what the best choice was, and virtually all of them said there were no really good options for them.

But I would argue that the question of whether women should work outside the home is the wrong question entirely. The right question is how much power we should give to the formal economy, and its presumptions, and to "public" life. At least as important as the question of what women with children should do is the far less commonly asked question, Should fathers work outside the home? And almost no one asks, as writer Wendell Berry does, whether it is good for marriages that husbands and wives work apart, outside the home.

The question for everyone then becomes, How much should we value the work we do outside the home, and how much should we value the work we do in it? That question, I suspect, might begin to get us somewhere that Mommy Wars cannot. Perhaps it might even take us to a good answer.

Berry answers this question in no uncertain terms in his essay, "Feminism, the Body and the Machine." He says, in answer to critics who accused him of sexism for having a wife who worked in the home and typed his essays,

> *I know that I am in dangerous territory, and so I had better be plain: what I have to say about marriage and household I mean to apply to men as much as to women. I do not believe that there is anything better to do than to make one's marriage and household, whether one is a man or a woman. I do not believe that "employment outside the home" is as valuable or important or satisfying as employment at home, for either men or women. It*

is clear from my experience as a teacher, for example, that chil-
dren need an ordinary association with both *parents. They need*
to see their parents at work, they need, at first, to play at the
work they see their parents doing, and then they need to work
with their parents.... My interest is not to quarrel with individ-
uals, men or women, who work away from home, but rather to
ask why we should consider this general working away from
home to be a desirable state of things, either for people or for mar-
riage, for our society or for our country.... But for the sake of
argument, let us suppose that whatever work my wife does, as a
member of our marriage and household, she does both as a full
economic partner and as her own boss, and let us suppose that
the economy we have is adequate to our needs. Why, granting
that supposition, should anyone assume that my wife would
increase her freedom or dignity or satisfaction by becoming the
employee of a boss, who would be in turn also a corporate under-
ling and in no sense a partner? (Berry, 68–69)

Will you forgive me for saying that I think Berry's is a damned good question? He goes on to observe that what is bad for his wife is also bad for her
husband — that men do not receive a greater share of independence, dignity or happiness by working out of the home, away from their spouses and
families, in the dehumanizing environment of corporations.

We are accustomed to debating whether the breakdown of the family
stems from the habit of women going out to work. But if the family broke
down thoroughly, it was around the time the baby boomer children were
young — the levels of alienation and misery, depression, anxiety and family
disruption among boomers are radically higher than among the previous
generation — and many of those families had stay-at-home mothers. So perhaps we need to look, instead, at what fathers were doing.

All of this focus on the impact of whether women work misses the basic
point that for most of human history, children spent much more time with
both parents than they do now, and that many of the negatives we attribute
to the separation of children from their mothers might equally or more be
said of the separation of children from their fathers.

Now, as my friend Mea reminds me, it is also true that in the past many
more children lived in blended families because of high death rates, and also
in extended family structures. So perhaps a more accurate way to describe
this would be that children mostly lived in families that included both adult
men and adult women who cared for them, loved them and modeled adult

work and behavior. I will, for the purposes of this conversation refer to them as parents, without assuming that all of the people taking primary parental roles were biologically related to the child.

Until 200 years ago, a vast majority of all children spent most of their lives with both parents every single day. In hunter-gatherer societies, the tribe often traveled together, and because hunting was generally a less common activity than gathering, male hunters often had considerable time to spend with their children. In most such societies in existence today, men do a considerable amount of parenting, especially of older children.

As agriculture came to predominate, children continued to spend their days with their parents. Young, nursing children were often with their mother, but by the age of weaning (four or five in most traditional societies, unless a younger sibling pushed it ahead), children might work or play alongside their fathers for part of every day. Boys would join their fathers in traditionally male work, but even daughters would often help in the barn or around the farm. Everyone would reconvene for regular meals, and the family would spend Sabbaths and festivals together. Remember, most societies worked much less than we do, so such interludes were frequent.

. . .

Teenagers need meaningful work and to feel that adults care about them and have confidence in them.

. . .

As the percentage of people living on farms and in small towns decreased, more separation arose, but it is worth noting that as recently as 1920 or 1930, nearly half of the US population farmed, ran small local businesses, or worked within a mile of their homes. All of which meant that children were involved in their parents' daily lives in ways that are hard to imagine right now. A family that ran a shop would have children playing in the back. By seven or eight, children would take turns assisting customers and stocking shelves. The family would often convene for meals (children were allowed to walk home for lunch from school), and children would join their parents in their work after school.

The level at which the family was integrated into one another's lives is hard for most Americans to imagine now; and it is not a coincidence that though the past was always imperfect, overwhelmingly this was part of a more sustainable, more environmentally sound form of family life than we have at present, as well as one that led to greater psychological happiness. Living at a scale that enables integration is almost always a better choice environmentally — but after decades of living apart, unsustainably, we have created a population of people who valorize apartness and who fear closeness.

Women say, "I wouldn't know what to do with myself if I was trapped with my kids all day." Men take their identity from their jobs, rather than their relationships. Children say, "I would never want to live that close to my family." And aging parents say, "I don't want to depend on my children." People don't want their neighbors to drop by, or "know their business."

We have created not only physical dependencies on cheap energy, but psychological ones, so that no matter how much harm our dependencies do, we now fear to live any other way. In her book *Holy Days,* writer Lis Harris observes how shocking it was to hear both boys and girls at a school for Orthodox Jewish children answer the classic What do you want to be when you grow up? question, with "A mother" and "A father." We are accustomed to taking identity from our careers. Only unusually "backward" communities like Chasidic Jews and the Amish seem to resist this convention and define themselves based on relationships.

In some senses, we have adopted a new theory of "separate spheres" — it is different from the Victorian notion by the same name, but structurally very similar. The Victorians imagined this in terms of gender roles — one had the "angel in the house" and the man out at work (a division that actually described significantly less than half the population during the actual Victorian Era), and each was supposed to have their own role. Now the division is not made by gender, but by age and work. Parents go off to their own separate jobs, away from their homes, and spend long hours there; or at best, one parent stays home and the other is away for much of the week. The children routinely spend long hours at school and activities designed to educate and entertain them, provided by professionalized adults. Children themselves, including siblings, are divided up by age, so that older children and younger ones rarely meet or interact.

The spheres are so separate that they rarely overlap — friends of ours, both with important careers, acknowledge that at times the only communication they have with one another is to list the necessary information about the children before one heads to bed, the other to childcare. The children, the parents, all are deemed to have important work to do, and it is almost never done together. Even leisure time is rarely conjoined. On weekends everyone has separate obligations and activities — one child has a birthday party to which siblings are not invited; another has sports practice; mother runs errands; father shuttles the children about.

This is not, I think, a good way to run a railroad — or more accurately, a family. We tend to focus on the costs to children, but Berry's emphasis that this is not good for marriages is important as well, given the nation's appalling divorce rate. The divorce rate has an enormous cost for children as well, of course, and the two things cannot be separated. No one has yet succeeded in finding a cure for the fact that we are bad at staying together. Is some of it perhaps the pernicious influence of the industrial economy that separates us and keeps us from creating the bonds that shared work and shared domestic interest create? Is it possible that marriages are better when husband and wife share whole and integrated life together? I can speak only from my own experience, but my marriage is happier when my husband and I are together than when we are apart. We both enjoy our work, but our preference is always for more time together with each other and our children.

I cannot say what impact thousands of years of human beings living together and working with their children had upon our biology or our psychology or our instincts, but it seems not wholly coincidental that an enormous body of unhappiness arose in our society precisely as parents began to separate from their children routinely and as childhood became a period enacted in isolation from family and without meaningful ways of contributing to the household, family and domestic economies. Children seek meaning. I think this may be the one great lost truth of childhood. We forget, as we become adults, how much children long to matter in the world at large.

I can remember from my own adolescence a passionate desire to do things that would matter to adults, to enter the world of adult work in some useful way, which was far more important to me than simply entering the cash economy. I noticed in my peers similar desires — and a willingness to engage in destructive meaning-making, if that was the only way into the adult world. Segregating children into their own separate spheres of school, music lessons, sports and homework is, at the very least, an experiment on a couple of generations of children that violates everything that human history has taught us about what makes a strong and healthy family. And it represents a tremendous change in how much we actually value the idea of a strong and healthy family. Now we are willing to sacrifice that in order to have other things.

The sphere we value least, of course, is the domestic one. We see it as a repository of our wealth — a home is a place to decorate, but it is not a place to do good work in. It is not a place that makes us better able to live in the world, but the thing that keeps us running on the rat treadmill to pay the mortgage and keep up the repairs. And because "labor saving" devices have stripped much of what was valuable and interesting from domestic work, home labor is boring. We are no longer engaged in the absolutely urgent process of feeding and clothing ourselves, nurturing and loving and protecting others. That happens at work, where we make the money to buy food and provide security.

Many of the laborsaving devices have been proven not to save us much time — or any at all if you count the time to earn the money to run and maintain them. A classic example is the vacuum cleaner. Research shows that when vacuum cleaners were developed, carpets got bigger and standards got higher, and time spent cleaning floors remained essentially the same. But what the reduction of domestic work to cleaning did was take away the fun and excitement, the meaning and urgency, and make it seem valueless, something always to be relieved by technology.

Helena Norberg-Hodge documents the ways that this happened in Ladakh, where she witnessed the coming of the industrial economy and the home/work division in a society that had previously looked like the society from which we came, at least in the sense that fathers and mothers both worked at home,

> Women ... do not earn money for their work, so they are no longer seen as "productive." Their work is not recognized as part of the gross national product.... Despite their new dominant role, men also clearly suffer as a result of the breakdown of family and community ties. They are deprived of contact with children. When they are young, the new macho images prevents them from showing affection, while in later life as fathers, their work keeps them away from home.... In the traditional culture children benefitted not only from continuous contact with both mother and father, but also from a way of life in which different age groups constantly interacted. It was quite natural for older children to feel a sense of responsibility for the younger ones. A younger child in turn looked up with respect and admiration, seeking to imitate the older ones. Growing up was a natural, non-competitive learning process.... Now children are split into different age groups at school. This sort of leveling has a very destructive effect. By artificially creating social units in which everyone is the same age, the ability to help and learn from each other is greatly reduced. Instead, conditions for competition are automatically created.... Now there is a tendency to spend time exclusively with one's peers. As a result, a mutual intolerance between young and old emerges. Young children nowadays have

less and less contact with their grandparents who often remain
behind in the village. (Norberg-Hodge, 126–7)

Norberg-Hodge documents how profoundly perceptions of what is valuable affect us. We view domestic work as unimportant, and thus women who do it are demeaned, in Ladakh and in the US. And because in most households, whether they work outside the home or not, women do the domestic labor — either themselves, or by paying poorer women — the work itself is seen as demeaning.

No wonder women who make different choices are so hostile to one another — one group attempts, against impossible odds to redeem something that the entire culture and economy attempts to dismiss, including dealing with her own created insecurities about it. Another woman has to choose both lousy options — working out and doing most of the housework, and cannot help but see the distinction between the things she gets paid for and rewarded for with cultural approval and those she does not. Everyone loses in this situation. I have spoken little about the losses of men, but there is no doubt that they lose out — having less time with their children and their wives, and having greater psychological pressure as providers.

That segregation and emptiness of meaning has meant that the industrial economy has leaped to fill the void we manifestly experience. We have filled it with processed foods, television and educational toys that teach children the alphabet so that parents do not have to. We have filled it with sports and other things that don't matter very much. We keep our children active by replacing meaningful labor with meaningless exercise, and what should be pleasurable athletic activity with intense competition. In effect, we have turned childhood over to corporations, and meaning-making over to advertising. And the kind of children such a world creates are ones that are disconnected — instead of their imaginary lives being connected to imitating their parents and integrating into their family life, their imaginations are shaped by shopping and the economy.

As David Orr has observed in his essay "Loving Children: a Design Problem," we endlessly repeat the claim that we love our children, but we do not live our lives that way, or enable our children to feel loved in the ways that time has shown are successful. Orr notes,

In an ecologically and esthetically impoverished landscape, it is
harder for children and adolescents to find a larger meaning and
purpose for their lives. Consequently, many children grow up
feeling useless. In landscapes organized for convenience, com-

merce, and crime, and subsidized by cheap oil, we have little
good work for them to do. Since we really do not need them
to do real work, they learn few practical skills and little about
responsibility. Their contacts with adults are frequently unsatis-
factory. When they do work, it is all too often within a larger
pattern of design failure. Flipping artery clogging burgers made
from chemically saturated feedlot cows, for example, is not good
work and neither is most of the other hourly work available to them.
Over and over we profess our love for our children, but the evi-
dence says otherwise. Rarely do we work with them. Rarely do we
mentor them. We teach them few practical skills. At an early age
they are deposited in front of mind-numbing television and later
in front of computers. And we are astonished to learn that in
large numbers they neither respect adults nor are they equipped
with the basic skills and aptitudes necessary to live responsible
and productive lives. Increasingly, they imitate the values they
perceive in us with characteristic juvenile exaggeration. (Orr,
designshare.com/Research/Orr/Loving_Children. htm)

How do we create a society in which we actually act like we love our children? How do we get women and men out of the ugly set of choices they
have — working too much in isolation from children and one another, or
one parent isolated at home with children in an environment that has been
degraded and stripped of its importance and meaning?

My suggestion, then, is not that mothers should stay home, but that
everyone should. Of course, in most cases that isn't possible, but it is a recog-
nizable starting point for thinking about what would be best for us and our
society. In more practical terms we might ask how we should, as Orr puts it,
"reconnect living with livelihood."

The first solution would be to need as little as possible. Studies find that
nearly everyone who is asked believes they need the income they have, or
just a little more. But would that actually be true if we treated our homes
and households as places that produce what we need rather than suck up our
income? If the costs of car payments, new clothing, much of one's food and
other items could be eliminated from the budget, along with daycare, would
one person in the family be able to cut back on their work or quit altogether?
Could both cut back? Could one person take a job making less that would
require fewer hours, less commuting?

Are you doing work that improves the world or work that harms it?
Because we need to make a living, many of us exclude our jobs from our

environmental and social consciousness, assuming that our work creating paper on some irrelevancy is not a negotiable issue. But that is a lie — we have to do good work, and model good work for our children, so that they will want to join us in it. Could you create a small home business? Start a farm or market garden? Work from home? Work less? Involve your older children in your work? Take a baby or toddler with you one day a week? Homeschool? Many of these things may not be feasible for most people, but have you seriously considered them?

Could you move, live somewhere cheaper or closer to family? Could you live with family and enable your parents, for example, to retire and help care for their grandchildren, or a sibling to stay home with her child and yours? Could you choose a new way of life, where part of your income involved some work that could be done with your children around? Could you both work part time? Could you find work that husband and wife could do together? Could you combine several of these options with increased frugality and self-sufficiency, and get by on only one part-time income? Many people will not be able to do these things — single parents, for example, often have limited choices. I do not mean to imply in any kind of blanket statement that there is one ideal solution for everyone. But if we could see as our major goal the reduction of the time we give to industrial society, and the increase of time we give to our home economy, how might we change the world?

• • •

Consider setting up your home so that older family members can live with you when the time comes.

• • •

Right now, many of us work for health insurance — but for an increasingly large number, such is not available at any price. It is true that being less of a participant in the industrial economy makes us less secure in that regard, if more secure in others. Ideally, we will find ways at the national or state level of ensuring that everyone can have equal access to medical care. If not, perhaps we could do as the Amish do and form mutual aid societies that cover medical bills for a group. Most states have insurance for children, and some have it available for those who have home businesses. This might be a starting place.

As for saving for retirement, I do not wish to presume too much about what my children will want for me, but in much of the world, and through much of human history, one's family — not money — was one's security. We all should know the danger of a lost pension fund, a stock market crash, a currency crisis. Money is often less secure than we would imagine. But it is absolutely necessary if we continue to live our lives, as Orr notes, as though we do not truly love our children. If we continue to live in ways that degrade the world and deprive children of family connection, we will have children who do not want to help us in our last years. Despite our cultural nostalgia for the 1950s, we should note that the children of the 1950s, who remember it so fondly, were the first generation to overwhelmingly stick their parents in assisted living and nursing homes. The mothers who were at home baking cookies weren't much valued in their old age.

None of us likes the idea of dependency, but we will be dependent, no matter what. Some day, unable to work, we will either be dependent on a collection of machines, the industrial economy and professional people doing a lousy job for minimum wage, or we will be dependent on the children we loved and raised and the grandchildren we adore. Which is better? I know which one I would choose.

As I finish this section of the book, I am cutting up old jeans to make quilts and rag rugs. It is dull work, but useful, because it saves me a little money every year as I patch my old jeans and don't have to buy blankets. As I work, my six-year-old is making a blanket for his stuffed animals out of scraps. My four-year-old is playing hide and seek with his two-year-old brother, hiding beneath a half-cut up jean leg, and my oldest son spins a long strip for braiding around and around. My toddler chews my knee and begs me to sing "Itsy Bitsy Spider." My husband does dishes at the sink.

The most precious moments of my life are the ones in which there is nothing at all to buy, moments whose value is increased only by their ubiquity, by the fact that we are together as we usually are in our accustomed ways, enjoying accustomed pleasures. The moments are precious in that sense because they are apart from the economy — or rather, because they are fully integrated into the most essential of all economies, the home economy.

Husbanding Our Resources

How do we find the time and money to stay home, if we want to? It is still enormously challenging for many of us to find more time to do things like preserving food, growing gardens or making and repairing things, as essential as that work is. We often live close to or beyond our means, and an increasingly unstable economy means that giving up income can be risky. So one of the ways to think about how we might find time and money to start participating more in the informal, domestic economy would be to try and keep as much of our money in the family and close to home as possible.

Teodor Shanin observes that in peasant societies, things like houses, cars and bicycles are not private possessions for the owners, but something to be passed down from generation to generation, and thus preserved. The "owner" is really a "steward of resources." How would our society's basic structure change if we saw ourselves as the stewards of our family resources, engaged in an intergenerational project protecting and growing what we have?

Consider the contemporary model of family. (Can we just skip ahead and assume that family is whatever you call it? I'm going to use a nuclear one as an example, but I'm not making any major assumptions, I promise!) For purposes of simplicity, we'll imagine that Mom and Dad have a couple of children and one set of aging parents, but we all know it gets more complex than that. Mom and Dad have a baby — how exciting! They are comparatively young, and both work full time, so they put baby in daycare at eight weeks, which takes up a large percentage of one household income. They save what they can to afford a down payment on a house, but it is a struggle to put anything away.

Meanwhile, Grandma and Grandpa have a house that is too big for them, now that Mom and her sibling have grown and moved out. Eventually, Grandma and Grandpa decide to sell their house and move into a smaller place. They'd like to retire, but can't yet, so they go on working. Meanwhile, Mom and Dad are expecting baby #2, and they go into tremendous debt to buy a house surprisingly like the one that Grandma and Grandpa just sold, but, of course, closer to Dad's job (which is regarded as fixed and sacrosanct, even though he'll probably be laid off a couple times in the next decade).

Grandma and Grandpa live to see their grandchildren, but don't spend as much time as they'd like with them, because they are still working and it is a long drive to Mom and Dad's place. A little later, Grandma and Grandpa retire. They'd like nothing better than to devote their time to their grandchildren (while also taking the occasional vacation), but the kids are in school/daycare all day. Grandma and Grandpa can't make the drive too often, and they have to live cheaply so they can someday afford assisted living and still leave money for their children's inheritance.

Mom and Dad still work full time, with the kids attending school and daycare. They are deeply in debt. They are also exhausted from home care, childcare and two jobs. If they ever have any spare income they spend it on having others cook their meals (takeout), clean their house, mow their lawn, entertain them (cable) and so on.

Move on a bit, and Grandpa dies. Grandma sells her house, gives up her familiar possessions and her relationships in her community and moves into assisted living, which gives her the exclusive company of her peers. Her grandkids don't visit too often because it isn't very kid friendly, and of course, it is a long drive. Mom and Dad are now constantly torn between the needs of Grandma and the needs of their children, with neither being able to provide any benefit to the other. Just now, the children are teenagers and begin saving money doing pointless labor completely unlike the labor their parents and grandmother are paying other people to do. Finally, Grandma dies, her saved money spent on assisted living. Mom and Dad can look forward to a decade of frantically working to pay for college, until they start the cycle over again.

Sounds stupid. Sure. And yet, that's the scenario our culture endorses as the norm, in the name of independence. How many of us see ourselves in that cycle? Changing the way we live and keeping our resources in our family and community would both save energy and money in general, and also enable us to transform our lives. Families, biological and chosen, could easily transform the situation.

Imagine that we did prioritize the well-being of all the people in the family over generations. Mom and Dad have a baby. They move in with Grandma and Grandpa, who have the room. Because they are sharing the house, they only need two full-time incomes, so it is agreed that Dad and Grandma will work full time, and Grandpa will take early retirement and Mom will stay home. He helps with the childcare, and Mom and he do the housework together. They both have enough time to pursue other ways of saving money, such as gardening and cooking from scratch, as well as pleasure activities. Grandchild grows up intimately connected to his grandparents. As Grandma and Grandpa get older, adaptations are made to the house, or another, handicapped-accessible house is purchased for the extended family, but with minimal indebtedness, because they have the first house as a stake.

Once Mom is done being pregnant and breastfeeding, she may go back to work part time, so that Grandma too can retire and devote herself to home and grandchildren, or perhaps they will find a way to live on a single income, with three adults caring for home and children. If they grow a bigger garden and live more frugally, this might be feasible, if the mortgage is paid off.

As the children grow, they take on domestic work too. If Grandma and Grandpa need help getting along eventually, grandchildren, now grown to adolescence, can provide it, along with their parents. In exchange, grandparents provide help in funding education and other needs with their savings, knowing that they don't need to prepare for a long life in assisted living — they will be cared for by their family. The pace of life is comparatively slow and relaxed — there are always enough people to play with the children, do the domestic work, earn an income and provide food, entertainment and affection.

Far less money is earned in this scenario, but total wealth is greater and indebtedness less because very little money goes out. Moreover, the family is happier (which is not to say that they don't get on each other's nerves sometimes) and everyone receives more and better care by virtue of it being done by people who love them. Are there problems with this scenario at times? Sure. Some families can't live together. Some arrangements would never work. Sometimes outside investment is necessary. But we could do far more than we currently do to ensure that we retain what we earn and that everyone benefits.

And we can create these scenarios with others than our biological family — perhaps if daycare is truly necessary, a neighbor can be enriched. Perhaps family conflicts can be resolved. Perhaps if we change our patterns of thought and create new models of the ideal, we can have what we need when things get hard. In the end we will have to find a way to recreate the extended family. Why not do it now?

This is the Way the World Ends... With Your Brother-in-Law Sleeping on Your Couch

The coming decades bring with them a whole host of reasons why the current system of everyone in separate vast houses, isolated from one another, will probably not go on much longer.

The first reason is simple demographics. Aging baby boomers will increasingly require help getting along, and the cost of that care will increasingly be shifted onto a smaller working population, particularly since most boomers have comparatively little saved for retirement. (The average personal savings was just over $24,000 as of 2004.) Most of their wealth is in housing at this stage, and that wealth could easily evaporate entirely during a recession.

Meanwhile the cost of providing elder support will quickly overwhelm existing support structures. The annual cost of Alzheimer care alone for the baby boomers will consume 98 percent of Medicare's entire present annual budget. That leaves virtually no money for anything else. Though we will certainly expand the amount we pay into the system, it is also true that

Medicare will probably get stingier and more limited over time; the nursing homes they will pay for will be worse, the resources fewer.

Assisted living is generally purchased with one's house — again, a very unstable resource, and people who live longer than their resources last are often evicted from assisted living, either into nursing homes or to families. The simple reality is that more and more of us will be taking in our parents, grandparents, aunts and uncles — or we will pass their care and needs off onto increasingly strained and inadequate resources. I know many of us find our relatives annoying or unlikable (and yes, I know some people genuinely have reasons not to be able to be around their families), but you'd have to dislike a family member quite a lot to voluntarily pass them off to a bad nursing home.

The next factor is Climate Change. For almost half a million people, Hurricane Katrina was an experience in shared housing, and we can expect similar disasters to increase in frequency. As Thomas Homer-Dixon put it in *The Upside of Down*, "...this won't be the last time we walk out of our cities." And, of course, in just this decade we've seen people walking out of New York City twice (September 11 and the 2004 blackout), attempting to walk out of New Orleans and being turned back by their own military pointing guns at them (Hurricane Katrina), and we will see it again — and probably again and again. Where will the denizens of Las Vegas go as the water dries up (a recent article suggests that this could be within this decade)? Where will the residents of Miami go as their fresh water is replaced by sea water? Where will the victims of the next disaster go? Or rather, let us not say "they" — let us say "we."

The simple reality is that as more and more disasters occur, and more and more people are dislocated, they will seek out family and friends to provide either transitional or permanent housing. Though all of us are not equally vulnerable, any one of us is a potential victim of flood and fire, hurricane and tornado, earthquake and tsunami. We will go to our family, to our friends — and that is as it should be. And hosts and victims will share the common problem of living together in a society of people increasingly unaccustomed to doing so.

More than five million additional foreclosures are predicted in the year that this book comes out, and it may be worse even than that. Many of us are going to lose our houses because we can't pay the rent or the mortgage. Many of us are going to find ourselves leaving behind old jobs and old houses and living on someone's couch until we get our lives back together — or perhaps we will permanently move in together, consolidating our houses so that we can afford to continue our lives.

The forces driving us out of our houses and into consolidation are about to become powerful, but we've also been driven by powerful forces encouraging us not to live together. It is important to remember how deeply our own sense of privacy, like everything else about us, has been shaped, not in isolation by our inner selves but by the marketplace and the social mores it creates. That is, one of the reasons for the housing boom is that we've been consistently told we need bigger houses, more space, and that we shouldn't live together. American culture is unusually solitary, with a heavy emphasis on individualism, privacy and not sharing things — and it is no coincidence that these tend to be characteristics that the growth economy encourages. If we don't share much, we need more things. If we believe it would be an intolerable burden upon our privacy to share space with a family member, we will buy or rent separate housing. The housing boom, which some economists estimate may have resulted in the manufacture of several million more homes than the market will support, was based on a combination of population growth and cultural pressure to move into ever bigger houses, in ever smaller family units.

I am not saying your relatives and friends aren't awful and annoying and impossible to live with. I'm not saying that need for privacy isn't real. But the reality is that, to some degree, our acute need for isolation from one another is neither natural nor personal but culturally created by our economy and the needs of our marketplace. Some of us won't be able to live with our parents or siblings, for real and serious reasons. But we can live with friends or more distant family. There are few, if any of us, who cannot accommodate others when the need arises, but we have been told otherwise so often we've come to believe it.

We saw this when my husband and I bought this house with my husband's grandparents. The responses of Eric's grandparents and other people of their generation, who had, after all, cared for their own parents, were uniformly positive. But the reaction of many of our peers and our parents' generation was naked horror that we would do such a thing. We were too newly married, we were told; it would take away time we needed for our children; we would find it too hard; we would have to give up all our privacy. The assumption was that all the benefits of the arrangement fell on Eric's grandparents' side. But that was not true. We benefited in a whole host of ways, from the financial (they helped us buy the farm) to the practical (I could run out and leave the baby with Grandma for a few minutes) to the emotional (I had supportive, loving company at home during the day; my children had an intensely loving relationship with their beloved great-grandparents).

Now, I don't mean to suggest it was always idyllic — sometimes it was damned hard, especially during end-of-life periods. I freely acknowledge that grandparents are often easier to deal with than parents and siblings, and long-planned and prepared-for arrangements are easier than those suddenly thrust upon us. But I like to think that there are some strategies we might use to make this easier, and that for most of us it won't be as bad as we thought. If I can prevent a single axe murder, fratricide or poisoning within our extended families, I will consider my time well spent. So here are my rules for advance planning for living with family — biological or chosen.

First and foremost, plan ahead whenever you can. If you have elderly or disabled family members, or if you are an older or disabled person, start talking now with your family about what the long-term future might look like.

• • •

Many seniors suffer from isolation while many young people need the skills seniors have. Build the connection.

• • •

If someone is likely to come to live with you (or you with them), my opinion is that it is vastly easier to make the change if you do it while everyone is still able bodied, rather than in time of crisis. I'm not saying that healthy 50-year-olds should give up independence, just that the worst time to do this is when a medical or personal crisis strikes. If you or your household is economically unstable and you may need to move in with family members, now is the time to bring this up in a gentle way, to talk about how it might work, how you would share things like chores and bills, and how you would get along.

Opening this subject can be particularly difficult for the person who may require assistance. That is another reason to consider consolidating housing while you are still in good health — instead of saying, "Will you take care of me?" you can offer something in exchange. Most seniors could help with the mortgage and the grandchildren, for example. Everyone on earth can contribute something to a household, no matter how elderly, ill or disabled. Eric's grandmother could rock a baby like nobody's business, even when she couldn't chase a toddler. Eric's grandfather was at the end of his life, but he could still tell stories to my sons that were infinitely valuable to us. Figure out what you have to offer, and offer it. Even if you aren't prepared to move in together yet, you might begin to arrange your life to suit such a set up — moving nearer family or buying a house that could readily be adapted to sharing.

I strongly recommend intergenerational living even for people who don't have to do it. It tends to combine the best of several possible worlds for everyone. In our society wealth is heavily concentrated among people in their 40s and above, while vigor and energy, hardly limited to younger people, tend to be abundant among people in their 20s and 30s. I think the lives of children are enormously enriched by growing up with older people in their lives. Right now, millions of seniors whose dream is to spend the rest of their lives comfortably in their own homes are wondering what they will do when they no longer can. There are also millions of young people who long for a little land — a small farm or even a good-sized suburban yard — and a chance to get ahead. These two groups have every reason to combine their interests and their futures.

Second, be prepared for the unexpected. Though some consolidations can be anticipated, there are plenty of reasons why many, probably most, of our housing arrangements will be brought on suddenly — whether it is a private crisis such as job loss, fire or foreclosure, or whole regions on the move. In some cases, people may have only minutes to leave their homes, or they may arrive traumatized, ill, injured or otherwise in bad shape. But there are still ways we can prepare to deal with all this. We should also understand it is we who may be moving.

Each of us should prepare in two ways. First, we should imagine the situation with ourselves as the refugees requiring family help. Second, we should imagine ourselves as the hosts, and prepare for an influx. If we've been preparing for Peak Oil and Climate Change, many of us may be more likely to end up as the hosts, but it is important to remember that all sorts of things can happen, and, as Robert Burns said, "The best laid plans of mice and men gang aft agley." If things can gang aft agley, they will.

So start looking around you and imagining scenarios. What would you need if a large number of family members arrived suddenly on your doorstep? Where would you go if a forest fire or a chemical leak required you to leave your house in minutes? Do you know where vital personal documents are? Do you have an emergency kit, a backpack or other bag of basic items — toothbrush, change of clothes, food, water, a supply of needed medications and maps so that if it takes a day or more to get where you are going you'll be okay? Do you have enough food to feed additional family in a crisis? Basic medical supplies so that you can treat minor problems, such as muscle injuries or mild dehydration, at home if emergency rooms are overflowing? Are you set up for babies, young children, pregnant women, the elderly, and disabled or medically fragile?

Think about the people you know. Who could you go to? We all know some people who would welcome us without question, but if there are questions, perhaps it would be wise to ask them ahead of time. Begin with, "In the event of a natural disaster, would it be okay if Mom and I came here?" Find out whether you can take your pets or livestock. If not, what will you do with them?

Think about who might see your home as a potential refuge and what issues might they have. Bring this up with them in a non-threatening way, perhaps by saying, "Since Hurricane Katrina, I've been thinking it might be useful to have a plan for an emergency." The more you think ahead on these issues, the better off you will be. One of the few virtues of the events of the last few years is that all of us have seen a concrete example of what can happen. The uses of things like stored food and emergency transportation plans are no longer the province of survivalists. All of us need to make these preparations and plans.

Crises don't always occur when we're all at home together. If things get suddenly dangerous, you should have a plan, for example, for gathering children from school or spouses from jobs — who gets who and where you meet up in the end. Have backup communications plans — cell phones might not work; the Internet connection might be down. Leaving messages with a centrally located family member, or even one out of the country, might make sense.

For me, the most important things to remember (and I didn't always remember them when Eric's grandparents were alive — something I regret) is that the people whose home you share, or who provide home to you, are the people who share, for all their imperfections, ties that matter, who are worthy of honor and respect. No matter how maddening they are, no matter how frustrated you are, no matter how difficult moving in together is, no matter how close the quarters or stressful the situation, these people are your tribe. It is in some ways easy not to love and appreciate the people who are always there, especially when you sometimes wish they would be elsewhere. It is also worth noting, however, that the world is not full of people who will share their homes with you, add water to their soup so your husband can eat, rock your child through a nightmare to let you sleep, give you the coat from their backs and the bread from their table, and say, in a thousand words and gestures, "You are one of us." If you have such people in your lives, treasure them.

EIGHT

Raising Kids in a New World: Family Life and Education

The eyes of the future are looking back at us and
they are praying for us to see beyond our own time.
— TERRY TEMPEST WILLIAMS

Why should I care about future generations?
What have they ever done for me?
— GROUCHO MARX

I Don't Know How She Does It!

THE FIRST THING EVERYONE SAYS TO ME, WHEN THEY HEAR I FARM, WRITE books and cut my emissions while raising small kids is "How do you do it all?" The only possible answer I can give is this — I don't. People know me because I'm a writer, and when I say things like "I canned nine quarts of peach jam and put up 200 ears of corn yesterday," it sounds smooth, blithe and relaxing. And even if I tell you otherwise, people mostly think I'm joking.

In fact, the process of putting up 200 ears of corn and making nine quarts of peach jam is nothing like it sounds like when I edit out the boring parts, like the 200 times I said, "Stop touching that!" while we were picking the corn and the kids wanted to play with the tractor attachments. Or the part where my husband did a very fast, very disgusting diaper-related crisis triage with a handful of corn husks. Trust me, it is better this way.

The reason I put up that food yesterday is that I blew off editing this book, replying to 50 e-mails and dealing with three-foot weeds in my garden. Today, I'm blowing off the still uncanned raspberry sauce, the weeds and the e-mails to work on this chapter and then homeschool the kids. Every time I am doing something, I'm letting something else lapse, usually something that probably shouldn't.

At the moment, I'm praying that the couple who are renovating our garage into a goat barn won't have to pee at all so that they don't see my bathroom. The house has been sacked. I have no idea what we are eating for lunch — we have tomatoes, eggplant and beer. I don't think good Mommies feed their children beer for lunch, so I guess we'll be having eggplant and tomatoes.

The reasons I can do what I do are that I have a committed husband who can do much of his work from home, because I'm always more than willing to neglect the housework, and because I work from home. But mostly because I'm comfortable with chaos. I could look at this day and see only the mess, the failures, the mediocre parenting, the fact that they didn't learn about evaporation the way we'd planned. Instead, I look at it and think "I got four sinksful of dishes done. I put up corn for the winter. We talked about how corn is different than other grains. The kids spent a lot of time picking. We took a long family walk. We ate homemade tomato and mozzarella sandwiches and three out of four kids wanted seconds. They helped time the canning of the peach jam. The boys picked chard for dinner. The boys got to play with a neighbor's kids, and Eric and I finished clearing the crap out of the garage. I answered two e-mails. I babysat the neighbor's son. We picked up 300 lbs of organic grains and transferred them into buckets. I did some research. I set pumpkin leather to dehydrate. Eric played banjo with friends. I got the kitchen made presentable. I made rice pudding. I watered the container plants. I went to bed happy."

That is a good day by my lights. If I look at what I didn't do, at the mess, the chaos, the exhaustion, the failures, it doesn't look so hot. So I try not to look, and hope to do better tomorrow. So if I have one bit of advice for parents of young children — and everyone who is facing hard times, a big learning curve and not enough time — it is this: do the best you can, trust yourself, and be pleased with what you do. Embrace the chaos.

Toys are Not Us

It was a parable, but I didn't listen. My neighbors gave their two boys a big Thomas the Tank Engine train set for Christmas. It had miles of track, a lot of trains, trees, buildings, bridges, everything you could ever want in a train set. It even had its own table to set up the track on and a drawer to store it in. This was no small piece of furniture, either. Bigger than a coffee table, it was a substantial thing, placing trains at the center of their lives. And on Christmas morning, a half hour after providing everything a train-obsessed child could ever want, my neighbor went in to see that her children had taken the trains away from the track and were running them along the living room floor and up over the "mountains" of the couch pillows. The track, the buildings, the bridges were all left behind as the two boys happily raced two small wooden trains around the room.

I should have listened. But a year later, when Grandma wanted to get my children a big gift for Chanukah, she proposed a train set, complete with table, and we encouraged her. My husband and I were excited — we had forgotten the parable. They could set up whole villages, we thought! It would be welcoming, exciting for any child who comes to visit. The kids would spend hours playing with it! And they did, for a little while. But half the time, they were racing the trains over the floors, or making up stories about the trains crossing bridges — not the premade wooden bridges that came with the set, but bridges they built themselves from blocks.

• • •

If a holiday gift exchange is part of your life, consider having a $100 holiday this year and making most gifts.

• • •

It turned out that the person who spent the most time playing with the trains, setting them up and arranging them "just so" was my husband. The kids didn't care about just so — they just wanted to play train. The box it came in, the table, the track and the accessories made clutter in my house. What my kids really wanted — four two-inch wooden trains — could have provided the same amount of pleasure for one one-hundredth the waste.

The thing was, it was Daddy and Mommy and Grandma who wanted the children to have the trains. We had a dream of providing them with something wonderful. And how often is it true that our gifts are more about what we want to give than about what the children really need and want?

If you are like many parents, you've spent a good bit of time in the past few years sorting through your kids' toy box, tossing out lead-contaminated toys, items made with endocrine-disrupting plastics and other dangers. It turns out that not only are our houses cluttered with toys but the toys themselves are often toxic. In the summer of 2007 there was an enormous outcry against Chinese toy manufacturers. How, we asked, could they dare to endanger our kids?

But of course, such anger is misplaced. All of the relevant toys were cheap plastic crap, manufactured in a poor country with lax standards on environmental, child and worker safety. They were being manufactured in a comparatively unregulated economy by people making tiny wages, often in poor working conditions, on a contract given to the lowest bidder. The average action figure that retailed for $10.99 actually cost far less than a dollar to produce, and only a few pennies actually went to the guy whose job it was to ensure safety. And every single parent and grandparent who bought one of the toys *knew that this was true* — or could have if they stopped to think for two seconds about where the toys came from. We either didn't bother to think or we trusted that other people, far away and with no incentive to do so, would care more about our kids than we care about theirs.

I'm not blaming anyone here — I'm as guilty as anyone of this. I buy toys at yard sales, but plenty of them started out as cheap new toys somewhere. The truth is that because we think our kids need a million toys, we need them to be cheap. That way everyone who knows them can afford to buy them a ton of stuff for Christmas, birthdays, and whenever Grandpa comes to visit. They can have gift bags at every birthday party, a toy in every Happy Meal, a bunch of junk for every occasion. And they can have toy boxes full, closets full, houses that look like stores. This is possible only if we cut every corner, pay no attention to the environment or labor practices or sustainability. The problem is not any particular toy — it is all the toys.

Cheap toys aren't just bad for our kids, they are bad for everyone — for kids, for workers, for the planet, for the future. The toys are made by impoverished people who didn't get to have toys themselves growing up, sometimes by children who are enslaved in factories instead of playing at home. And for all that the lead paint on Elmo's face is dangerous for our kids, it is worse for the workers who make the toys. They are the ones who work 12 hours a day with lead paint — many of them young women at the beginning of their reproductive years. The factories emit greenhouse gasses that warm the planet and use up limited supplies of petroleum for what? For a toy that will be broken in a matter of days or hours? And their destruction is inevitable, because children with a million toys simply cannot understand the value of a thing — and children who own only cheap plastic junk are not making a mistake when they imbue it with no inherent value.

> Don't entertain your children all the time. Even older babies (1 year +) can be expected to amuse themselves for periods of a half hour or so, assuming their basic needs are met. Help older kids learn to guide and watch out for younger ones.

What's the solution? There is only one answer I know of, and I hope that parents and grandparents will begin to take this seriously — many,

many fewer toys, made to much higher standards. That is, toys made of natural materials that are demonstrably nontoxic and made without waste. Toys you make yourself or that your children make. Toys made from non-toxic recycled things. But most of all, fewer of them for every child. That means not 50 dolls, but one or two. Not 100 stuffed animals, but two. A set of blocks. Some old clothes for dress up. Pots and pans and empty cans and boxes for playing store. A blackboard and chalk. Some crayons and the backs of paper you've already used. A few balls. A bat. A glove. A few games. Lots of books. Perhaps one big thing — a dollhouse or a battle cruiser or some trains and track.

But not everything under the sun, not even if it is educational. Nothing with batteries, as little made of plastic as possible. Nothing cheap — we have to pay the people who make them enough to live on and to give them a powerful incentive to keep our kids safe. Better fewer good toys than more cheap ones. And greater generosity on our part, so that those who can't afford to pay well for toys can still have some good ones that won't poison them or deplete their future.

I have a doll that my grandmother bought when I was a little girl. It was my favorite throughout my childhood, so much so that "Big One" went through three cloth bodies, each one replaced by my mother or grandmother. When I outgrew the doll, my sister claimed her. By that time, the doll was bald and had permanent gouges in her cheeks. After my sister had also outgrown the doll (now named Andrea), my mother cleaned it up, replaced the body again and dressed it in the dress I wore home from the hospital when I was born. For a decade and more, she sat on a shelf in my closet until one day I brought her down and showed her to my youngest son. To him, she is "Baby." He holds her as he nurses to sleep each night, and she accompanies him to bed. I suspect I will have to replace Baby's body again — and I wouldn't be surprised if someday, my son sits over a needle and thread and does so for one of his children.

If we're honest about our motivations for giving our children toys, I think we'll find that this is what we're seeking — the child inside us who loved a particular toy, or a few particular toys, and felt powerfully about them. We give our kids toys because we want them to have that magical and imaginary space in their lives with a toy that feels real to them. So we give and give and hope that the next one will be the one. But the reality is that it is more likely that we will create magical experiences for our children and grandchildren if they have fewer toys, rather than more. The experience we remember is in part a consequence of limitation. That is, we imagine better when we have more reasons to imagine, and fewer real things that substitute for imagination. Our toys are real to us precisely to the same extent that we make that possible by limiting them.

Childhood in a Changing World

In his book *Last Child in the Woods,* Richard Louv argues that American children are suffering from a lack of connection with the natural world. It is a brilliantly reasoned book, and worth reading. On one level, support for his contention can be justified by simply walking through most suburban neighborhoods. The children are mostly in enclosed spaces — in playgrounds or ball fields being organized by parents and coaches in the best scenario or in the house playing video games or watching TV. Very few are out in their ecosystem, even when the ecosystem is as processed as the suburban lawn.

So is it any wonder that most American children may have generalized fears about things like global warming, drought, dangerous storms, but don't have either the educational background to understand what is going on or the practical experience with nature, agriculture and the environment to understand their own connection with the earth? A few years ago, for example, a study came out that suggested the average American child could recognize only 13 species in their own little ecosystem. That is, walk out onto your lawn, and the average child would be hard pressed to tell you whether the tree by the window is an oak, locust or cedar, to recognize which of the driveway weeds they can safely pick (and even eat or make a whistle or daisy chain with) and which are poisonous, name the birds that come to the feeder, or identify whether a carrot comes from a tree or under the ground.

There was a time when children had relationships with the trees on their property — when they climbed them, swung on them, named them, talked to them, took a hammer and nails and made precarious houses in their branches. And they knew something about them; perhaps a child might even have tapped the sugar maple in the yard or collected acorns from the white oak. It is hard for all of us to grasp the stakes of global warming, for example, but children who know what a sugar maple is, have a relationship to one and a taste for the syrup can begin to understand the tragedy of the idea that will be no more of these trees in our place again. The more that children understand about ecology in general and about the biology of their specific, beautiful, particular place, the more stake they have in the future.

Contemporary education has failed to give children what they need in two ways. First, most of us were taught when the Battle of Hastings was but not the slightest thing about the history of our agricultural system, other perhaps than when the plow was invented. We were taught to read poetry but never to wonder what the "eglantine" that Shakespeare mentioned actually looked or smelled like. We were taught the periodic table, but nothing about soil microbiology. We were taught about Mendel's peas, but nothing about specific peas — not how they grow, what soil bacteria they depend on, which varieties suit our climate or how to cook them. That is, our education has prioritized the distant and abstract, rather than the local and concrete. We were not trained to think of ourselves as part of history, biology and literature. And this means that we often have no way of connecting our abstract knowledge of distant places and histories with the concrete reality of our future — or even our present.

In many cases, we have no ability to use history to predict consequences, or to understand the connections, say, between one fact (that 50 percent of all reptiles are expected to become extinct before 2050) and another fact (that our own food web depends on reptile species) and a third fact (that a particular species of reptile lives here and needs these conditions). This gap in part explains the inability of adults to understand what is happening to their world — and thus, our inability to teach children how to absorb the changes they face.

We need to add an ecological and agricultural education to our children's lives. It would be nice in some ways if public schools would do this, but the reality is that we need to know these things now, and parents must take up the burden, assisted by friends and family members and any adult who can do this work. For many of us, this means taking up ecological education ourselves. We have to ask, What is that tree? Why do thistles grow here but not plantain? Where does my water come from? What does corn syrup have to do with global warming? We need desperately to become literate in a host of areas we've never been familiar with, and teach our children as we learn.

And we need to get our children out onto the soil and teach them by doing, by touching, by growing, by *being* in the world. That doesn't mean taking trips to "visit" nature. The occasional visit to a national park is inspiring, but we cannot connect with nature by taking long trips that warm the planet and destroy what we seek to visit. The hypocrisy of doing so is bound to be detected by your child. If there is anything one can count on it is the magical ability of children to spot hypocrisy. Thus, we all must find a way to make nature present where we are — plant some trees in a vacant lot, start a garden on your roof, call for setting aside land from development, build a community garden. Because your children need to grow up with a relationship to nature that intersects their everyday life in the place they live in.

All of which means that we have to preserve nature in our man-made landscapes. We must, in some literal and metaphorical way open up the boundaries of the enclosures and let our children out into their own world. We cannot expect our children to be attached to a nature that is majestic, transcendent, and "over there somewhere." If they are to be invested in the preservation of their future, they must grasp that nature is them — it is their world, their lawn, their garden, their park, their food, their souls. And they must get to know it in concrete, direct and real ways — both knowing about it and knowing it with hands and mouth and nose and body.

And, of course, our children need to be inculcated into our environmental practices. They need to see us valuing the environment over our convenience, not occasionally, but every day. Those brilliant hypocrisy sniffers need to see us doing things, understand that we are doing them from real commitment and grasp the moral terms of that commitment. They need to learn how to do these things hand in hand with their parents — baking bread with us and understanding why we aren't driving to the store, shopping in thrift shops with us instead of at the mall and understanding why buying used is better. They need to see us fixing things and preserving things, instead of throwing them away. They need to be wholly integrated not only into the natural world but our relationship to it. The things we do to preserve the world are the things we do to preserve our children and their lives. They need to feel that what they do matters, not just in child ways, but having a real and material effect on the world.

This responsibility does not apply solely to parents. Aunts and uncles, grandparents, neighbors, friends — children need adults in their lives who care about them and who will teach what they have. The children who live around you may not get this from their parents, but they will remember all of their lives the neighbor across the street who invites them to look in the worm bin and shows them the garden soil the worms create. They will take with them a little taste of the aunt who bakes pies with them and lets them decide whether blueberry-banana is a good flavor. They will someday, as grandparents themselves, remember that grandpa named the trees, and do it for their own grandsons. If we do it soon, the trees will still be there to be named.

School and Energy

Our family homeschools — sort of. At six, Simon is in his second year of homeschooling, reading miles ahead of grade level, enthusiastic about math and science, still struggling with writing. His four-year-old brother is in his second year of what he calls "kindergarten" — still working on his alphabet while leaping ahead in math. Two-year-old Asher is a full-time pest, but he colors along and sings the ABCs with gusto. But we're also public schoolers — sort of. Our autistic oldest son attends a private school for children with autism — paid for by the school system because they don't have a class for Eli.

Now, a lot of homeschoolers do what they do because of a passionate dislike of public school options or from strong religious convictions. That's not our motivation. Instead, we've made our educational decisions both for the benefit of our kids and for environmental reasons.

In Eli's case, school is the best option for him, and the fossil-fuel energy he uses to get there is a long-term investment — a chance for him to be able to function better as an adult. Our society mostly recognizes that we're all better off when disabled children achieve their full potential. There will probably come a time when local school districts can no longer afford to provide expensive edu-

. . .

Have you considered homeschooling? It is legal in every state and can be enormously satisfying. Even if you don't homeschool, consider "afterschooling" — teaching your kids useful skills and providing a critical perspective they won't receive in most schools.

. . .

cations to disabled children. For example, most of the disabled children of New Orleans experienced extended disruptions of their education and periods of regression and loss of continuity due to Hurricane Katrina — in many New Orleans schools, services for the disabled were not fully restored a year later.

Although my other children are better able to adapt to a generalized, one-size-fits-all program, I'm not sure they are better served by such a thing. The notion that an education should be customized to fit non-disabled children as well doesn't seem that radical to me.

My six-year-old is as unique as, and in many ways as different from, other children as his "special" brother. He learns better in some ways than others; he has things he needs special assistance with and things he is radically ahead in. School tends to reduce all these distinctions to sameness, as though they do not matter. And though my son will not always find himself in a world customized to his needs, I'm not convinced that, as some people have argued, he must prepare himself for "real life" by living in the unfettered harshness of the "real world" from five on.

Thus, we homeschool. But of course, there's more than that. One of the reasons we do so is that it is an environmentally wise choice. We live in a large, rural school district. My sons would cover many miles on the bus each day, on a bus that wouldn't otherwise come down our road.

The push to regionalize and expand schools has led to a number of consequences that are potentially troubling in a lower-energy world. Students are traveling more miles on the bus and in cars, and more children are traveling that way, rather than walking or bicycling. Streets and communities are often less accommodating to walkers, and schools are often in inaccessible neighborhoods that involve crossing busy streets or highways. Many towns and neighborhoods no longer have their own school systems — they are now in large consolidated districts, and school districts all over the country are struggling to provide busing for their students; some are ceasing to bus entirely as higher energy prices make transportation expenses difficult to bear. As we are less and less able to transport children long distances, many children will be less and less able to go to school. As heating and cooling the schools becomes a bigger burden, regional school systems may simply collapse — or become non-functional as they cut back to bare bones.

• • •

Create local educational systems.
Resist regionalizing schools
and advocate for neighborhood
school and library systems.

• • •

There are psychological and cultural problems associated with large-scale education as well. Classrooms of 28 kindergarteners (as friends of mine in an affluent suburb have) simply can't have the same degree of individual attention that smaller groups can. Thus, there is an enormous amount of pressure to conform. I live in the school district that has the honor of having been the very first (but hardly last) in the US to try to legally force a family to administer Ritalin to a child whose parents didn't think he needed it. Such things are far more common now — a friend of mine who is a school psychologist in a low-income school district in Massachusetts observes that many of the teachers he meets recommend drugs for nearly every difficult child because they simply don't have the time or energy to deal with their difficulties in more productive ways.

The reality is that large chunks of public school educations are about conformity and not about critical thinking; and some features are actively destructive. Moreover, children are being pressured to conform in particular ways, to transform themselves in the image of a future that is not going to happen. Much of what is being taught is preparation for (as almost every school says) "being part of the global economy." Lucky kids, who get to be cogs in that wheel! But how likely is it that our current state of depletion will allow a global economy to continue?

Our school is definitively not preparing our children for a local, but not parochial, society. In fact, the curriculae that I've seen in areas such as patriotism seems to be quite the opposite — we are trying to create a parochial and globalized society. That is, we are teaching children that they are supposed to participate in a "global" economy but also to believe that Americans are better than other people. My own goals as a home teacher are to have my children experience a wide world through the lens of their particular place, precisely the opposite goal.

But for all of this, I'm also a proponent of public education — just a better public education. My children have the luxury of homeschooling and a better education than could be provided to them locally because their parents have the luxury of time, comparative wealth, and a stable two-parent family. We are not willing to have our own children get less than the best education available, but we also want other families, with different circumstances, to have the same choices.

I believe that public schools are important, and I strongly believe in participating in them and helping to shape the curriculum so that it better mirrors the realities of our world. We believe that we do not serve our community if we completely absent ourselves from the institution that does so much to shape what our kids understand about the future. We see homeschooling as a necessary corrective, but we also believe good public schools must be available.

Some homeschoolers say that all parents should home educate. This is clearly not possible. For example, millions of parents have to work two or three jobs; millions of parents — including a minimum of 84 million Americans who are functionally illiterate — lack the basic ability to teach their children. Teaching your children at home when you can barely read in any meaningful sense is not like staying two piano lessons ahead of your students — it is impossible. Indeed, since nearly half of all American adults say they never read for pleasure, it seems clear that many parents, literate or not, should not teach their children at home — because it is impossible to teach a love of reading to children if you do not understand that love yourself.

As well, there are tens of thousands of disabled children like Eli who will benefit more from school than home, and millions of developmentally typical children who love and benefit from good schools all over the country. And we also all know the simple truth — that there are millions of children in the US for whom school is a far better place than home. It does not do to romanticize too much here — there are millions of households where violence, drug and alcohol addiction, and other factors simply mean that children are better and happier at school than at home. There are millions of children whose only hope to escape their bad homes and lives is for them to get lucky enough to have a teacher take an interest in them or for education to take hold in their lives. So we need not just good home education, but much better public schools.

Blanket dismissals of the value of public education are wrong. Blanket assumptions that we cannot home educate are wrong. In fact, most of what we think about schools is wrong, I suspect. As Ivan Illich observes in *Deschooling Society,*

> *The pupil is thereby "schooled" to confuse teaching with learning, grade advancement with education, a diploma with competence and fluency with the ability to say something new. His imagination is "schooled" to accept service in place of value. Medical treatment is mistaken for health care, social work for the improvement of community life, police protection for safety, military poise for national security, the rat race for productive work. Health, learning, dignity, independence, and creative endeavor are defined as little more than the performance of the institutions which claim to serve these ends. (Illich, 3)*

I do not think the importance of this point can be underestimated. Neither the current model of public education nor any at-home alternative, can, on any vast scale, allow us to enter a new world and prepare us for a new society without our first understanding that we are not the industrial process — and finding a new alternative.

What is that alternative? Just as population turns out not to be the root cause of our environmental crisis but a symptom of it, I suspect any meaningful change will begin by integrating home and school more than public school or homeschooling currently allows. That is, the first thing that school teaches us is that home is insufficient, that we need more than the domestic world where we spend an (increasingly small) part of our infancy and childhood, that we must be separated from home and family to learn.

What if home and family and school came together? What if cooperative, neighborhood education were normal, and children could still go home at lunchtime? What if we began our school years in small, mixed-age class-rooms in walkable areas? What if merging home and school were not a choice, but a logical necessity, if we began our understanding of the world, of history and biology and ecology on our own lawns, in our own town, among our own neighbors?

One strategy we can use while there's still time and resources is to advocate against larger district schools and in favor of local, walkable, smaller schools designed to serve our neighborhoods. This will be difficult because it is buck-ing the consolidation trend, but it is also important. As oil prices rise, busing becomes a larger and larger portion of the town or district budget. Small, community schools can cut those costs enor-mously. They also can bring about other ben-efits. A small community school with simple infrastructure can also serve, in many ways, as a community center. Here, after all, is where the parents congregate. Here is a kitchen used every day to prepare meals. Perhaps it could be

• • •

Get together with neighbors and create an at-home summer camp for your kids. It saves money and kids can learn useful skills!

• • •

adapted to become a community canning kitchen during the weekends; or perhaps a school cafeteria that used local food ingredients could also send home pre-made, local-ingredient, healthy meals to be reheated by commu-nity members, or the cafeterias could be opened on weekends. It is not an accident that in many small towns, the school is the center of communal life — and that it could be in larger places as well.

All of us can help shape the education children receive in public schools, both by voting and by participating in discussions about educational culture. Teachers are generally overstretched and have enormous demands placed on them, and schools generally welcome community participation. There is no reason an energetic and devoted person couldn't get a school garden started or a cooking program using seasonal ingredients. Certainly you could offer to teach ecology or how to build a solar oven. Most importantly, we can lobby to bring back agricultural education to our schools. In elementary school and high school we need to be teaching our kids to grow food, and how cook and eat that food.

As I've said, the line between homeschooler and public schooler can be quite fine. Any of us may find that our child wants to go to school, or that we have a child whose abilities or disabilities are better suited to public school than to home. That is, instead of thinking in terms of "public educa-tion vs. homeschooling" I think we need to consider ways in which we can integrate the two. Ways in which we can meet our own needs whenever possible, but also offer a good, responsive and public-minded education to people for whom homeschooling is not a good choice.

What does that mean? First, in practical terms, I think simple preparedness means that those of us who have children should have a plan for a long-term disruption in existing educational services. That doesn't necessarily mean buying a curriculum, but it does mean having easy access to (either in your private library or at your local, walkable public one) a good variety of educational materials. It means parents picking up textbooks and other materials at local library sales and being prepared to introduce algebra if the schools are closed for a while because of a natural disaster or the inability of the district to afford heating oil. And it means knowing what your local educational resources are — it isn't necessary for every parent to be able to teach physics or Latin poetry if there's someone in the neighborhood who can help. Educational services are just one of the cottage industries we can create.

• • •

Expand your library by buying books at yard sales, library sales and used bookstores. Besides books on gardening, farming, building, cooking and other useful skills, add light reading to distract your mind from difficulties, material on history and politics to help you understand what is going on, and plenty of books, educational and pleasurable, for children to learn from.

• • •

But what if there's a longer-term disruption in services and you can't homeschool? Even if you can personally homeschool, the neighborhood may be full of kids whose parents can't school them. That's when parents should get together to consider collective home education. Generally speaking, it will not serve your community to have kids hanging around doing nothing (or worse yet, coming up with creative and undesirable things to do). It certainly won't serve the long-term good to have kids miss years of education. And though the unstructured life has some advantages, in a crisis, those are likely not to be the salient points. So getting together with your neighbors and dividing up the teaching makes sense. There's no reason a child shouldn't come to your house on Monday to study history and botany and learn about herbs, and go to the neighbor's house on Tuesday for cooking and arithmetic.

That doesn't necessarily mean that one should mimic the schools exactly — public schools have valorized some kinds of education while neglecting or rejecting others. For example, we've long emphasized that "smart" people don't need "vocational" skills like fixing things, building things, growing things and making things. This, of course, is errant nonsense. We need to teach our kids to think critically, to write well and compellingly present their ideas, to read complicated material and understand it, to be able to grasp the science and math they are encountering and to recognize the literary, philosophical and historical origins of things. But we also need them to understand how nature works and how science is as yet only a thing that describes one aspect of nature, but is not nature itself. They need to know the limits of book knowledge as well as the potential of that knowledge. And they need to have experience with the basic work of providing for one's own needs — growing and making things.

In his seminal book *The Archaeology of Knowledge,* Michel Foucault argues that the way we organize our knowledge always and utterly transforms our relationship to it. And just as Peak Oil and Climate Change are in the broadest possible sense "market failures" — that is, failures that illuminate the deep inadequacies of our present economic system — they are also "education failures" — that is, profound revelations about the inadequacy of how we organize knowledge.

The way we categorize our knowledge, segregating artificially into pieces, separating "reading" from "art" from "mathematics" and "ethics," has led us to this particular point in history. The idea that we can sift out ecological impact from something like "work" or "sex" or "science" has driven us to a real crisis. That, if nothing else, we must change. That is, we have to teach our children new ways of looking at the world and of imagining our future. We need to naturalize, from birth, the connections between moral principle, science, history and our daily actions.

I sometimes wonder if the breakdown of our existing educational structures might not be one of our best hopes for the future. Because, in the end, it will all come down to education — the education we offer at home and in schools, the self-education of billions of adults who transform their lives without any real guides to help them, and the messages we pass on to the next generation. It will all come down to what gladly we would teach and learn.

Four

[*Home Economics,*
Home-Land Security]

NINE

Little House in the Suburbs

Who has not found the Heaven below
Will fail of it above.
For angels rent the house next ours,
Wherever we remove
— EMILY DICKINSON

I've never loved any earthly thing so much.
— BARBARA KINGSOLVER

Home is Where You are Now

ONE OF THE THINGS THAT HAPPENS WHEN PEOPLE REALLY GRASP THE implications of our coming collective crisis is that they immediately think, "I have to grow all my food, cut all my own wood, mine salt from my backyard, grow flax so I can weave my own underwear and blacksmith my own automatic weapons!" The first reaction we all have is to try and protect our own, and to imagine that the right solution is to claim as much land as humanly possible on which to do it.

Speaking as someone who did move out of an urban location to begin a farm, I think for some people that's a really good response. If you love growing food, have some experience with it (although even that isn't wholly necessary — I didn't have very much), want to live the country life and don't have ties keeping you in the city, then moving to a rural area and becoming more self-sufficient can be a good idea, and far be it from me to discourage you. (But you can probably reuse your current underwear for some time to come, and even if you have the forearms for blacksmithing, maybe start with a nice trellis instead of an automatic weapon.) We are going to need more

145

farmers if we're going to have real local food systems. Living in the country can be much cheaper than living closer to cities.

On the other hand, a big chunk of land often costs a lot of money, and not all of us have that. And living in the country has its downside. You may be more car dependent because it is harder to walk or bike to things and there are fewer public transportation options. There isn't always a large selection of jobs. And not everyone is cut out for a life in the woods.

That, however, is no bad thing. Because the simple fact is that there isn't enough land in the world to give everyone 20 acres, or even 10. And even if we could, it isn't necessarily a good idea — the "use what you have" thinking that this book is based on suggests that people should mostly live in the houses we've already built and adapt existing communities rather than building new houses in new places. We've already covered an awful lot of our precious arable land with housing — we can't afford to do much more of that.

Estimates suggest that over the next few years, Americans are going to have to produce more and more food on less and less land. In a 1994 paper, Cornell Professor David Pimentel and Mario Gampietro demonstrate that by 2050, most Americans will have only 0.6 acres of arable land available to grow their food. At the time of the study, the average American's basic diet used 1.8 acres, and to keep it more or less the way it is requires a minimum of 1.2 acres, according to the study's authors. According to Gampietro and Pimentel, by 2025, the US is likely to cease exporting food because of a rapidly growing population and falling land availability. What does that have to do with anything? Well, it means that it is more and more important that we make use of the arable land connected with suburban houses, growing gardens on existing properties rather than moving onto new land.

An enormous amount of rhetoric in the Peak Oil movement has been expended in attacking the value of suburbs. The film *The End of Suburbia* and James Howard Kunstler's books *The Long Emergency* and *The Geography of Nowhere* all represented powerful analysis of the disaster created by our move to suburbia. Kunstler argues passionately and compellingly that the suburbs are doomed; he calls them — not without excellent reason — "the greatest misallocation of resources in the history of the world." The conclusion of *The End of Suburbia* is that we will become an urban people, living in communities where we can walk to jobs and shopping. And to some extent this may be true. Kunstler's ultimate prediction for suburbia is this:

> *If large numbers of people cannot unload their suburban McHouses and McMansions, then sooner or later many of these*

buildings will simply be abandoned, or become the slums of the future. I don't think the transition will be long. Lawlessness may make the continuation of life in the dysfunctional shell of suburbia extra-difficult. The national chain stores will be dead. The supermarkets will not be operating. None of the accustomed large-scale systems we depended on for the goods of daily life will be operating as they did, if at all. It is hard to conceive of any kind of social reorganization that might overcome the practical limitations of the suburban development pattern minus the fuel needed to run it. Many people might try to hang on there, but their lives may be Hobbesian. (Kunstler, 249–250)

It is hard to underestimate how deep the impact of this rhetoric has been on people's thinking about a low-energy future. Because Kunstler and that film were many people's first contact with the idea of Peak Oil, and because Kunstler is so enormously persuasive, I think the ideas here have had more currency than perhaps they deserve.

Now to be perfectly clear, I agree entirely with Kunstler's critique of the *project* of suburbia — it was an enormous misallocation of resources. It did create incentives for people to consume and pollute. It often is both wasteful and ugly. However, I do not agree that the suburbs will be abandoned — in fact, I think they cannot be abandoned, if we are to continue eating. We need to grow food; we need to grow food in places near where people live now; and we cannot afford to move 50 percent of the American population (that lives in suburbs) back to cities and small towns and build new housing for them. Having wasted resources in suburbia, we have no choice to use what we have and make the best lemonade we can out of our lemons. Most of all, we cannot abandon suburbia because of the simple mathematical problem of feeding people — without the arable farmland we turned into suburbs transformed into gardens, forests and food producing areas, our kids and grandkids will starve. So we must find some way to make suburbia sustainable.

So instead of everyone picking up and moving to a farm, or building some new society, what we need is a "Little House in the Suburbs" model — a way of making what we already have usable in a much lower-energy and -emissions world. We need to wholly rethink our houses and the places we live. I'm going to start by talking about suburbs, because that's where most Americans live now. We tend to think of the suburbs as rich places, but, in fact, more poor people now live in suburbs than live in urban communities. And even among those in urban areas, many now live in cities that are essentially designed like large suburbs — that is, they are heavily car dependent, with residential areas separated from everything else. So, much of what I have to say about the 'burbs applies to sprawl cities like Atlanta as well.

The most troubling design feature of suburbia and sprawl is that it is tremendously car dependent. You probably see this in your neighborhood — you live in one place; shopping is in a different place; and your job is probably somewhere else. The average American commuter now drives 41 minutes round trip to get to work and 28 minutes round trip to shop. The same commuter shops three times per week or more. Many people drive much longer. Supercommuters, those whose total daily commute exceeds two hours, are the fastest-growing group of commuters. Many people simply can't afford to live close to their jobs or their families. The closer you are to places with a lot of work and services, the more expensive things are. So people move further and further out.

Now, the standard advice has been that the best way to live sustainably is to be as close as possible to your job. That is probably good advice if you are a tenured professor, a Nobel Prize winner, the owner of a business or the child of the owner. That is, if you have serious job security or are in some way indispensable, moving close to work is a good idea. If family and shopping are located near your job or you already conveniently live near your job, great. But things are changing in the housing market. Right now we are in the middle of the collapse of our housing system — foreclosures now outnumber new home sales in many regions, it is increasingly difficult to get a mortgage at all and the housing crisis crowds the business page with scandals. Housing prices are dropping rapidly, and many houses simply can't be sold at all. So it might not be such a good idea to move at all. Most of us might already be stuck with our houses.

But if you were going to move, should you move near your job? It really depends on how likely it is that your job will be there in the long term, and how likely it is that you might be able to get another job in the same area. Because in the best of times we tend to change jobs quite a bit; and these will not be the best of times. Widespread unemployment is one possible consequence of the coming changes. It is also possible that we will experience short-term growth in some areas, such as manufacturing, renewable energies and the building trade. But these are guesses, and I don't have a crystal ball. What I would say is that much of how we will cope with what is coming for us depends on our recognizing that our jobs in the official economy are not very stable, and we are better off making decisions about where to live based on family and optimal geography, where we can afford to live well and where good communities are.

Could this come back to bite you in the ass when you are priced out of your job by high gas prices? This may be true, but there are a number of ways that you can minimize the likelihood and the need or cost of commuting. If you work in a white-collar, computer or information-based job, you may be able to telecommute. Certainly, you could cram many more people into your car and share the costs of commuting. Pat Murphy, of the Community Solutions advocacy group, has put together a program called the "Smart Jitney" solution to the transport problem. Murphy argues that the most energy efficient way to adapt is not to try and replace all our vehicles all at once, but to change how we use our vehicles.

. . .

Now is a great time to discuss telecommuting with your boss.

. . .

Right now, a majority of cars at any given time have only a single occupant. Changing this so that cars are mostly full most of the time would do an enormous amount toward allowing us to use our infrastructure more efficiently. A midsized car, getting 30 mpg with five people crammed into its seats gets mileage roughly equivalent to the best that electrified passenger rail can accomplish. Since most people commute to broadly the same few areas for work, this shouldn't be too hard to accomplish in most places.

Electric-assist bicycles can allow even lazy people like me who are carrying too many pounds to get on our bikes and cover long distances. Even without an assist, a bike ride of five to ten miles round trip with a trailer to haul groceries is doable for most healthy people under 60. And it is possible to combine car and bicycle, carpooling to a central location near jobs and biking the rest of the way. Electric assists for bicycles cost a little money but can effectively replace cars in some cases.

New urbanism and similar designs that emphasize "walk to shopping" have their merits, but there are other solutions available to those who don't live near shopping. The first is to shop only occasionally. Grow a good-sized garden, plant some fruit trees, get practiced at eating seasonally and you'll rarely need to stop for fresh produce. Get a couple of small Nigerian dwarf goats for a section of your yard, or get together with your neighbors and share a Jersey cow who rotates around yards, and you'll have milk. A couple of chickens and you've got eggs. Yes, I know your zoning doesn't allow that yet. Give it time. Add a few more hens and some rabbits for meat if you eat it. Or if you don't want to do that, maybe someone else does, and you can buy your neighbor's eggs and pick up milk at the farmer's market from some other suburban five-acre plot turned into a small farm.

Buy staple foods in bulk and learn to cook whole grains, beans and fresh vegetables. Guess what — you now need to visit the grocery store no more than once a month. Learn how to repair your clothes and fix your house, and ta da! You now only have to shop once a month; and you can drive with three neighbors or take your bike and trailer.

But even that probably won't be necessary, because remember, more and more of us are going to have to move into the informal economy. And we're not going to be renting office space for that, we're going to be doing it out of our homes. So one person may be telecommuting in a spare bedroom and fixing shoes in the garage. Another person will sell bulk goods out of the spare room, and the garage will be the hen house. All the infrastructure of suburbia can be adapted to our new way of life. It will be harder, of course, to adapt ourselves and to push our zoning regulations aside so that we can start this now, rather than later, but that work is achievable, low cost, and makes the best possible use of what we have.

• • •

Invest in a small cart that you can pull behind you so that you shop and carry your purchases on foot. Or add a trailer to your bicycle so that you can run errands while biking.

• • •

Ultimately, the question of how to get to work and shopping is one of the smaller ones facing us. The larger questions are how do we keep our homes in hard times? And how do we adapt them so that they aren't absorbing most of our resources? We need to change the way we think about our houses, the way we use them and they use us.

Since at least the 1950s our homes have been expressions of our lives — and costly ones. It isn't just that we pay mortgages and property taxes. Our homes are furnished and decorated and managed to keep us shopping and spending. It just keeps costing us and costing us. But we're not going to be able to afford anything as costly as that in our lives. Instead, home should be multifunctional — it and the land it is on should provide you and your family not just with shelter, but with fuel for heating and cooking, food to eat, space for money-making cottage industries and money-saving projects such as storing food and sewing. Or if it doesn't, then it should be very small and cheap, perhaps a rented room or two in a larger house, so that you can afford to get those resources other places. The coming decades are going to transform our entire relationship with our homes.

How do we do this? We begin by rethinking and reorganizing and opening up to even the most basic questions, such as, Should I own a home? Should I keep my present home? How should I adapt it? And most of all, we ask the question, Where will I stay? Our society's tremendous mobility has been heavily fueled by fossil energy. We've always been able to pick up and move far from family and friends, knowing they are only a plane ride away, knowing that we can always pack up and move again if things don't work out. But the environmental cost of all that mobility is catching up with us.

If the meaning of home is about to change, then our relationship to our homes will also change. Home is no longer just a place to decorate and stop in between trips to the mall — it is the source of our dinners and the place that our family lives. The house you own now may be the house your children grow up in, that they live in as young married people, and that your grandchildren run through. We're heading back to a culture of permanence, so the very first question is not, Where do I go? but, Where will I stop and stay?

Staying Put

It almost doesn't matter what you believe is the central problem of our present society. Whether you are focused on economic instability, Peak Oil, Climate Change, poverty and inequity or just the decline of community and standards of behavior, when you filter out the details and get down to brass tacks, much of my advice in this book can be summed up as "go home and stay there." And not just mine — if you sort out the advice of most books on getting along during Peak Oil, an enormous amount adds up to the same message.

Think about how much of what we need to do involves simply being at home. Home is where you cook dinner instead of buying it. Where you put that money away so you can donate it. Where you talk to your neighbors and build community. Where you grow your food, and where you bring the veggies after your trip to the farmers' market.

Home is where you advocate for zoning changes at your town meeting and where you hold the local emergency preparedness society meetings. It is where you sort through your extras to give to the needy. When you walk and bike, you stay closer to home. When you make things instead of purchasing them, or do without, you do it at home. Home is where you turn down the heat and put on your sweater, where you chase your kids or play soccer with your neighbors instead of going to the gym. Where you talk with friends, sing with your family. Home is the soil where you plant trees, the dirt you practice permaculture on. Home is the root place of simplicity, of quiet, of the economy, which literally means "domestic management." Home is where your roots lie. But we cannot do these things unless we go home and stay there.

You cannot build community, have an orchard or depend on others for the things that you need, unless you actually stop moving around and stay somewhere. And most of us are not very good at that — the average American moves every five years. That doesn't give you enough time to pay off the mortgage, see that standard apple tree grow to fruition or get to know the local issues well enough to have an impact on your town. In five years you can get a carpool together and get some bartering going, but you'll leave just as things get good. It gives you just enough time to begin acquiring that wonderful quality, "known-ness," in which you know your neighbors and understand how they are connected to other people (that the postman is the nephew of the woman in the third house down, and that the woman in the green house is worried about her mother at the nursing home) and how you fit in (you are the weird one who composts and has chickens).

Then you move — for the best of reasons: because this was a starter house and you need something bigger, to build your own passive solar place, to be closer to your elderly parents, so the kids can walk to school or to downsize now that the kids are gone. And you start again with a new garden, new soil, new trees and new neighbors, new friends for the kids and new everything.

Now, I have a lot of natural sympathy for people who move a lot. I would be one of them, but I'm not allowed. Eric feels about moving much the way I feel about toxic chemicals, only not so positively. If it were left to him, we would probably still be living in the same apartment we lived in during graduate school. But now that he's here, he's happy, so he's never, ever moving. Add to that that this is the house we lived in with his beloved grandparents, and we're here forever.

On the other hand, if three months have passed since we moved here that I haven't looked over the local real estate listings, I'd be shocked. I'm a grass-is-greener kind of person. I've never been anywhere that I didn't think (however briefly) "Could I live here?" And often, when I'm most frustrated with my life, my first reaction is that we should do something drastic — and what could be more drastic than relocating?

It has been a long, long struggle for me to realize that I am staying here forever, if possible. I still fight against that reality sometimes. I do love my house, but I love it the way I love most of my relatives — that is, I'm not always sure that I actually want to live with it. If you were to describe the ideal sustainable house, I suspect you would not choose a 3,800-square-foot rambling, under-insulated farmhouse with a bat collector (er, cupola space). It is a pain in the behind to keep clean (and I am an indifferent housekeeper at best), drafty, too big even for our four kids (we had hoped Eric's grandparents would be with us much longer), and because of its size the taxes are appalling. And, of course, there are a host of other things that make it much more difficult and annoying to make efficient than would a new, green-built home. That is, it is imperfect like every other house, except the ones in my imagination.

I'm going to bet that most of you live in the wrong house too. Statistically speaking, the odds are with me when I say that. But, no matter how imperfect our houses are, we are not going to replace our 90 million dwellings with brand new, perfectly designed ones. Think of what we'd waste in doing so! A few people will build new, green-design houses, but most of us will make do with what we've got, or, as most of us do, buy another house and another house, trying always to get to the point at which our house will fulfill its dream functions for us, but never succeeding. Some of us will move in together, putting more people in our oversized suburban houses.

. . .

Reconsider how you are using your house. Could you add a roommate? Share with a family member? Work from home? Do projects more efficiently? Add a greenhouse? Work with what you have to make space more useful.

. . .

However, all this moving that we do exacts a price. First, there's the economic price — realtors' fees, advertising, moving costs and buying new things at the other end. We lose an average of 6 to 8 percent of the purchase price on each house. Even in a good housing market, most of us don't keep much of the profit we've made from "flipping" our houses — we give it away to other people. The people who make money tend to be those who stay in place a long time, long enough to pay it off and enjoy the profits from it.

And all this mobility sets us back on every goal we have in creating local economies, local communities and local cultures. Every time we move, we lose a year or two of high quality work, because while we're adapting to a new place, meeting people, finding out about local resources, getting used to the new job, seeing where the sun falls in the yard and testing the soil, we're spending time that could have been used for gardening and working at the shelter and bartering with the neighbors. It also costs energy. Moving our stuff, sorting and organizing it, buying new stuff, flying on airplanes, renting trucks — these are not low-energy activities. They raise our personal energy footprint.

Now, sometimes we have to move. But over the coming decades, a lot more of us are going to have to stay put. We are, as author and Post-Carbon Institute founder Julian Darley puts it, going to have to change to a foot economy and "relocalize." But we cannot relocalize if we are dreaming of the day we will move to our perfect house, dreaming that we will find the perfect community of people just like us. We can't wait until we can all afford the perfect place. Some, perhaps many, of the places we're in are going to have to become perfect because they are ours. We're going to have to learn to "bloom where we're planted."

With the crash of the housing market, it isn't going to be economically feasible to trade up all the time. No matter how good your insulation, the building materials in your dream house come with a big energy footprint. No matter how annoying your neighbors, maybe it is time to share with them, rather than dreaming of the perfect community in which everyone is wonderful and perfect. Even if the house is too small or too big, doesn't have the garden space you dream of or is down the street from weird people, it might be the best place for you. Perhaps you could take in a roommate or family member, or rent a room for office space in a neighbor's house. Perhaps you could garden in an elderly neighbor's yard or start a garden at the school or park. Perhaps the weird people might become friends some day. Perhaps the truth is that all houses lack something, all yards are imperfect, and ultimately, all neighbors are a little weird — even you, even me.

• • •

New houses are being built and old ones renovated. Ask permission to scavenge free building materials, cinder blocks, and old windows and scrap wood for your own projects.

• • •

Taking a look at your "here" and accepting it as your home is a big step. It's a hard one for me, but I'm trying. Instead of crying, "But shouldn't we move to where we can bike everywhere?" I'm looking at bikes that can handle four kids, and we're debating whether we could get rid of our car and make our community more bikeable. Instead of complaining that the house isn't perfect for what we want, we're concentrating on retrofitting it to make it as perfect as it can be.

Buy or Rent?

This really depends on your circumstances. Generally speaking, I think comparatively few tenants will have the option of really adapting their rented spaces for the future — too many of the changes are visible and not conventional, and may be difficult to get by a landlord. But renting can be so vastly cheaper than buying (in some regions) that it may be a good deal for you. And if all you can afford to buy is a condo or housing with substantial deed restrictions that make it impossible for you do things like hang out laundry, put up rain barrels and plant edible shrubbery, you might be better off renting.

Generally speaking, I think if you can afford to buy outright, you should buy. If you can pay down a mortgage rapidly by scrimping and saving, then getting on your land and starting gardens, home improvements and fruit trees can be advantageous. But I would not recommend buying simply to buy. And if you can rent from someone with great flexibility who won't mind your gardens, that can also be a good choice. Personally, I would rather rent than buy a house with tiny down payment, large mortgage or adjustable rates in this market.

I'm going to guess that many of the people who are reading this own a house already, or will be moving to a house owned by friends or family. A larger question for more of us may be whether we *can* and *should* hang on to our houses in difficult circumstances.

Where to Live?

First let us dispense with the obvious. I assume you know that the north is cold, the south is warm and that this is mostly a matter of personal preference. That is, you can live quite well on little or no energy in the very cold north or the very hot south. You might not like it, but it will not kill most people.

Every time I say this, someone argues that heat and cold do kill. Yes, there are some medical conditions that make you especially sensitive to one or the other. And yes, you can die from both heat and cold. But even without powered heating, people are designed to tolerate a lot of cold — if they weren't, we'd never have survived until the invention of central heating. If you dress warmly, bundle up when sleeping, wear a hat, layer, sleep with another human or a dog, and move around during the day, you can live with no supplemental heat, even in Saskatchewan. You probably won't like it very much, but you will do fine. People who freeze to death in their homes are generally elderly or children and don't know how to respond to growing hypothermia — they may even feel warm and take off their clothes. The best cure for this is being together, with adults watching over the very vulnerable and making sure they get enough calories and are protected from the worst of the cold.

The same is true of heat. Yes, people die of heat stroke — but mostly they are elderly or disabled people who are alone, muddled by the heat's effect on their bodies, and who lack the ability to do simple things like put their feet in a bucket of water or hydrate adequately. Most people who die of heat stroke or cold, die because they are isolated, not because of the weather per se. Have close communal ties and a system of support for those without family, especially those with medical conditions, infants and the elderly, and such deaths could be greatly reduced or eliminated.

All of which means that temperature in and of itself is largely a matter of personal preference, one of those pick-your-poison issues — snow, ice and cold or heat. You should be aware that all regions will get warmer gradually, so be prepared to live with not just what it is now but what it will be in a few decades. In the meantime, if you like neither extreme, there are some options there, too — the Pacific Northwest and the southern Appalachians, for example.

Then there's the matter of neighbor prejudice. Information on this you can get in bulk at various websites and in books, so I'll keep it to a minimum. The idea that right-thinking people don't want to live near conservative Christians, that scary Asian pirates will depopulate the Pacific Northwest, that Latinos will rule the Southwest with an iron hand, and that inner cities will be filled with "them" rioting and shooting all assume that a) we are not whatever "them" we're worrying about and b) this is going to be the defining feature of the future. I don't swear it isn't true, but I also think the whole thing is probably rather overstated. There are some people who probably will have good reason not to pick certain regions — but there will be many people who find those regions compelling precisely because of a scary-to-others immigrant population or religious culture. Because I know there are various "thems" of all sorts among my readers, I'm going to suggest that instead you find a community where you feel secure, are comfortable and have a supportive community. Pick your poison.

So what should you care about when choosing a place to live? Here's my personal list of the most important factors:

A PLACE TO STAY — one to pass down and that you believe will be good for you and your family for the long term. The coming changes may well involve a great shift in how we regard natural resources like land and water. We are moving from a society that has invested enormous economic value in things far removed from the origins of their production to a society that is probably going to be hyper-aware that wealth = natural resources. In a society where food is scarcer, water is short and resources are stretched to their limits, land and the resources on it, along with the capacity to grow food and wood, are likely to be intensely valuable.

In many societies, ordinary people have been sustained by their access to the land and their long-term ties to that land. Generally speaking, poor people cannot buy much, if any, land. Instead, they inherit it — families steward land and pass it down from generation to generation. We do not do this in the rich world very much, but I think we may go back to it. Although for a short while we may become a mobile society, with many refugees relocating, over the long term we may become more fixed, more bound by our investment in a place and the community ties we depend on.

So the first factor I take into account is a place to stay. This is not a perfect solution, of course — no one can know the whole future, and migration is always possible. But unless we stop and stay, we will not be able to feed ourselves from our land, and we will never become truly native to anywhere, with a native awareness and love for a place. So I would recommend an area that you have reason to believe will continue to be a good place to live not just next year, but in 50 and 100 years. This is difficult, given the impact of Climate Change — projections are uncertain. But generally speaking, if the map shows that your home will be under water in 25 years, you might want to consider moving before the rush devalues your home. Take a serious look at the long term.

WATER — and lots of it. I can't stress this one enough. Anything less than 20 inches of rainfall a year is impossible to farm without extensive irrigation — and don't bet on having the power to do this. Personally, I wouldn't take less than 30 inches of rain per year, evenly distributed. If you have a dry season, where it doesn't rain for months on end, be absolutely sure you can fill your tanks sufficiently to get through.

Now, I know there are people who worry about water less than I do. I have a friend doing remarkable things with dry land tree agriculture in Israel, and she, among others,

• • •

Learn about your local watershed and encourage local water conservation efforts.

• • •

has great hopes. I, however, have my doubts. The reality is that most very dry places have never supported large populations. Moreover, in such places, the foodshed is extremely large — Gary Nabhan, author of *Coming Home to Eat*, required a local diet of 250 miles, rather than 100, simply because of limited availability. Though some people will undoubtedly do very well in the dry plains, deserts or other low rainfall areas, what kind of population will the area be able to support?

I personally would be very reluctant to live in much of the dryer parts of the American Southwest, parts of Australia and the driest parts of the plains of Canada and the US, unless I had full legal rights to reliable sources of water. Riparian water rights, as practiced in the Western US, make water issues contentious, and I would want to be absolutely sure that I could draw water from my source for a long, long time.

In addition, look for comparatively clean water. This is increasingly difficult to find all over the US — there is almost no drinkable groundwater or freshwater that I'd like to take a lot of fish out of. We've contaminated our most basic resource beyond compare. Make sure you test water from any well you might consider using, understand the basic pollutants in your area and have a good idea what and who you are downstream from. And I would recommend that everyone have a high-quality water filter, ideally gravity fed, such as the British Berkefeld or Kataydin filters. Even if you have to eat beans, dandelions and rice for a month to afford it, I'd consider this a worthwhile investment for anyone who has any spare cash at all.

· · ·

Practice extreme water conservation during hot weather. Mulch gardens to reduce the need for irrigation, use gray water from sinks and showers to irrigate gardens and flush toilets, bathe less often and use less water.

· · ·

At a minimum, unless your house has a spring as pure as ivory, I would never permit children or women who are or might become pregnant to drink unfiltered water from any source that has not been thoroughly evaluated. We cannot afford to damage future generations, and if we are to have fewer children in the future, their lives and health will be all the more precious.

NOT SITTING ON TOP OF MAJOR ENERGY RESOURCES. The next few decades are going present reasons to try to extract the last drops out of old oil wells and coal out of areas previously deemed too populated or dangerous to touch, etc. I do not want to be on top or very near any major energy source — natural gas, uranium, coal or oil. The toxic, environmentally disruptive nature of extraction of all sorts means that my own basic goals of reasonable security, minimal medical interventions, food self-reliance, can be destroyed by one nearby mountaintop removal or uranium extraction. These projects contaminate water tables and streams, generate toxic air, noise and water pollution, and generally make life miserable for the people around them. They are the price of our insatiable desire for energy.

So if the words "old coal mine" or "natural gas well" apply to your proposed property or anywhere near it, run like heck, unless you own every single mineral right and are sure that there is no other way to get at the resources (such as digging in from the next property over). The Supreme Court's recent removal of restrictions on eminent domain means that I would be very, very cautious even if I did own all the rights to minerals on my land. I've reluctantly come to the conclusion that my New England ancestors were probably right — the best land out there may be the land that nobody really wants too badly.

LOCAL FOOD SECURITY in a place where you can eat a diet you like and where the region can mostly feed itself. I think we will find as we live and eat more locally that our diets change — sometimes dramatically. Most people who live regionally eat a few staple foods every day. They have other special foods, but if we live regionally, our cuisine will become localized as well. This is not a bad thing — people travel all over the world to experience local cuisines and their specialties. When you are picking a spot, pick a place where you like the food, since food is a factor in quality of life. If you are "from" tortillas and chilies, the potatoes, baked beans and fish of the Northeast may not be appealing to you. You can cook almost anything almost anywhere, with variations, but you will have to make do with what grows. Your kids will, to some degree, end up adapting to the culture.

You also should probably think hard about where your food is coming from. That doesn't mean that we all absolutely have to live in regions that can be self-supporting, but it is a matter of rational bet-hedging. If you live in the I-95 corridor of the US, say in New York City, your 100 mile diet will run into the hundred mile foodsheds of heavily populated suburbs and large cities such as Albany, Stamford, New Haven, Hartford, Newark, Trenton. That is, there is simply no meaningful way that these regions can be fully food self-sufficient — their food is going to have to come from less populated areas.

This in itself doesn't mean that everyone has to leave these areas — but you do need to have a local system for food, water and energy that can be sustained in the long term. It isn't enough just to say "Oh, great, we'll get our food from nearby." Make sure you know that it is possible. You want to choose places that have the potential to produce a great deal of food.

NEAR THE PEOPLE YOU LOVE — the times that are coming are going to make us depend on one another more than we have. If there are people in the world who have your back, who love you, who you care about, be near them. Transportation is getting expensive, and all of us are going to need all the help we can get. This factor, in the end, may trump everything else.

Sufficiency Plan for a Suburban Home

I wanted to give an example of how adaptation might work in different places. As a suburban model, I chose as my example the home of a college friend of mine, who has become aware of Peak Oil and asked for my advice not long ago. Emma (not her real name) lives in an exurb of Boston, with no direct public transportation (there is a train line 15 minutes away), in a fairly conventional suburban home with her partner and two children, 2 1/2 and 6.

Emma's house has slightly over an acre, of which half is wooded, the rest being open yard with a few raised garden beds. Her neighbors have similar lots, often quite shady, but with fairly good tree cover. The population is quite dense there, but there are few lots of less than half an acre. She is not terribly connected to her neighbors, but they get along reasonably well.

My friend wanted to know if she could feed herself and her family from the land she has. The answer, I think, is not quite. But Emma could make an enormous reduction in the amount of food she has to purchase, and within her limited budget, adapt her home to use less energy.

The first major project is to ensure a reliable water source. The house has a well, in addition to town water; she might consider putting a manual pump on the well so that she can bring water into the house if necessary. Because she lives in the wet eastern part of the US, she can do this — her water table is less than 200 feet down. If she lived somewhere with a lower water table, I'd recommend rainwater harvesting or solar-powered well pumping, which is more expensive. If she had no well on site, I'd recommend putting one in or adding a cistern. In fact, if my friend can afford it, it might be more pleasant for her to dig a large cistern and put a manual pump on her kitchen sink, so she can get water without going outside in bad weather. In a pinch, she might get away with a narrow well bucket of PVC pipe and let it down into her well with a string; but drawing all your water that way would get old, very fast. The cistern and pump would probably cost $2,000–$3,000. A well pump would cost about $800. A well bucket might cost $30. Direct water pumping using solar power would cost several thousand dollars, and a deep well in a dry climate could cost as much as $30,000.

The next issue is supplemental heating, which is necessary in central Massachusetts. Emma has enough woodland to take perhaps a half cord of wood (with coppicing and very careful management) every year, possibly less. Preserving her wood supply should be a high priority — the woods provide long-term heating fuel, cooling and shade, food and other value. She has a woodstove in her finished basement. The finished basement could become the family's winter quarters, as it would need far less heat than the rest of the house (being at least partly below the frost line). Her wood supply would probably not be sufficient, but it would minimize what she had to purchase, and in the worst degree of extremity, they could live with it, heating the stove only to cook. No one would enjoy living in a 40-degree basement, but they could survive.

It is important to remember that every item for which she is self-sufficient makes it more likely she will be able to purchase supplemental wood. Sufficiency here does not always mean meeting every single need but rather ensuring that you can use your limited funds for the most urgent purposes. Summer cooking will be outdoors, to keep from heating up the house. I would recommend building a small masonry oven using the rocket stove model (see bibliography), which uses minimal fuel and cooks quite well.

Emma has two cats, one of which is an excellent mouser. I suggested she keep the cats, as long as her economic situation permits her to feed them, especially if she's going to be living in the basement for a lot of the winter. The cats will provide both warmth (they sleep with the kids) and rodent protection. I would stock up on at least a year's supply of cat food, stored in metal bins, and make long-term plans for feeding the cats.

I would add meat rabbits (three does and a buck), four hens and perhaps a pair of geese as livestock, which is close to the maximum she could hope to feed on her property. At present she is permitted to keep only poultry, but rabbits are often classified as pets, and she need not tell anyone otherwise. A portion of each year's garden would be put to growing alfalfa hay, both to restore garden fertility and to feed the animals over the winter. In addition to gathering edible weeds from the garden and property margins, she can grow a small amount of wheat, oats and corn in the garden. About half would go to the maintenance of the animals and growing their young for meat and breeding replacement.

- - -

Grow some food in your garden for your animals. Alfalfa, root crops, even wheat can be sowed in garden beds.

- - -

Or they might choose to go vegetarian, but a recent study from Cornell University suggests that a small amount of animal protein integrated into one's diet makes the best possible use of the land available. My friend is going to have garden weeds and grassy areas in her yard by necessity, and if she can get some meat and eggs from those weeds, she's improved her family's food security.

Most of my friend's sunny, open half-acre will be taken up with a garden, nearly half of which will be in cover crops providing fertility, hay and mulch.

Remember, she may not be able to run out to the garden center for fertilizer. Maintaining soil fertility is the key to feeding her family. Storing some fertility boosters like greensand and bone meal would be wise. The ashes from the woodstove will also go on the soil, as will composted animal manures.

The remainder of the land will be heavy on perennial edibles. Landscaping is with edibles — blueberries replace rhododendrons, raspberries replace privet, and several small ornamental trees should be replaced with fruit trees. The diet will be low on grains, but high on potatoes and other roots. A large portion of the garden will be planted in these crops to maximize calories and nutrition for the available space.

Potatoes, cabbage and rose hips from existing bushes will provide vitamin C in winter. All roots can be stored in a walled off, insulated area of the basement after the furnace stops burning. I estimate that with good management, my friend will be able to have half a loaf of bread a week and fresh meat once a week, in addition to what staples she can buy. She should get about 450 eggs per year, heavily concentrated in the warm weather. The eggs, one or two slaughtered geese per year, and occasional bits of extra chicken fat from older hens will provide most of the fats in their diet. If they go vegetarian, sunflowers and oilseed pumpkins might be grown to provide fats.

. . .

Plant high-vitamin C fruits like Aronia, seaberry and rose hips.

. . .

In her woods are a number of sugar maples — she should be able to take several pounds of sugar (or liquid maple syrup, although sugar stores better) from them, which would be the year's sweetener. She might also be able to keep one or two hives of bees, which would provide sweetener and candle wax and improve fruit set and vegetable yields.

Emma is an experienced gardener, but has more practice with ornamentals than with edibles. She will not be able to grow all her family's food on a half acre at first, and the odds are good she won't be able to do it for a family of four at all. But she can probably produce the majority of their produce, some of their staple foods, and again, arrange things so that much needed cash is reserved for other foods.

In the meantime, I strongly recommend that she store enough food for at least two years, including enough for her family and anyone she anticipates might come to live with them. Stored food, judiciously used, will also add to the grains in her diet and provide balanced nutrition. I would recommend weighing storage heavily toward dried foods such as grains, beans and salt along with storable fats and flavorings.

The poultry will live in a tightly built pen attached to the back of the house to minimize theft and predation, and will have a yard to forage in each day. A large amount of green food, grass seed and weeds are available on the margins of the neighborhood, and I suspect that few of her neighbors will be wise enough to use them. Rabbits will be kept on the screened-in porch in summer and can be brought into the house in the winter. All animals should probably be moved to the garage for security and warmth over the winter.

The woods can provide small quantities of firewood, acorns (for rabbit feed, although humans can eat them too), a small number of mushrooms and leaf mulch, but must be carefully managed. Again, I suspect all of these things will be able to be acquired in her neighborhood, since most people will not be aware of their value. Scavenging weeds for the rabbits and chickens to eat, wood for cooking and acorns will be useful work for the children after school.

Emma has a large library but might want to begin accumulating educational materials and books for older children now, in case her regional school shuts down. Yard sales and library sales should provide a collection of useful materials at low cost. Children should also be taught useful skills. Emma might consider inviting other neighborhood kids to come to school with her children, both to provide them with companionship and as a way of establishing good neighbor relations.

If she can store enough food, I would recommend that Emma acquire a mid-sized dog to alert the family to night visitors, human and animal, and to assist with security. I would also suggest she get stout locks and deadbolts for the doors and get to know her neighbors well, to provide local security.

Emma is an excellent seamstress, and to insulate her family against economic shocks, she might begin a mending and sewing business to provide supplemental income. She also teaches childbirth classes and offers her service as a doula, both needs that will continue whether formal employment does or not. Her husband works as a computer technician but also brews beer and does simple construction. I would encourage both of them to put a foot in the informal economy because her husband's work is particularly vulnerable to market forces.

Will everything work out perfectly? Not necessarily. Emma has a large mortgage, and may not be able to stay in her house for the long term. But because the house has many advantages, she might prefer, rather than losing her place, to rent out two of four bedrooms to keep up mortgage payments.

Because she and her older son's father are divorced, and the father lives in the neighborhood, Emma will have a powerful incentive to keep her house, even if space gets tight.

In the end, this is not a perfect system. There is no perfect system. But I have high hopes that Emma — and most of us — can go on from where we are, with what we have.

·

TEN

The Beauty and Necessity
of the Low-Energy Home

A man is rich in proportion to the things he can afford to let alone.
— HENRY DAVID THOREAU

It can hardly be a coincidence that no language on
Earth has ever produced the expression "As pretty as an airport."
— DOUGLAS ADAMS

Why the Lights Go Out and What to Do About It

SOME PEOPLE WORRIED ABOUT PEAK OIL AND CLIMATE CHANGE ARE concerned about the potential collapse of the electrical grid and the possibility of having to live entirely without power. Richard Heinberg, for example, makes the case in *The Party's Over* that the electrical grid is extremely vulnerable to disruption because of short supplies. He argues,

> At a certain point, demand for electricity will begin to exceed
> supply. From then on, the electrical power grids may become
> threatened. Periodic brownouts and blackouts may become com-
> mon.... Within years of the first widespread blackouts it may
> become impossible to maintain the grids at their present scope,
> and efforts may be made to reduce the size of the grids and to
> cannibalize components that can no longer routinely be replaced.
> Eventually it might no longer be possible to maintain the elec-
> trical grids in any form. (Heinberg, The Party's Over, 204)

There are signs of this already happening. Brownouts and blackouts are becoming routine in places like California during periods of peak electrical demand. If we do not build more coal plants (something we should not do under any circumstances), thus exacerbating the climate problem, it is unlikely that electrical availability will meet demand for much longer according to many analysts. We might build nuclear power plants, but these have a long lead time to build, and uranium too is in danger of reaching its peak point. An industry insider recently reported that even if all barriers to nuclear construction were suddenly removed, shortages of experienced nuclear engineers and the fact that only a few companies have the resources to build them would itself remain a limiting factor.

In addition, electrical generation is tremendously water intensive. Studies suggest that areas of both the American southwest and Australia may soon have to choose between water for drinking and water for electrical generation. And among the aging infrastructure we are not main-

• • •

Make sure that emergency supplies such as first aid kits and flashlights are readily available and can be easily located in the dark in a crisis.

• • •

taining is the grid itself. We have not preserved our existing infrastructure, much less provided for enough expansion for many of the techno-solutions we imagine that would convert rail transport, cars and heating to electric generation. In many poor-world countries, the electricity comes on only a few hours a day — if that. Unreliable power is characteristic of places as diverse as Iraq, Albania and Mozambique. When the power comes on, you do laundry, fill every container with water and check in with the world on the Internet; and the rest of the time, you do without it.

I am agnostic on the question of whether the grid will continue to function as it has in the future — this is not my area of expertise, and there are simply too many variables to know for certain. But what I do know with some certainty is that we can expect to see whatever mitigation strategies we use raise the price of electrical generation dramatically. So there's a more insidious and serious issue that means that many of us may have to live without power part or all of the time in the future. That is, we're going to be poorer, and it doesn't take a grid crash to leave us without power — all it takes is the utility company shutting you off.

As I keep saying, Peak Energy and Climate Change, for most of us, will be less about geopolitics and large-scale infrastructure crisis than it will be about what I call ordinary human poverty. Even economists who dismiss Peak Oil acknowledge that significant oil shocks of any kind, caused either by depletion or by political crisis, would cause a major economic crisis and that most energy sources will rise in price along with oil.

During the last depression, Herbert Hoover famously said, "At least no one has starved," only to be caught out as cases of starvation appeared around the nation and mothers in cities rioted because they had nothing for their children to eat. The classic image of stockbrokers selling apples on the street and bread lines going around the block doesn't even quite convey how desperately poor many people were. It is not unlikely this view of our past is part of our future. This is what we face.

One of the useful things about having been crazily poor for some years during college and graduate school, which I don't generally remember with fondness, is that I now have experience to draw on with all sorts of unpleasant things like eviction notices and having your power shut off. The defining characteristic of poverty is never being able to pay all your bills. So you play bill roulette. You pay the one with the most urgent exclamation points and potent threats first, and then you pay the next one. You can go on like this for some time. But that is very hard to maintain when you don't have enough money to meet your basic expenses. And eventually, you get caught out — the check bounces, the next payment doesn't arrive in time, you have an unexpected crisis or the bill collectors threaten you into paying out of order, and something happens. And when you let one of the balls fall, the next step will set you back even further. Because getting your vehicle back from the impound, having your phone turned back on, contesting your eviction or whatever is expensive. Those things cost money you don't have, and you end up further behind.

Peak Oil and Climate Change will hit most of us where it hurts — in our jobs, in our pocketbooks, in the homes where we won't be able to make the rent or mortgage payment, in our health because we'll no longer be able to afford routine care, in our choices. Instead of "vacation fund or 401K," many of us will be wondering "shoes or groceries." Add in that we can expect the price of electricity to rise steadily — carbon sequestration is expensive (if it even works, which seems unlikely at this writing); nuclear power is expensive initially and dealing with its wastes is very expensive; much of the easily accessible, cheap coal is gone; investment in renewables is not cheap either. At this writing, US electricity prices have risen by 29% over last year, and British prices are even higher, with further increases projected.

So whether from electrical infrastructure problems or economic crisis, lots of us will be having our power turned off. And because electricity for the most part runs luxury items such as refrigeration and lights (although we are not accustomed to thinking of them as luxuries), if it comes down to hard choices like food or electricity, lights or medicine, we should all recognize that electricity is not essential to (most) human life and prepare to function well and comfortably without it.

Now, private renewable energy is an option for some people. But the systems are expensive and somewhat complicated, and in the northern part of the country, we can expect periods where there isn't enough sun to run our solar systems. I am not trying to discourage anyone who can afford it from investing in renewable energy systems, in fact, quite the contrary. But the process of adapting our homes to operate on less is a large and expensive one. In a nation with a negative total savings rate, enormous quantities of mortgage and credit card debt and a shaky currency, a lot of us, probably a majority, aren't going to be able to go solar, and probably shouldn't, because it really doesn't return the most bang for our bucks.

If you have $2000 to spend, you could choose among several things. For that money, you could add significant insulation to your house, make or purchase insulating curtains for windows, buy four solar lanterns, a couple of battery-powered lanterns, a solar battery charger and some rechargeable batteries. The insulation and curtains would provide a lifetime reduction in your heating and cooling needs; the rechargeable batteries and the lanterns would provide you with light and music for your existing CD player. Or, for that same $2000, you could get a battery-backup solar system that sat on your roof, and run four lights and a CD player. Oh, and you'd still need the rechargeable batteries for when the sun wasn't shining. I know which seems the better deal to me.

For those who are way ahead of the game and already have their insulation and everything else they need, great. And if you have tens of thousands of dollars to spend on your house, you don't need my advice on how to use it. But for the rest of us, solar panels or a wind generator is probably not the best use of our money. (If you have the right spot for microhydro, you might have a better deal, and I'm envious). As we try to find the most bang for our limited dollars and avoid indebtedness, we generally find that lower-technology, human-powered systems are almost as good, and infinitely cheaper.

Most solar systems generally cannot heat houses, run conventional refrigerators (the kind they can run are usually well above $1000, and the cost of the system to run them is quite significant as well), run toasters, electric stoves or, except with the largest systems, air conditioning. So even after dropping thousands of dollars on your rooftop solar system, you will still also need to buy non-electrical backups for every system if you live in a climate where there are cloudy periods. You will also still have to cover many other basic needs — besides the solar system, you'd need a method of preserving food, heating or cooling or cooking, if you felt yourself in danger of not being able to afford electricity and gas or heating oil.

If you are like us, that's just out of the question economically. We can't afford to preserve electricity at all costs. To do so, we'd need a generator, which is pricey, depends on outside gas and produces a lot of carbon, or on a giant solar system with a large array of toxic batteries. We cannot afford to have both low-technology and high-technology solutions. We'd have to have non-electric backups for the times when the skies were cloudy or the wind wasn't blowing. I think that's true of many or most people.

A lot of us have instinctively believed that our future is going to involve new, fancy high technologies. If that's the case, we're going to have to be able to afford to pay for them outright (remember that credit crunch), probably without lots of subsidies from the government. And most of us won't be able to do that — it is hard enough just to pay the bills.

Instead, what if we all took Wendell Berry's rules for the use of technology seriously and chose our technologies on the following grounds:

1. The new tool should be cheaper than the one it replaces.

2. It should be at least as small in scale as the one it replaces.

3. It should do work that is clearly and demonstrably better than the one it replaces.

4. It should use less energy than the one it replaces.

5. If possible, it should use some form of solar energy, such as that of the body.

6. It should be repairable by a person of ordinary intelligence, provided that he or she has the necessary tools.

7. It should be purchasable and repairable as near to home as possible.

8. It should come from a small, privately owned shop or store that will take it back for maintenance and repair.

9. It should not replace or disrupt anything good that already exists, and this includes family and community relationships. (Berry, 219)

What kind of tools would we have in our lives if we obeyed these rules? I think most of the "intermediate" technologies that are powered by hands, animals and very simple solar energies would make sense, while many technologies that are being proposed to solve our problems would simply fail the test.

The good news is that solar panels and wind generators aren't the only, or even the best, options anyway. For those of us who need the most bang for our buck, we need to prioritize. Electricity is nice — I'm very fond of it. But most of us should have homes that function well without it, just in case. And non-electric, human-powered solutions and stand-alone renewables (things like solar calculators, solar battery chargers, solar radios) are overwhelmingly more reliable, cheaper and more secure than dependency on the grid or on house-sized renewable energy systems.

In cold climates we need water, heat, light, a source of food and some way to prepare it, and toilet and washing facilities. A means of keeping food cool is helpful too, but a bucket of water taken from the ground and a mason jar will keep your dinner overnight — just put the food in the jar, seal it, and put it in the cool water. Laundry facilities would be great, but if you don't get to that, you can wash your clothes in a bucket, using a plunger to agitate them. Or wear your clothes longer and rinse them out in the sink by hand, like you do when you travel. Or you can put them in your tub, cover them with warm water, get in the tub with clean bare feet and stomp on them until they come clean. (Kids love this.) Then you can hang your clothes on a $2 clothesline. Many places sell a small, hand pressure washer for clothing for about $40. Or if you are ambitious, I've heard of people converting their washing machines to bicycle power. Many things we take for granted we don't need, but want. That's not to say there aren't good reasons to want these things, but our instinctive panic and sense "I must have this thing" is often just a lack of awareness of our options.

• • •

Put in a composting toilet. They don't smell; some of them flush; and they need not be expensive.

• • •

If you are good at scavenging, willing to endure some inconvenience and handy, you could probably provide yourself with non-electric heat, light, cooking facilities, food storage, toilet and washing arrangements for under $2000 — maybe much less, depending on where you live, what you are prepared to go without, and how good a sense of humor you have. Buying new, and hiring someone to install them for you, you might need to spend as much as $5000, but that can be done gradually, over time, and it will allow you to live comfortably without electricity. Many of these items are portable and compatible with living in rental housing — that is, you can take them with you if you go.

What might break the above budget is water in the dry west. Most of the rest of us can capture rainwater, but horribly, in some places in the west, it is illegal to capture the rain-wash off your roof. Very deep wells cannot be pumped manually. For you, solar direct pumps are probably the best option, or perhaps we will return to windmills. Either will cost you several thousand dollars. It might be wise, if you get sufficient rainfall, to spend that several thousand on a large cistern and collect rainwater. Changing the water laws so that you can collect your own rainwater would probably help.

In the hot states (an expanding number), cooling is a much bigger issue than heating. And though a lot can be done with good insulation, heavy curtains and shades, and a good solar attic fan, some people may still need air conditioning. In this case, if air conditioning is a life-or-death issue, house-attached solar might make sense. But for poor people, swamp coolers (which use water to cool the air) and battery-powered fans, changes in lifestyle (do work in the early morning and evening), cool baths and showers, and a change in pace will probably do it.

Our plan is to make our house functional and comfortable without electric power. We live on a fairly low income for a family of six, don't believe in debt and do believe that whatever changes we model should be accessible to most people. Now, I'm wholly aware that a few thousand dollars' investment is a huge thing for many people. Those folks will probably have to do without some of the things that would make them comfortable.

But we have found that it is possible to be surprisingly happy and comfortable without electricity. This mirrors the experience Eric Brende describes in his book *Better Off: Flipping the Switch on Technology*. Brende describes his family's eighteen-month sojourn living in what he calls a "Minimite" — that is, Plain People's (not all members were Amish) — society with very strict rules about outside technologies. His conclusion?

> *My quest to discover how little technology was needed for actual human comfort and leisure was now over, and I believe I had an answer: no more than the Minimites used. Maybe less. As Mary's mother is our witness, even in the busy season we had more time. This was another way to say that we had fallen in time, taken our time.* (Brende, 216–217)

It is hard for many of us to truly believe that doing things by hand can give us more time, but it is true. Industrial society steals time from people. Doing things without power, besides making us secure, can give a little of it back by costing us less. It is a whole package though — if you just try and pump the water by hand while still running the kids to soccer three nights a week, it will cost you time. The low-energy lifestyle is a whole thing, a whole life, and a good one. But it isn't the same as the energy-intensive one we live now.

By declining to use power now, we are preparing for the days when we can't use it. And that does mean an investment in simple tools.

For us, that involves a manual pump on our well, as well as a cistern with a hand pump at my kitchen sinks (because I'm lazy and want water in my house so I don't have to carry buckets in February). We have two solar lanterns, two solar battery chargers, and a crank/solar radio for lighting and music. (We consider music an essential.) I can do my laundry in a bucket, but I'm coveting a manual washing machine because I still have kids in cloth diapers. Refrigeration will be water bas d during the summer and natural during the winter. (We have an insulated area that stays plenty cold but does not freeze.)

It will also mean changing the way we cook in warm weather, but that's no tragedy — the planet is full of people without fridges, and they created some of the best cuisines on earth. We have a wood cookstove and a woodstove for heat. We had a homemade outdoor masonry oven, but we'll need to build a new one this year. I've got two homemade solar cookers. I am coveting a professionally made one, which will achieve higher temperatures, but I could get along with my homemade ones, constructed from tinfoil and cardboard boxes.

Our baling-wire-and-glue composting toilet setup, made from an old commode, is about to be replaced with something new and pretty; but the original worked fine, the bucket was free and the commode bought at a yard sale for $5. We buy sawdust now and then but could make do with leaves if need be.

We're reinsulating, which is not cheap, but we could, if necessary, just get used to the cold. It would not kill us. Homemade insulated curtains, tapestries or blankets hung over underinsulated walls, reusable bubble wrap on windows, even Styrofoam insulation covered with bookshelves, and handmade draft dodgers would do the same job for much less money, as would moving more and faster and putting on more clothes and having plenty of warm blankets for unheated sleeping areas. We should not confuse issues of comfort with issues of necessity.

My writing requires I have a computer. I could, if worse came to worst, write in longhand or on the ancient typewriter I inherited. But I suspect we may purchase a stand-alone solar panel and a laptop for me eventually, if I keep doing this work. But that, again, is a matter of convenience and having the money, not necessity.

For transportation we have the land to support a horse and buggy, and we own bicycles. Unfortunately, as yet our kids are too young, or in one case too disabled, to bicycle long distances. Bike trailers or fancy Dutch-style "bakefiets" bikes could move our whole family around. We have yet to go for either horse or family-style bikes, simply because of the cost. But even in our rural area, we could meet most of our needs by distance biking. It would be tough on us — neither of us is in perfect physical shape, but biking 10 to 20 miles per day is well within the realm of what most healthy adults can accomplish. The transition would be hard. It would also doubtless be good for us.

What Life in Our Low-Energy Home Looks Like

I wrote this "Day in the Life" piece on a cold day in November. I wanted to give people a glimpse into what life was like using only a fair share of energy resources. A hot, sunny July day would h. ve been completely different. But what is most notable to me is how happy and content that day felt to me as I recorded it. There are parts of it I wish were different — among them that my children would sleep later in the morning. But generally speaking, that's not a consequence of any change we've made. It wasn't anything special, just an ordinary day in the life of boring people using as close as possible to one tenth the energy the average American uses.

4:08 AM: Dear freakin' g-d, what the hell time is it? 4:08! Oh, noooooo! But yep, that's the sound of four boys bouncing, chatting and wide awake. My boys are very early risers — usually between 5 and 5:30 am. That part is okay; we live on a farm and they are in bed by 7, and we're morning people. But this hardly qualifies as morning. My autistic eldest child hasn't had enough time to adapt from dayligh⸱ savings time, and he got his brothers up.

• • •

Play "heater chicken" — compete to see how long you can go without turning on the heat or starting a fire.

• • •

Worst of all, it is my day to get up with them. Eric was out playing banjo last night, and it is my turn to take the morning watch. So I haul myself out of bed, throw on a thick, fuzzy robe over warm pajamas, visit the composting toilet briefly and open the kids' door. They are, of course, bright eyed, bushy tailed and ready to start the day. I, on the other hand am surly, despite the sweetness of their cheerful greetings.

4:15 AM: If it were really cold, I would start the cookstove, but it isn't that bad downstairs. Even though we didn't keep a fire going overnight, the lingering warmth of the heat in the cast iron stove is enough to make the house comfy at 60-ish. No one is cold — all four boys wear long johns under their fleece pajamas. So the first order of business is to let the dogs out, perform a cloth diaper change for Asher, and then get breakfast for the boys. I'm still not conscious enough to eat anything. The kids drink milk and eat rice pudding that I baked last night with local milk, jasmine rice, bulk almonds, vanilla and honey. This is a favorite breakfast and I get a lot of compliments on it from the kids. My surliness fades a little.

4:30 AM: Story time. Isaiah and Asher both have a selection of books for me to read. We do nursery rhymes, an Inuit folktale, a book about Chinese cooking and Chicka Chicka Boom Boom which I read three times. I decline a fourth repetition and go off to light the cookstove. I get it on one match. Things are looking up!

5:00 AM: Water has boiled. I have drunk my first cup of bulk, fair trade Earl Grey. Things are really looking up. I punch down the bread dough that Eric made last night before bed, grease four bread pans and dump the dough in. I set them to rise in the warming oven above the cookstove while I get the oven hot enough to bake bread. I dress Asher and help Eli dress himself. The other two are okay getting themselves dressed, although I do supervise clothing selections. Because our house hovers in the low 60s with the cookstove going at this time of year everyone puts on a sweater.

5:15 AM: Bread is baking. I'm doing dishes in the dishpan to conserve water. Brief and best-forgotten disciplinary crisis involving Asher's enthusiasm for hurling objects at his brothers.

5:30 AM: Okay, I'm picking up speed. The kids are listening to *Wee Sing Nursery Rhymes* on Asher's toy CD player, using batteries charged in the solar chargers. (For the rest of the day I will be humming "Did you ever ever ever in your long-legged life/See a long-legged sailor/Kiss his long-legged wife?" I fail miserably to resist the temptation to transform the lyrics into something far raunchier in my head.) I run out on the front porch to check the temperature and bring in yesterday's laundry off the line. Today's load of wash is in the machine. Eli's school lunch is ready — leftover Thai noodles with tofu and greens that Eric made yesterday, a local apple, homemade cookies, and water in his water bottle. Will I get the giant pile of half-folded laundry on the guest bed sorted out today, finally?

• • •

Put up a clothesline! And consider hand washing your clothes outside in cool water in the summer, as everyone will enjoy getting wet anyway.

• • •

5:45 AM: Nope, not a chance. Asher is singing his favorite song, "Mommy, Mommy, stay with me." I leave the laundry, and Asher settles himself firmly on my lap. Eli joins him and there is some wrestling over possession of my right knee. It is still quite dark, and there are lights on in only two rooms. After a short snuggle, we decide to go outside and see the stars. The kids fight over who gets to carry the flashlight. The dogs join us and help keep us warm in the cold morning. We see some bats flying around too. The light breaking over the spruces is transcendently beautiful.

6:00 AM: My contemplation of this beautiful, peaceful moment is interrupted by an argument over the Halloween candy inventory, and whether there are still any Smarties left. Since Eric and I have both been sneaking them, there may not be. I remain resolutely neutral on this subject, and when we go back in, pretend to need to feed the fire so that my guilt goes unnoticed. I wonder whether I have to count the Smarties and mini-snickers bars I ate from the kids' Halloween bags as non-local food, as I didn't purchase it?

6:30 AM: Okay, I let them watch a video. I know a good environmentalist wouldn't even have a TV. It is a constant battle at our house (not with the kids, between me and my husband), but since we've got it, I cave and let everyone watch an old (from when I was a kid — it really was better then) *Sesame Street* episode. The TV is a small portable model with a built-in DVD player that draws only a small amount of energy. I watch too for a few minutes, drinking that second cup of tea. When the bread comes out of the oven, we all eat some hot and fresh while singing "Draw a daisy that's dee, de-lightful.... When D is handy, it's fine and dandy." I'm enjoying myself disturbingly much.

7:00 AM: Eli goes out to play on the play set in the front yard — I check to see that the gate is locked (he wanders). The other boys are still engrossed in Super Grover. Time to wake up Eric — three hours of extra sleep is enough. (To be fair, he got up super early the previous day and is the one who does this more often.) Exchange of data about kids, food, diapers, laundry and today's homeschool projects. Eric gets dressed and scavenges the rice pudding the kids didn't eat, and then we get the kids all together to sing "Modeh Ani," the Jewish morning prayer.

I make a third cup of tea (herbal this time, lemon verbena, nettle and oat straw — way better than it sounds), add more wood to the stove and wander off to the computer. I'm within a few weeks of the book deadline, so I'm spending much more time in front of a screen than I really like. Today won't be too bad, though, because Eric is working and I've got other commitments.

7:30 AM: I'm logged on. The boys are starting on homeschool math with Daddy. I'll work until 10:30, when Eric has to head to SUNY. Eric and the boys will do manipulative math and practice doing problems in their heads. At 8:15, the bus arrives and Eli heads off to school. This is his big energy consumption — school is 16 miles each way, and in the morning, he's the only kid on the special needs bus. The rest of us *might* make our 90 percent reduction goals; Eli won't — he'll probably come out at about 30 percent of the national average. That puts him way ahead of most of the country, but still is a nut we haven't been able to crack.

8:30–10:30 AM: I work on my book; Eric and the boys take a walk in the woods, collect kindling, chop some wood for the stove, hang up the newly washed insulated curtains that help keep our heat in (it was too warm to want them until recently), clean the living room and have spelling practice. Simon reads poems aloud for a while. I hide. It is best if Asher is not reminded of my presence.

10:30 AM: Eric departs for his 17-mile drive to work. He carpools one day a week, but he works so much from home and such odd hours that it is hard to find a carpool. Before he leaves we verify that there's nothing we need — he goes past a grocery store, hardware store and most everything else. We're generally pretty organized about keeping stocked up, though, so nothing is needed. Eric grabs his homemade lunch, his water bottle and backpack and goes off to teach "The Exploration of Space." I take over at home and turn off the power strip on the computer.

11:00 AM: Asher is ready for his nap. I lie down with him on the futon in the back bedroom and nurse him and read a novel while Isaiah and Simon play quietly (mostly) together. Acknowledging that although a two-hour nap seems a perfectly wise and rational way to spend the mid portion of a day that began at 4 AM I'm not going to get one, I get up once Asher is settled and go make lunch — noodles reheated in the cookstove oven. We keep the leftovers in containers in our coolers. We have a freezer, at least for now, so every night I put the day's ice packs back into the freezer and take out a new, cold set, and put them in the cooler with the leftovers, the milk and various other things that need to be kept cool. But we're getting to the end of that — pretty soon we'll be able to put things on our covered porch or in a cooler outside. Natural refrigeration!

11:30 AM: Lunchtime. Everyone enjoys their meal, and the boys and I walk out to get the mail. I must, must, must do more to get rid of my stupid catalogs — if nothing else, they are ruining my garbage/recycling totals. I resolve to make more calls asking companies to take me off their mailing lists. Soon.

NOON. Homeschool time with the boys. We read a fairy tale, practice handwriting, talk about how wetland plants and animals survive the winter, and then, as a reward, play two games of Candyland. I cheat to let the kids win — maybe not the best moral lesson if they catch me, but cheating at Candyland does make the game slightly less monotonous. I take the chicken carcass we ate on Friday out of the freezer and stick it in a pot of water with some onion, garlic and ginger. We'll have Laotian style chicken soup tonight.

1:30 PM: Asher is up and wants lunch. Everyone has a glass of local apple cider, and Simon nibbles off Asher's plate when he's done. While they eat, I sneak outside, hang more laundry and split a bit of wood to build up the fire. I even manage to get a load of wool diaper covers and linens soaking in a bucket — they need to be hand washed.

2:00 PM: Everyone cleans up. The kids tidy their toys and help scrape food scraps into the compost bin, and we all go upstairs to work on cleaning our rooms. Mine needs it worst. We mostly pick everything up but get distracted by the pleasure of playing "hide the penguin," where Coltrane, their giant stuffed penguin "hides" and we all pretend we can't find him. It sounds stupid now, and it is, but we like it. Oh, and there's an extended game of "The Minister's Cat" and a discussion of what an adjective is. Isaiah and Asher don't quite get it, but they contribute gamely anyway.

3:00 PM: Eli's bus will be here soon. We all troop outside, bundled in sweatshirts, and visit the bunnies. The chickens and ducks are roaming around, and we take the angora rabbits out of their hutch and put them out on the lawn in our "bunny tractor," a little chicken-wire cage that lets them eat grass without getting eaten by something else. The kids bring parsley from the garden to feed them.

• • •

Choose breeds of poultry that can set and hatch their own replacements. Orpingtons, Cochins and most Bantams are wonderful mothers.

• • •

We recently had one of the birch trees that shades our house during the summer taken down. Sadly, they aren't long lived and the tree was at the end of its life. We discuss why we need another tree to provide shade there and what kind of fruit tree we need. The kids help me move some of the wood under cover to dry for next year's fires.

3:30 PM: Eli is home, and we all indulge in our post-school totally unsustainable ritual — popsicles. Eli is addicted to them and gets one every day after school. About two thirds of the time I make them from organic juices, sometimes organic juices I make myself and preserve. This time, they are eating red dye # whatever popsicles from the grocery store. What can I say? Everyone follows up with milk and an apple, except Simon, who eats dried blueberries from our garden.

4:00 PM: I should have planted the garlic a month ago, but I'm behind. Everyone helps me get it done, which means it takes twice as long, but we plant four garden beds of garlic and mulch the beds with leaves we picked up on the roadside during our forays into town. The kids love the leaves and are excited by how warm they feel from the process of decomposition. We talk about decomposition and heat. This is a good chance to visit the various compost piles, and I bring out the humanure bucket and take it out to the bin. Isaiah walks with me, and we see some yarrow, discuss its medicinal uses and spot a wild turkey in the woods.

5:30 PM: Dinner time. The kids are flagging, so we don't all eat together. They've had a long day. They get the non-spicy version of the chicken soup, which is made with the tomatoes we've been ripening on the windowsill, the bits of chicken I pulled off the bones, lime juice, keffir lime leaves (I keep a lime tree in the house), lemongrass (I keep a plant going over the winter), and onions. It is a wonderful, tart soup. The kids eat it with gusto, except for Isaiah who is in a picky stage. He eats brown rice and stir-fried cabbage and carrots, while the other kids eat everything. It is dark already, and we have the lights on in the dining room and living room, but the rest of the house is dark. After dinner each kid gets to pick a piece of Halloween candy, which they do with much excitement and discussion of the merits of each kind.

6:00 PM: Boys back into long johns and pajamas, and we march upstairs to do bedtime. We take a flashlight, because the lights are off downstairs while we get the boys settled. I read a chapter of *The Long Winter* with Simon and one of *Mary Poppins* with Isaiah. Asher gets two repetitions of *Goodnight Moon,* and Eli elects to have me sing his favorite song "Chelsea Morning." I don't sound like Joni Mitchell, but I don't let that stop me. Normally, the boys are in bed around 7, but by 6:30 Isaiah is asleep, Asher snuggled on my chest and halfway there, and Eli keeps saying "Goodnight" which means "Go away and let me sleep." We do. Despite the fact that we have four beds in their room, the kids all sleep together on one futon, like a pile of puppies.

6:30 PM: Eric heads outside to do the "critter chores" — I feed the dogs, start some laundry and bank the stove. Our soup is ready, the cabbage and rice are set. I go back to the computer for an hour or so before dinner, while Eric sweeps the dining room, wipes down the oilcloth, puts the cloth napkins in the wash, sets beans to soak for soup tomorrow and tidies the kitchen. The house is dark, except for the kitchen and the computer room. It is also cooling down (stove is banked for the night) so I put on a sweatshirt.

8:00 PM: Dinner. The food is terrific, even if I am the one saying it. We elect to eat on the couch in the living room, and we sit companionably and read while we eat, talking occasionally and enjoying the quiet together. The rest of the house is completely dark, except for the glow of the fire in the cookstove.

8:45 PM: Dishes set to soak (will do them in the morning), food put away, ice packs rotated, stove given one more attention, curtains closed for the night, draft stoppers against the doors, lights out, dogs in, boys tucked. We take a quick shower together to save water. And perhaps we'd better close the curtains here.

Food and Health:
The New Basics

ELEVEN

The Bountiful Home:
Grow and Preserve What You Need

What I stand for is what I stand on.
— WENDELL BERRY

*One evening our three and four year old daughters are
playing and I am working halfheartedly...Suddenly, I overhear them.
"God is made out of sky and wind," says the older
in a voice of absolute assurance.
"No," the other is equally firm. "A flower. God is a flower."
....They come to me and I stumble, caught up short and unpre-
pared....They want certainty....
At last in a burst of stentorian authority the
younger gathers herself and bellows out "God's in the garden!"*
— LOUISE ERDRICH

*Thou shalt not be a victim. Thou shalt not be a perpetrator.
Above all, thou shalt not be a bystander.*
— DISPLAYED ON THE HOLOCAUST MUSEUM IN WASHINGTON DC

The Crazy Lady and the Garden

WE WERE CRAZY, OF COURSE. WE PACKED UP OUR THOUSANDS OF BOOKS, OUR
cats, our 15-month-old son and my pregnant belly, stopped occasionally for me
to vomit by the side of the road and moved to the country to grow food. Twelve
years of public education, four years each of college (history and literature
for me, physics for Eric), seven years at Harvard studying astrophysics (Eric),
six years at various Boston institutions studying Shakespeare (me), had left

us with copious education, absolutely none of it applicable to anything we were planning on doing. All my classes on Shelley, Eliot and Renaissance drama had included nothing on seed saving, soil humus levels or tomato hornworms. Eric's years of higher mathematics had included no time spent on compost, carrots or pressure canning. And yet, we went. As I said, we were crazy. But it has turned out to be a wonderful sort of crazy, a necessary sort.

It turned out to be a joy, the most wonderful choice we could have made. It gave us lush pleasure in our food and time together, working companionably side by side. It gave my children an appreciation for food and nature, animals to touch and love, and an understanding that everything has an origin. It made us happy; it made us laugh with the sheer pleasure of discovery. And it turned out that it didn't matter that our training was in other things — this was the most fundamental, ordinary work of human beings. Until the past 100 years of human history, finding, growing and preserving food was what people did. It took 40 or more combined years of education to erase food lore from our lives — it took only a little time to get it back.

• • •

Grow an ornamental and useful garden full of flowers that have value as medicinal, dye and fiber plants, seasoning herbs, natural cleaners and pest repellents, such as dye hollyhocks and coreopsis, soapwort, hip roses, bee balm, bayberry and Johnny jump ups.

• • •

Over the past few years the idea that we ought to be eating more locally grown food, maybe even growing some of it ourselves, has gained currency all over the US. Books like *Fast Food Nation, Plenty,* Barbara Kingsolver's *Animal, Vegetable, Miracle* and Michael Pollan's *The Omnivore's Dilemma* have exposed the disaster that is our food system and also proposed an alternative. "The 100 Mile Diet" has clubs all over the nation encouraging people to eat more locally, focusing on foods grown and produced within 100 or 200 or 250 miles of their homes.

This is, of course, an enormously important step. Because in an energy-depleted world, where shipping and transportation constitute the single largest sector of the economy and the single largest cause of global warming, getting our food and other goods from our local region is increasingly essential. With our economy destabilizing, we can't afford the enormous energy costs, much less the environmental ones, of having everything come from far away.

Right now the average meal covers 1500 miles, and takes about 10 calories of oil and other fossil fuels to produce a single calorie of food. We are figuratively eating oil and natural gas, at a tremendous price to the environment and to our own personal food security. We are now tremendously vulnerable to famine from a combination of soil and resource depletion, growth in biofuel production, Climate Change and rising energy prices.

Dale Pfeiffer has perhaps done more research than anyone into just how vulnerable our food system is. His definitive book *Eating Fossil Fuels: Oil, Food and the Coming Crisis in Agriculture* lays the issues out quite clearly.

> *Modern Industrial agriculture is unsustainable. It has been pushed to the limit and is in danger of collapse.... [W]e have already appropriated all of the prime agricultural land on this planet; all that remains is a very small percentage of marginal lands.... Even without considering energy depletion, our agricultural system is ready to collapse. (Pfeiffer, 39)*

Pfeiffer exhaustively explores the limitations of industrial agriculture arising from depletion of soil, water, fossil energies and other resources, and falling yields because of industrial practice. He comes to the obvious conclusion — we face a true and deep food crisis. Since the publication of Pfeiffer's book, additional information has emerged about the impact of Climate Change on food yields (30 percent or more reduction in most grain yields — and that excludes the impact of water shortages, flooding and natural disasters) and about natural limits on phosphorous, a mineral essential to agriculture.

In 2007, world grain yields were at their lowest level in decades, and the world's stored food was enough for only a few weeks in a disaster. Biofuel production has driven up food prices all over the world and increased hunger. In Swaziland, 40 percent of the population is starving while cassava, the staple food of the region, is turned into fuel for export. And more and more grain goes to feed livestock worldwide. In the rich world, 80 percent of all grain goes to cows and pigs and other animals. Among the poor, 80 percent of all grains are eaten directly. The sheer injustice of this system is bound to create both hunger and violence. At this writing food riots have occurred in Italy, Mexico, Guinea, Mauritania, Yemen, Senegal and Morocco.

And, of course, as economist Amartya Sen has demonstrated, most famines are not caused by food scarcity at all. They are caused by the inability of people to buy food. That is a growing problem, both in the poor world, where globalization has driven millions of farmers into the cities, where they are especially vulnerable to rises in the price of food, and in the US, where working families are increasingly finding it difficult to make ends meet. As food prices rise, food pantries and other support programs are in a bind — donations are down because people who normally donate are finding it hard to meet their own needs, and the dollars given buy less food for the pantry. Meanwhile, demand is up by 40 percent. One food pantry in Vermont was reduced to giving out just stale Doritos and flour, while Alaskan food pantries closed because there was so little food that lighting the building wasn't worth the cost.

As we saw in a previous chapter, the US cannot hope to feed itself without more gardens and small farmers making use of land with houses on it, and this is almost certainly true of the rest of the world as well. All of us need to share in the project of creating food security in our communities and around the world. Every bite of food we raise for ourselves cuts back on global warming in several ways — every vegetable and fruit we raise is one that isn't grown with heavy applications of nitrogen fertilizer (which produces nitrous oxide, a gas that warms the planet far more than carbon), that isn't trucked across the country and wrapped in plastic. Every bit of compost and organic matter we add to our soil enables us to sequester carbon in the ground. Every tree, bush and plant we raise takes up carbon. Every bit of independence we earn from the supermarket makes us richer and more secure.

The 100 Mile Diet was an excellent start to thinking about local food security, but it isn't a sufficient place to end the conversation. So far, the 100 Mile Diet works in part because there are comparatively few people eating locally. Thus, the small numbers of local farmers can support them. So far, the growing niche market of "locavores" is encouraging new farmers — but slowly. That's great, and enormously important, but real food security will require that each region be able to support a large portion of its population eating locally.

Food security is going to be the central issue of this century. We are coming to the end of a great era of centralization in which most people have little or nothing to do with their food. That has to end. As mentioned earlier, studies on land use show that by the middle of this century we will have only 0.6 acres per person of arable land to grow food on. At present we lose 3 million acres of American cropland a year — 2 million to desertification, soil destruction and other problems of industrial agriculture, and 1 million to housing and development. Our current diet takes 1.8 acres per person; and a more basic, vegetarian diet would require 1–1.2 acres per person.

But the situation is not hopeless. It will be difficult to feed America on 0.6 acres per person, but we could nearly double that figure were we to make use of all the arable land that we have turned into suburban lots, golf courses and corporate lawns. That is, there would be enough and to spare if we went back to growing food everywhere that it can be grown. But that requires the participation of ordinary Americans. It means that probably 100 million people need to get involved in food production. We need more farmers, but we also need ordinary people to start producing food in their yards and in community gardens, on urban rooftops and on their church lawns. The more food we produce in our own regions, the more secure we are when hard times come.

What does "food security" really mean? The UN defines it this way:

> "Food security" means that food is available at all times; that all persons have means of access to it; that it is nutritionally adequate in terms of quantity, quality and variety; and that it is acceptable within a given culture. Only when all these conditions are met can a population be considered "food secure." (UN FAO)

To meet these requirements, then, there has to be enough food to go around. That seems obvious but will not be true if we continue our rush to biofuels or if most of the world's population eats a heavily meat-based diet. If we take these principles seriously, availability requires that all of us begin to eat a diet that ensures that other people have equal access. For most people in the rich world, this means reducing meat consumption to a few meals a week and voting and working to discourage biofuel production.

Access means that food cannot be rationed by price, as it is in the US. Such a policy, where food prices rise out of control as they have recently, is discriminatory; it harms the health and hope of poorer people. It also harms our overall goals; that is, when we don't have enough nutritionally adequate food, our health care costs rise and are borne by the rest of us. It also affects population; food security, along with other kinds of security, enables families to choose to have fewer children. And then there is the long-term problem of access. Our current access to food is based on theft — theft of soil and water that future generations will desperately need. We cannot provide short-term access to food without a long-term strategy for feeding the future.

• • •

Grow only open-pollinated seeds that reproduce themselves exactly. Practice saving seeds.

• • •

Nutritional adequacy is a huge concern in Western nations, where it is perfectly possible, even common, to be obese and suffering from malnutrition. Nutritious foods are more expensive than foods with minimal nutrition, and study after study has shown that organic produce may be many times richer in nutrients than cheaper conventional produce. Many North Americans who do not go hungry have insufficient access to nutritious food — in poor neighborhoods there are more McDonalds than vegetable stands.

Finally, acceptability is also a real concern. Food is tied up in culture. Our diets are tied to family structures, and the ways we eat are tied into the economy, community, faith and spirituality. Food is a holistic issue, and approaching it in pieces, as we have been, is doomed to failure. We cannot change our food system without changing our lives.

The Bull's-eye Diet

So how do we know that local food production and gardens will mitigate hunger? Well, first of all, access to land to grow food can give poor people a greater degree of total food security. Growing food locally can also help stabilize skyrocketing prices by ensuring that supplies remain stable. Gardens improve overall diet — vegetables are expensive, so growing them yourself is more affordable; and home gardeners and small farmers need few, if any pesticides, so they cut total chemical exposure. But most of all, local production ensures that transportation disruptions and disasters don't leave people hungry.

One useful example might be the research that Michael Hamm and Monique Baron did for the state of New Jersey. In order to feed every man, woman and child in the state a healthy vegetarian diet, they estimated, New Jersey would require 115,000 additional acres of land, above and beyond the current land in agricultural production, the equivalent of 3.4 million 200-square-foot gardens. For those of you who don't garden, a 200-square foot garden is quite a manageable space — ten 4' x 5' raised beds would do it. A combination of existing yards and community gardens make this entirely feasible. In this space, the whole state could feed itself, and most likely produce some food surpluses to help feed neighboring New York City.

Fall is a great time to try out the 100 Mile Diet or the Bull's-eye Diet.

But this would require some substantial changes. We would have to eat much less meat, far more vegetables, more local and seasonal foods. We would need a generation of new farmers to take over the work being done by existing farmers. (The average farmer in the US is nearly 60 years old.) And millions of people would have to take on the project of gardening. This is well within the realm of possibility, but it does present some challenges — and we will need a useful model to enable us to begin to rethink our whole food systems.

This is one way we know that simple things like gardens can help us feed the world. Another way we know it is that the UN's Food and Agriculture Organization estimates that small-scale, largely organic farms and gardens are, at present, feeding 2 billion people in the world. That is, almost a third of the world's human population relies on small plots of land, many no bigger than a large garden, to feed themselves. They are feeding themselves and their families without expensive chemical fertilizers and pesticides because they cannot afford them. And they are doing it often on marginal land because the best land has gone to corporate agriculture. Again, I am not speaking here about models and possibilities, but the simple truth that feeding yourself is an ordinary and human project.

If local eating is to become a way of life, if most of us are to eat mostly from our own regions, we need to develop some new ways of thinking about this subject. My friend Aaron Newton proposed that instead of thinking in terms of 100-mile regions, we begin to imagine our foodshed (that is, the places our food comes from naturally) as a dartboard, with a bull's-eye in the center. Aaron and I call it the "Bull's-eye Diet."

The center dot would be your home. The first question is, How much of my food can I produce here? For some people, the answer will be very little — only sprouts and a few window boxes, perhaps, or maybe nothing at all. For the average suburbanite, the answer is a lot. Those who don't garden will be shocked at how much food can be produced in a quarter-acre lot. Often, it is enough to provide a whole family with all its needs except perhaps some grains.

This work of putting food-producing gardens, trees and shrubs on our existing properties may be the single most powerful thing any of us can do to save the world. If you do nothing else I suggest in this book, I hope that all of you will begin to garden, whether in the smallest window box or on an acre or more. There is nothing potentially more transformative on the earth.

The first step is to evaluate your home for food production possibilities. Be imaginative. You think you can't keep any livestock, right? What about rabbits for angora wool or meat? What about bantam chickens kept like pet birds for eggs? What about bees or worms? All of these animals can often be kept in towns or even large cities — I know of chickens in Seattle, Dayton and Washington DC, and have even heard of apartment dwellers keeping tiny bantam hens or quail for eggs in New York City and Boston.

Perhaps you can't have a traditional vegetable garden in your front yard because of zoning regulations. How about landscaping your front lawn with ornamental edibles — blueberry bushes, grapevines trained to an arbor, a pecan tree. Got shade? Rhubarb and gooseberries will tolerate it, as will many medicinal herbs. And the bottlebrush beauty of black cohosh will look just like you planted it to look pretty. Don't forget to work to change those zoning regulations

— gardens are beautiful! In the era of Victory gardens, front yard gardens were de rigueur. Tell your zoning board you are bringing back the Victory garden!

It is hard to imagine that your three basil plants would make a big difference in the world, but they do — the composite effect of everyone in a society growing as much food as they can is enormous. During World War II, both the US and Britain grew more than 40 percent of their produce in home gardens, including urban gardens. Hong Kong and Singapore, two of the most densely populated cities on the earth, both produce almost half their produce and more than 20 percent of their meat within the city limits.

We all know that small-scale food production is important, but it is necessary to realize just how important. Industrial conventional agriculture is an ecological disaster. Industrial organic agriculture is increasingly organic only in name — and is just as dependent upon petroleum as industrial agriculture. Agriculture of all kinds is a major contributor to greenhouse gasses. Moreover, food yields are leveling off and falling because of Climate Change. North Africa lost two thirds of its grain crops in 2007; Australian grain crops dropped by more than 50 percent; in 2008 a substantial portion of the American Midwest corn crop ws lost to massive flooding. The world has its lowest food reserves since measures have been taken. This is a recipe for famine — large scale, worldwide and even here, in your family. We must start growing more of our food locally, or we may not have much to eat.

Equally importantly, our dependence on foreign crops has been enormously destructive to the agriculture of many nations. The leveling of rainforests to raise bananas and coffee for Americans, for example, has left millions of people less food secure because they are vulnerable to market shifts for these items. If we grow more of our food locally, we can afford to pay fair prices for fair trade, and we can ensure our own food security. We can eat better food — both because the vegetables we grow taste better and are fresher and more nutritious, but also because we can spend our food dollars on the good stuff rather than on the cheapest. When we don't have to buy vegetables or fruits, we have money for other things — the good olive oil, our favorite vanilla, traded fairly.

The smaller the plot of land you work, the more productive it is (after some practice). A person with one garden bed who manages it inch by inch can produce yields per square foot that dwarf anything a conventional farmer can produce. A farm of two acres is often two to 20 times more productive than a conventional farmer's use of land, according to Peter Rosset's seminal paper "Small is Bountiful." Similar results have been found in studies all over the world. Even the World Bank, long a proponent of industrial food production, admits that industrial agriculture is far too inefficient in its land use to risk continuing it.

Up to now, we've thought of efficiency in terms of less labor — if fewer people could produce more food, that was "efficient." But it was efficient only because energy was cheap and abundant, and we're at the end of those days. Now, with a growing world population, Climate Change and falling yields, we need to return to efficiency per acre — the project of generating the most possible food from each bit of productive land we engage with. Doing so means land for wildlife habitat, the chance to restore stripped soils, the hope of arresting some of the ecological crisis we've encountered, and most importantly, enough to eat for all of us.

The key, then, is getting as many people involved in farming and gardening as possible. We need about one third of the American population to take real responsibility for producing some of their own food. That means

• • •

Now is the time to convince your business, school, church, mosque, synagogue or community center to add a garden on that empty lawn.

• • •

most people in the US need to get out and find a plot of land they can grow food on — their lawns, community gardens, public space. If need be, we should be guerilla gardening, growing food on unused public land. Food is simply too important to take risks with.

The good news about this is that gardening is a great deal of pleasure, something that millions of Americans already do for the sheer joy of it. Now you get to add the joys of seeing your children pick cherry tomatoes off the vine and pop them into their mouths, the joys of spending time in nature and seeing birds nest in your corn stalks, the joys of fresher food and better health and time spent together as a family working and playing in the garden. A recent scientific study suggests that there's a chemical in dirt that actually makes us happy, so that people who spend time with the soil are happier than those who don't.

This doesn't only apply to healthy adults. Children can and should manage their own plots. My boys have grown an alphabet garden (one vegetable or herb for every letter — we cheated for X) and a pumpkin patch of their very own; and four-year-old Isaiah gets up anxious to go out and harvest. Gardening with kids is one of the greatest pleasures in life — they are endlessly fascinated with the miracle that transforms tiny seeds into plants and then into food.

The elderly and disabled can and should garden as well. When you use mulch to suppress weeds, raised beds to bring gardens up to their level, and rolling garden seats so you can slide along up and down rows without getting up and down, gardening can be an accessible practice, helping you keep mobility and stay in good health.

My friend Pat Meadows is in her 60s and disabled by lupus and degenerative disk disease. Her husband is also disabled, and they live alone. Because they live on disability and have spent much of their life savings on medical expenses, they are extremely poor. If anyone has an excuse not to garden, it would be Pat. But she and her husband grow an enormous quantity of vegetables every year, almost entirely in containers. They hire help to do heavy work a few times a year, and Pat does the rest of it, starting seedlings indoors, transplanting them into self-watering containers and producing vegetables that could easily win prizes at the county fair. Last year Pat reported that she had 22 self-watering containers built by her husband, with a total of 44-square-feet. In the ground, that would be a plot of less than 7' x 7'. In that area, Pat grew:

*   *   *

Get serious about redesigning your landscape. Sit down and thnk hard about how you can get the most food, fuel and fiber from your yard.

*   *   *

- 6 full-sized (indeterminate) tomatoes
- 2 early tomatoes (determinate — smaller plants)
- 16 Swiss chard plants
- 6 peppers
- 4 eggplants
- 4 orach plants (an edible green in the spinach/beet family)
- 3 (huge!) fluffy top Chinese cabbage plants
- 2 bush cucumbers
- 4 basil plants
- 1 tomatillo
- 18 bush bean plants
- 4 bush zucchini plants

This represents hundreds of pounds of produce for Pat and her family, all grown in containers in a tiny space, about the size of two hammocks in your yard. If she can do it, almost anyone can. (There is information in the references section of this book that can help you do this, including a link to Pat's Container Gardening group.) Pat asked me to tell my readers that she wasn't really trying that hard to maximize food production — she could have done more if she'd planted earlier, interplanted more and worked a little harder.

Although the 100 Mile Diet is important because it helped create demand for local, sustainable agriculture, demand creation in and of itself isn't sufficient. More is going to be asked of us all than simply wanting a thing — we have to take more responsibility for our future than that. If we're to raise food on a small, highly productive scale, we need much more participation by everyone. This is a huge part of the New Home Front. And because small-scale home production is the most efficient way to grow most vegetables and fruits, we need as many people to participate as possible in this new Victory Garden movement.

Back to the Bull's-eye Diet. The next ring would be the food in your neighborhood. Is there a community garden? Could you create one in a public park or on a vacant lot? Is anyone else growing food? Could you enable someone else to grow food? I got my neighbor to start a food-producing garden by offering to put one in for her as a thank you gift for some help she gave us. Aaron gardens on the land of his elderly neighbors, growing food and sharing it with them. My friend Laurie is growing a garden on her church grounds for the local food pantry. Are there churches, businesses or other folks with land you could engage with? What about getting neighborhood teenagers involved?

What about foraging in your neighborhood? Even in Manhattan, Wildman Steve Brill offers foraging classes to teach people to eat their local weeds. How much of your food could you get from the neighborhood that way? You'd be surprised by what kinds of wonderful edibles grow in parks and vacant lots.

The next step would be your town. Are there right-to-farm/right-to-garden laws? Could you get some instituted? How about changing zoning to permit livestock or front yard gardens? Are there any local farmers? Can you patronize them? Have you considered advertising? Put up a sign saying "I would like to buy organic produce from within my community." Maybe someone will start a market garden. Or perhaps you could start a CSA yourself with a neighbor. Community Supported Agriculture doesn't have to be a big farmer with 40 customers. It can be you saying to your neighbor, "If you'll pay for the seeds and share your wheelbarrow, I'll split the produce with you."

Check into local immigrant communities — many brought their agricultural traditions with them. Many home gardeners have extras — perhaps they'd like to make a little extra cash. Are there old farms with retiring or aging owners — does your town have a plan for protecting that land from development?

So the first three bull's-eye circles are probably within 10 miles of you. The goal is to get as much as possible as close as possible and to do everything you can to build up local food *systems*. That also means finding ways to sell and distribute local food in your community and to develop markets. For example, you might, besides your garden, start a Victory Gardener's club or local bulletin board that allows gardeners to advertise extra produce. You might bring in a teacher to show people how to can and preserve.

Some people will be able to get a lot of food very locally. I can get milk, eggs, meat and most of my produce within that ten-mile circle in my rural area. Someone in Phoenix or Manhattan will be able to do less. But a gardening movement that gets food back on people's properties means that this will be increasingly possible — every person should be able to get some food very locally, and the amount available should expand every year.

The next step would be your immediate bioregion — perhaps 25 miles from your town. This is your extended local region. If you live in a large town or small city, you might need to go here for meat and eggs and some vegetables. If you live in a very large city, 25 miles might provide only a little local produce from a few truck gardens. But everything you can do to build local food systems increases your security. Check out your local farmers' markets and connect with local food producers. Or start a farmers' market in your town.

From there, we might move outward to our larger bioregion, then our state, then neighboring regions, always keeping in mind that the goal is to get as much as we can as locally as we can. Remember, as you move outward, every community, every region has a foodshed (like a watershed) that has to feed it. The further out you go, the more likely you are to bump into someone else's foodshed. For example, if you live in Manhattan, by the time you get 100 miles in any given direction, you've bumped into the foodshed for at least one other medium to large city, as well as a number of heavily populated suburbs and small cities.

Can 8 million New Yorkers, or 8 million people in Tucson/Phoenix have a 100 mile diet? The answer is probably not, so the foodshed for the region will have to expand. But the only way we can do that fairly is to ensure that as much food as possible is being grown where the people are. That means Victory Gardens on every lawn, in city parks, in neighborhoods. And it means prioritizing food from your very immediate foodshed — from the center circles of your bull's-eye. Thus, while New York City may need to import grains from the Midwest, it may also get some of its grains from the Schoharie Valley, in my region, which was the breadbasket of the American Revolution. Few people raise grains there now, except for cow corn. But that could change if markets grew.

New Yorkers probably could produce as much as 10–20 percent of their produce and even some meat, eggs and milk were we to change the nature of New York City life. Much of their produce could come from New Jersey, Long Island and the Hudson Valley, including staple crops like potatoes and sweet potatoes. Meat and milk could come from those regions as well. A recent study by Cornell University estimated that New York State could feed one third of its population using conventional agriculture and no gardens. If we were to use all the land that has been converted to suburbs, we could almost certainly double that. If we were to have more people farming more intensively on a smaller scale, could we make it possible for New York to almost feed itself, with only supplemental grains coming in from the Midwest? It is possible. Even the harsh region of Montana was once 70 percent self-sufficient for its produce and meat.

• • •

Join your local garden club or street beautification society and encourage the groups to replace street trees and public landscaping with edible trees and shrubs.

• • •

That won't be easy for many people, and it is a long-term project. We can't necessarily do it today. But the local food movement is growing fast, and demand alone won't ensure that hunger never strikes Americans and that we always have enough excess to offer hunger relief to the people who are running out of food because of Climate Change we caused. If we're to burn carbon by sending grains around the planet, they should be going to the world's hungry, not to us, whenever possible.

As in a darts game, you won't always hit your circle. But with practice, you can get a little closer every time. The more food you create in your community, the better off we all are. Hunger in a world that can have plenty may be the greatest tragedy in human history. Let none of us be a bystander to that tragedy.

How to Start Your Garden

This is a huge subject, and one that I'd have to write a whole book about. In fact, I am writing a whole book about it right now with Aaron Newton. So I'm not going to try to cram everything you need to know about growing food into a couple of pages. The references in the back of the book will include a number of places to start. But I'll be blunt — there is no one magic book about gardening that will tell you everything you need to know. Every gardener has strong opinions, most of them shaped by where she lives and her personal experiences. Every garden writer thinks his way is the best, me included.

The people who know the most about gardening where you live are other gardeners; local fellow gardeners, your extension agent and certified master gardeners are among the best resources you can find. You will need other information as well, but these should be your primary resources. In fact, that's true of almost all the new skills you'll acquire over the years — the best possible way to learn is to find someone near you (remember, we're working toward a local life) who knows what you want to learn.

The best way to get started is to get started — join a community garden or a garden club, talk to people at the extension service, read some books, and then plant some seeds. You can do it!

Squirrel Time

It is autumn here, time for us northerners to be putting things by for winter. I get kind of "squirrelly" this time of year, wanting to gather up my nuts and be cozy and secure for the winter. But while I'm filling my pantry, I'm doing it with locally grown, small-farm products whenever possible.

* * *

Learn to preserve food. If you don't garden, check out your farmers' market at the end of the day for large quantities of produce they want to get rid of.

* * *

Food preservation and gardening must be tied together. Almost every place in the world has a season where not much grows. It might be winter if you live in the cold, snowy north, or summer if you live in hot, dry Texas. It might be too rainy or too dry, but very few places allow you to grow everything you need all year round. So at the same time that we must begin producing our food, we have to begin storing and thinking ahead through the cycle of seasons.

As our homeschool focuses on "how we get ready for winter" we're splitting wood and canning tomatoes, replenishing our supplies of basics like soybeans and popcorn, digging potatoes and onions and picking apples by the bushel at our local orchard. Mom and Dad both knit when we're sitting quietly, and three-and-a-half-year-old Isaiah has started his first scarf and brought in his first pumpkin. The older boys take (heavily supervised) turns with the axe.

Now, some of this "winterizing" is prompted by the weather. If you live in cool places, there's something about shaking off the lethargy of summer and beginning the transition to winter. Some of it is necessity — our heavily local diet means that if we don't preserve food, we'll have a very boring selection of foods all winter.

Now is the time to plan ahead. Most of us have a tough time with this one, and I'm no exception. When you live in agricultural time, life is circular, and you are always thinking to the next season and the next year. If, for example, you want to enjoy peaches in the summer, you prune your trees in late winter, thinking of the fall harvest. If you want milk next year, you breed your goats or cows in the fall to give birth at the end of winter or beginning of spring. Living in the agricultural mindset means simultaneously taking the very long view and very short one — you might be planting maple trees for your grandchildren to harvest sugar from while you deal with the surplus of peas today, putting some aside for the time when there aren't any.

For all of human history, hunter-gatherers and farmers prepared for the cold or the dry season for months ahead. But in the past 100 years, in our move to urbanize, most Americans have moved away from an agricultural worldview. It is important to realize how enormous a change this has been. We've lost that way of thinking, and we desperately need to regain it.

Most of us are going to have to go back to thinking the way we once did — with the seasons. The good news is that there's some evidence that we might be happier that way, and I suspect we might also be better at taking the long view if we had to do it a little more often. And more than that, the next step in our food and agricultural transition means that it isn't enough to eat locally or seasonally — we have to live local lives and seasonal lives. It isn't just our diet, but a whole way of being that we're recreating.

Local eating and local food production, then, require us to think, not just to the weekend or next week, but into next year. In the fall, we eat apples until the rhubarb and strawberries come around in spring, So when they are local, we buy bushels of apples, which get eaten fresh, made into sauce and dried for snacks. That way, we never have to eat sprayed apples from China.

Instead of buying a big sack of sugar, how about local honey, sorghum or maple syrup? Instead of 50 pounds of generic white beans, how about local tepary beans or Jacob's Cattle beans that are indigenous to your area? If you eat meat, consider local lamb, beef, fish or poultry. What about wine or beer? Can you pick your own berries to be made into a winter's jams and pie fillings?

Explore your local options, and if you can't find something locally, at least buy direct from farmers whenever possible. Instead of grains as your primary staple, consider potatoes and other root crops that grow in your region. Consider adapting your diet to a truly regional one — that is, focus on crops that grow well naturally in your area, not ones that require green-houses or extensive irrigation.

Storing may not be necessary if you live in easy walking distance of a year-round farmer's market or co-op that pays farmers fairly, but for the rest of us, storing cuts down on driving to get local food, saves us money by buying in bulk and when availability is greatest, puts more dollars into the pockets of local farmers and the local community, and enables us to have personal security, more to donate to local charities and a freedom from the supermarket.

A lot of this is mostly just planning — figuring out what you will want and need through the long winter and getting it now, from farmers who will make a decent profit on your purchases rather than from a supermarket chain where most of the money will be taken by middlemen, and where your food will travel countless miles, producing emissions all the way.

Where do you put all this food? I know that those of you who live in apartments may not have a lot of additional room. Nevertheless, I suspect the long-term security and savings might be worth the inconvenience of making storage space — even if you have to take out your couch, put down five-gallon buckets, cover them with couch pillows and a sheet, and make a food storage couch. (I've sat on one, and it wasn't half bad.) Under the bed is great for buckets of dried food or squash and pumpkins (which like to live where we do), a cooler or old fridge in an unheated garage or shed will keep apples, potatoes and other roots (don't store them together if possible — apples speed up rot in most root crops). Even a closet with a small vent cut into an outside wall will do. Many basements will work. If you rent, consider asking a friend or neighbor nearby with more space or more options to store your food for you. If you buy meat, perhaps you can barter some for space in a freezer if you haven't got one.

Stored food can also beautify. I collect glass mason jars and store much of my immediately accessible foods in them, an idea I stole from my step-mother. The jars, on wooden shelves built into the kitchen, look lovely, and everyone who sees them comments. I also use old large metal popcorn tins to store grains — these are often available at yard sales for a quarter. Consider building something to store potatoes and onions. A pantry is a beautiful thing, and should be treated as such. A house kept cool in the winter will store much food quite well in the spaces people live in.

I have wondered for some time if one of the reasons we as a society don't seem to be able to look far ahead to a future that isn't immediately visible is because we've gotten out of the habit of thinking further ahead than tonight's dinner. I can't prove it, of course, but I occasionally suspect that if we could just grasp again the habit of cyclical thinking, perhaps we might be able to see a little further on the horizon.

This, of course, is merely speculation, the speculation of a squirrel in pursuit of her own nuts.

·

TWELVE

The Hand that Stirs the Pot, Rules the World

Food is not fuel. It is not nutrition. It is fun, educational,
horizon expanding, delightful. It is consoling, transporting
and a comfort. If you want a happy eater, run a happy kitchen.
These things take time, but so do all good things.
Rejoice in what you have, be it rice and beans or baked Alaska.
— LAURIE COLWIN

Since Eve ate apples, much depends on dinner.
— LORD BYRON

To those who hunger, give bread.
To those who have bread, give the hunger for justice.
— LATIN AMERICAN PRAYER

It's All About Food

HOW POWERFUL IS FOOD, REALLY? IS IT TRUE THAT THE WAY WE EAT COULD matter that much? Is it true that what we have for dinner has so much power? It can be enormously difficult for us to grasp this fact — that the most powerful acts in the world are the ordinary ones we perform every day, that as my friend, magazine editor Peter Bane put it, Who eats? is the central question of our times. And, I would add, What do we eat?

We have been, as Wendell Berry put it, the most thoughtless eaters in human history. We must begin, for the first time in decades, to apply more thought to our food, to recognize that it is in the garden and the kitchen that we are most connected to our fellow beings, that in the kitchen we enact policy; in the kitchen, we change the world.

It is no accident that the foundational story of Christians, Jews and Moslems is about eating. In fact, we live out the story of Eve and the apple over and over again, not totally unlike this:

There's this apple, and it's hanging on a tree, and along comes a snake — anyone heard this one before? Well, in the story, the Boss tells this nice boy and his girlfriend, "Don't eat that apple. It is bad for you. You could die." And of course, the snake comes along and he's the first marketing consultant, and starts talking up the apple. "Now this apple," he tells them, "is no ordinary apple. It isn't like those regular apples that grow on regular trees. This apple is special — maybe even genetically modified, to contain extra nutrients, plus all the knowledge you could ever want." And the snake (who later went to work for Monsanto) assures the young woman that this whole dying-from-it thing has been totally overblown. "I mean, who cares about a little death or the hope of future generations when you could have the supercool, ultra-rad, tree of knowledge apple?" And the girl, she says, "Well, now, that does look tasty. Does it come in honey-barbecue?"

Now, does anyone here want to take bets on how this one comes out?

The reality is that we're living that one out over and over again. Most of us don't have much more willpower than Eve and Adam did with their apple. Most Americans have read and seen enough information to know that what we're eating is killing the planet, is killing us and hurting our children's health, and crushing the hope of future generations. But we're still listening to variations on that snake saying "But it's new and improved! And doesn't it look good?!" So yes, food really, truly is that powerful.

. . .

Rethink your seed-starting regimen now. Instead of depending on bags of purchased potting soil, electric grow lights and plastic flats, consider making use of more sustainable options like hotbeds heated by composting manures, homemade wooden flats, your own compost.

. . .

Getting Over Picky

Yesterday's project was a serious strawberry harvest, and today I'll make lots and lots of jam. Strawberry is the kids' favorite jam, so we grow lots of berries. The kids helped (hindered, really) with the picking in their own ways. Eli plopped himself down on the straw and began a two-fisted strawberry-eating project, with an occasional languid toss of one into a basket. Isaiah took his bucket and began a quest for only the biggest, reddest, ripest strawberries, which meant his picking rate was about six an hour, four of which were promptly eaten. Asher likes to pick, but by the time the strawberries get from his fat little toddler hands to the bucket, they often must be discretely disposed of, while you dispense lavish praise for his help. Only Simon really picks at this stage, and he takes great pleasure in bossing people around while he does it. "Don't step there, Eli, you'll squish the strawberries." "Isaiah, no eating!" (Here Mommy intervenes to say that Eli is fine and so is eating — her mouth is full, so she's no hypocrite). And when Asher accidentally ate a green strawberry and said "Yuck," Simon erupted in outrage. "No saying yuck!"

Now, this last is a firm rule in our household, although there are exceptions for babies eating truly gross things like green strawberries or dog food (don't ask). But my kids are powerfully enjoined never, ever to complain that food is "yucky" or "gross." They can say, "This isn't my favorite." They can say, "No, thank you." They are not required to eat anything they don't like (although seconds and dessert, if any, depend on eating a reasonable amount of everything). But the first "ugh" or "yuck" gets you a very stern warning; a second means you leave the table and don't eat again until your next meal. The same is true about discussing food that is not present in the same terms. None of my children have ever had to have this happen more than once.

This rule also applies to regularly visiting children who I babysit and has been applied by Isaiah (to Mommy's horror and embarrassment) to a visiting adult guest who was describing a meal she strongly disliked. Though we had a long talk afterward about being a good host and not embarrassing guests, I've never been sorry about this rule. My children can recite our reasoning as well. "This is very important to Mommy. All her jobs are about making sure other people have enough to eat, so we don't waste food and we don't say mean things about it, and we do say a blessing before we eat."

The world is a hungry place. Millions of people world wide don't get enough food — 2 billion are food insecure, including 30 million people in our own country. Hunger and its associated illnesses kill millions of people every day. Saying "gross" to food that is good for you, nutritious and just doesn't happen to suit your palate seems to me to be wrong. Everyone has food preferences, but the notion that there's an inherent ickiness to anything someone considers food is just wrong.

I was talking about strawberries to a friend the other day. She said she buys them year round for her daughter because they and bananas are the only fruits her daughter will eat. We, on the other hand, eat strawberries like mad for a month in June and then enjoy dried strawberries, strawberry sauce and strawberry jam until the next year's harvest. When the first strawberries ripen, everyone eats the few bites with reverence. A few days later, when there are enough, we gorge until the juice pours down our faces. By the end of the month, we've eaten strawberries every day, canned dozens of jars of jam, lived with the scent of dehydrating strawberries, and we're ready for something else. And here come cherries, peaches, plums, raspberries and blueberries to take up the slack.

But, of course, my children *eat* cherries, peaches, plums, raspberries and blueberries. A child who eats only strawberries and bananas can't eat a seasonal diet — even imagining a modest importation of bananas, that's a tough, fruit-free life. And for a child who also doesn't eat whole grains, chicken in non-nugget forms, greens, peppers, carrots, broccoli or any vegetables other than corn, peas and cucumbers, that lack of fruit is a real problem, health wise.

Why don't kids eat these fruits? Well, it is possible that there's a real underlying issue to some pickiness — sensory issues, unrecognized food allergies or some other deep reason. But in most of the families I know, the parents are picky too. If Mom doesn't eat cranberries, eggplant or beans of any kind, brown rice or brown bread, guess what message the child will get. And Mom, perhaps because she knows the pain of eating something she doesn't like, doesn't require her kids to try things, and gently passes along her own prejudices.

Most picky parents don't really admit the connection. A friend's son suddenly went from eating all vegetables to nearly none, but his dad ardently denies it has any connection to the fact that Daddy eats only lettuce and peppers. Other friends wince when their kid complains about the food at my house (not because we make a big deal about it — they don't even know about our rule), but I've heard the mother say, "No, honey, you won't like that. I'll get you something else." Hmmm ...

I'm going to take the risk of ticking off a lot of people by saying that in the absence of aggravating conditions (sensory stuff, toddlerhood, etc.) at least 80 percent of food pickiness is of parental creation. We're tolerating it, even encouraging it — and there's a real and serious price. We've somehow got the wacky idea that our children's health is less important than that they screw up their courage and eat some brown rice. Yes, it is fine to hate lima beans. Everyone is allowed a couple of things they don't eat simply because they don't want to. But if you also don't eat tepary beans, black beans, soy beans, pinto beans, adzuki beans, you've significantly cut back on your ability to adapt to a changing world and diet. Dealing with children's picky eating, which is really important, starts with dealing with adult pickiness.

In children, elderly people and the sick, sudden, radical changes in diet can actually be fatal. Studies done in World War II Britain on dietary changes caused by the war showed that young children, elderly people and sick people will, when confronted with a major, sudden, crisis-induced dietary change will simply stop eating. The medical term is "appetite fatigue," and it is a real and serious phenomenon. Most of them eventually adapted, but periods of malnutrition can have long-term consequences.

So given a possible situation where favorite foods became suddenly unavailable, people in your family who don't have a wide-ranging diet or who depend on foods from far away could really suffer. The solution is to get used to eating your local diet now, trying lots of new things — new grains, new tastes, new ways of eating things, particularly those that suit your area.

• • •

Try a new springtime food you don't usually eat — ramps, fiddleheads or something else.

• • •

How do grownups get over long-ingrained habits of not eating things, of thinking "yuck?" First we realize how high the stakes are. If we lived in a world where our emissions didn't matter and we were all rich enough to buy the three vegetables we like every week, and if we could afford to waste food, it wouldn't matter. But none of these things is true. We don't live in that world any more. Pretending we can is lying to ourselves and to our children, who may have to bear the consequences.

But if you've hated broccoli for 50 years, it will be a challenge to start eating it. Now, if you have plenty of locally available, healthy green options you love, there's no reason to choose the broccoli over the kale. But what if broccoli is it — if the bugs got the kale crop? You need to eat it and you might as well like it. Or what if you are a meat-and-potatoes person, and now you are told that you can eat only grass-fed meat, and not that much of it? How do you get there?

The good news is that you have to adapt your tastes only for local, seasonal, sustainable foods — if you think McDonald's hamburgers are vile, you don't have to do anything about that. No worries about your extreme distaste for barbecue chips. And go right on hating anchovy pizza — in fact, we encourage that. The other good news is that the things you are learning to like — whole grains, fresh vegetables, less meat — these things are really good for you. There's really no down side.

The first thing to remember is that you have overcome instinctive food preferences before. Comparatively few people loved coffee, beer, wine, tea, sushi or strong cheese the first time they tasted it. It took a while to develop a liking for these flavors. Similarly, I'm going to bet that your idea of a perfect day no longer involves candy for breakfast, lunch and dinner, as it did when you were seven. Tastes change. You can change them. You just have to do the work. They say a toddler often has to see a food 20 times before it seems familiar enough to eat it. Grownups might have to try it even more times to get over their long-ingrained prejudices.

What's the magic trick? Lie like a rug. Lie to yourself. Lie to your kids (but don't do it in an obvious way — kids are really not stupid). Explore your acting talent. You are not only going to convince yourself to eat hated foods (one at a time), you are going to enjoy it. So the first step is to tell yourself you will like it, and to eat a little. Trust me, it won't kill you. Try the kindergarten method — three bites. And then keep putting it on your plate. Smile at it. Think how wonderful it is to try something new. Think how lucky you are to have it. Find something you like about the taste, the smell, the color or the texture.

Join a CSA if you don't garden and learn to enjoy the bounty of a seasonal diet.

Perhaps the problem is the cooking method — do you cook vegetables until they are grey? Do you like highly seasoned foods, and most veggies are kind of bland? Try a quick steam, or eating it raw. Or perhaps you should add hot sauce, lots of garlic or herbs. Learn to cook your food well. Throw it in with something you do like — put the greens in with the bacon, or toss the peppers in with your pasta salad.

A lot of this is simply attitude adjustment. Maybe you'll always prefer turkey to baked beans, or no kale to kale. But being able to eat the kale and the baked beans enriches your life.

Don't complain about your food. Be grateful for it — don't call it names, and if you can, thank someone or something for it — God, the farmers who grew it, the soil it came from. Food matters in this world. We can't afford to treat it lightly.

Teach your kids the same lessons. Remember, no matter how many faces they make, it won't kill them to eat rhubarb or chard. It is a time-honored tradition to torture your children with green vegetables, and as far as I know, no one has died yet. Don't over-sympathize with their distaste — kids' tastes are much more malleable than yours, and you aren't doing them any favors.

How do we handle the complaining? Don't allow it. What about the wasted food? The firmest method is simply to keep serving the same meal until they eat it. Won't eat beans? Okay, but nothing else is offered, and there will be beans again for dinner. When they get hungry enough, they'll eat. Loving every bite is not a prerequisite for life, and missing the occasional meal won't kill anyone.

I admit, I'm usually not quite that firm. But you don't get seconds or dessert unless you eat everything. You don't get snacks between meals — if you are hungry, that plate of beans is still there. And you don't, under pain of getting to know just how yucky hunger is, complain about the food.

But a hard line alone isn't enough to make your kids really good eaters. They also need to know what's wonderful and fun about food. That means getting them involved — bringing them into the kitchen, the garden, the farmers' market. Get them involved in the process — where did that carrot come from? Take them to the pick-your-own farm and let them get their own apples. Let them have their garden and help in yours. Let them care for their own chickens and be in charge of the eggs.

There's something really different about food you've grown yourself. Kids who wouldn't touch a zucchini or eat eggs normally will beg their parents to help them cook zucchini frittata if it is *their* zucchini and *their* eggs. Simon and Isaiah were very resistant to salad, but they've invented their own — rainbow salad. It has chopped nuts, dried fruit, greens they pick and edible flowers — Johnny jump ups, daylily petals, begonia petals, borage flowers, nasturtium blossoms. With lemon-herb dressing they'll eat their weight.

Food is, after all, fun. It tastes good. If it doesn't have to compete with sugar frosted flakes, there's really nothing not to like about a ripe peach or a berry. If you act like you like homemade tofu marinated in garlic sauce as much as steak, your kids will never know that the two aren't supposed to be equally good. And since they both are good, your kids will grow up liking them both, most likely. Who knows, after a little practice at this deception, you might even believe it yourself.

Food Preservation and Democracy

I was lucky enough to know one of the people on the earth who knew the most about growing and preserving food, Carla Emery, author of *The Encyclopedia of Country Living*. Before her death in 2005, Carla was traveling the nation trying to help people get ready for a life with much less energy. She'd done almost everything in her book (and it is a big book) at least once. Here's what she says about how she makes sure her family is fed,

All spring I try and plant something every day — from late February, when the early peas and spinach and garlic can go in, on up to mid- summer, when the main potato crop and the late beans and lettuce go in. Then I switch over and make it my rule to try and get something put away for the winter every single day. That lasts until the pumpkins and sunflowers and late squash and green tomatoes are in. Then comes the struggle to get the most out of the stored food — all winter long. It has to be checked regularly, and you'll need to add to that day's menu anything that's on the verge of spoiling, wilting or otherwise soon becoming useless. Or preserve it a new way. If a squash gets a soft spot, I can gut it out and cook, mash, can or freeze the rest for a supper vegetable or pie, or add it to the bread dough.

You have to ration. You have all the good food you can eat right at arm's reach and no money to pay ... until you run out....

People have to choose what they're going to struggle for. Life is always a struggle, whether or not you're struggling for anything worthwhile, so it might as well be for something worthwhile. Independence days are worth struggling for. They're good for me, good for the country and good for growing children.

Her "independence days" were the ones in which her family ate from their own land and gardens. She was right in this — that sort of independence is well worth striving for. Not only is it worth striving for because we may need to depend on that knowledge someday, but also because right now, we might have a better, stronger country if we preserve and store our own food. Perhaps that sounds crazy — but I suspect that, like many crazy-sounding things in this book, it might just be true.

Americans tend to believe that hunger could never come our way. We forget that just two generations ago, during the Great Depression, as many as 25 percent of urban school children were malnourished, and people stood in bread lines. In fact, pretty much all human beings, starting with our grandparents and going back, knew periods of food insecurity, and the majority of people in the world know hunger at some point in their lives. Should we bet the farm on the notion that this magical immunity to the plague of hunger will go on forever? In fact, we have bet on it. The average American household has less than three days' worth of food; the average grocery store depends on daily deliveries. There are no community stockpiles or reserves. Most of us suffer from a tremendous vulnerability to hunger.

Growing your own food is one part of the project. The next is preserving it. And then there's the job of resource management — if I left things up to my kids, I'd have strawberry jam every day until there wasn't any more, and then they'd complain until the next year's strawberry harvest. Someone has to be the one to say, "Okay, apricot this time — let's save some of that strawberry for spring." Someone has to look at the apples and the pears and take the ones that are getting soft and make them into sauce before they rot and spoil, literally, the whole barrel.

The thing is, being involved with your food means revisiting a life of seasonality, with a time to plant, a time to sow, a time to harvest and a time to rest. It isn't just a song or a Bible verse; it becomes a way of life. And that's okay, because that link to nature may be the thing that we've been missing in our lives. There's growing evidence that people who work in the soil, live with the seasons and connect to nature are happier and healthier than those who live in more artificial circumstances.

Preserving food is everyday work. It begins with the first rhubarb that will be dried or canned or made into sauce (and with a reminder that I still have a bit left of last year's rhubarb sauce to eat). Next come the strawberries and nettles (which grow wild and are very nutritious in tea). And then the cycle begins in earnest. It really doesn't take much time, once you get into a routine, and is well worth it. There are always some busy days in the summer, but it isn't too hard to put berries in the dehydrator after work or mix up pickle brine while making dinner.

> • • •
>
> Early spring was famously the "starving time" when stored supplies ran out and people went hungry. As you look back over the food you stored and preserved last year, would there have been enough if you needed it? Plan next year's food production to take into account early spring limitations.
>
> • • •

Even if you don't grow your own, preserving what is seasonal and fresh can provide you with a great deal of economic and food security — if you go to the farmers' market at the end of the day, you may be able to get bushels of produce for almost nothing. Then comes the dehydration, canning or pickling. But the work is worth it — both because it enables you to eat a local diet and frees you from dangers in the food supply. And it does something more — it frees you from the power of corporations.

That last point may be the most important. Food preservation and food production are keys to democracy. We accept that a politician who is dependent on the money that special interests provide cannot be wholly independent in their thought, and we know that no matter how much personal integrity they may have, their intentions are fundamentally corrupted by being beholden to others.

Well the same is equally true of individuals — as long as we depend on large corporations to meet our basic needs, we'll never be able to judge them fairly or eliminate their power in our society. That is, we cannot simultaneously call for an end to multinational monoliths and also pay them to do something as basic as feed us. As long as we admit we are dependent on corporations, any attempt at reform or culture change will fail, because we ourselves are corrupted by that dependence. We cannot deplore McDonalds and then complain because poor people cannot buy their food from the equally troubling industrial organic producers who sell through Whole Foods. We need to recognize that our food dependence affects not just what we eat, but the fundamentals of our democracy and our political power.

We should not owe our lives to entities we deplore. And the only possible escape from that bind is to declare food independence — to meet as many of our basic needs as possible ourselves and through small, sustainable farms with which we have real and direct relationships. And that means not just growing food, but ensuring a stable food supply, reasonable reserves and a dinner that depends on no one. Worth struggling for indeed!

Frugality, Economy, Preparedness

It has occurred to me that by suggesting people store food and stock up on items that may rise in price in the long term, I'm implicitly suggesting that people engage in consumerism to preserve their economic status. If you have a limited food budget and need to store food, I think it not unlikely that you will end up shopping at Wallyworld or somewhere cheap. The problem with doing that is that the act of shopping at Wal-Mart (or its many equivalents) is as antithetical to our security as not storing food at all.

By that I mean that it is completely natural, when faced with a threat to our security, to think of preserving "me and mine," and to focus on that first. When we first started storing food for ourselves and our families we were thinking largely about personal self-preservation, and we bought our food wherever we could find it most cheaply. Our primary concern, besides palatability, was that we get the most food for the least money. We bought large quantities of things like peanut butter and rice at the cheapest price we could find, in addition to things we put up ourselves. For folks without gardens, I imagine canned goods from Sam's Club sometimes look pretty good.

The problem with that is that in many cases the cheapest forms food comes in are not either the best ones for you or the ones that best support the other most basic need for human security — strong communities. And generosity to our neighbors begins with creating communities that support what we value and then putting our money where our ethics are.

That's why most cultures that knew hunger had customs, practices and taboos designed to ensure that food was shared. Thus, for example, Jews were exhorted to make sure their Sabbath bread was always *pareve* (that is, made with neither meat nor dairy) so that if a stranger or a neighbor were to come to your house, he could at least partake of your bread. We are required to have festival meals at which we invite anyone who has nowhere to go, to the point that at Pesach we cast open the door and call out that all who are hungry must come and eat. Well, in a poor society, where feasts are rare, opening your door represents a deep and primal risk — if too many are hungry, there might not be enough for yourselves. But there's a risk, too, to not opening the door — the risk being the anger and resentment of those who are hungry. Your community is made up of the people you depend upon, the people who share your circumstances, and the people who eat with you when you have food, are hungry when neither of you has food, and who share what they have with you when they can.

Fairy tales and stories from every faith contain the tale of the selfish rich man, the family that did not welcome the stranger, or the good woman or child who shared her last crust or welcomed in the hungry wanderer. The generous are rewarded; the stingy are punished. These tales were meant to teach the urgency of generosity, even in times of scarcity. These are moral tales, and their morals are ones we've forgotten. As inequities increase between poor and rich, we've missed the point. We have forgotten the messages of the fairy tales — good things come to those who share. People buy cute little plaques about angels, but they have forgotten that angels, if they exist, arrive unexpected at our doors and must be greeted and fed.

Joetta Handrich Schlabach, in *Extending the Table: A World Community Cookbook,* writes the story of a friend who was visiting Lesotho. The friend went to visit a neighbor, 'Me Malebohang. They discussed the bad pumpkin harvest, and how 'Me Malebohang had only eight pumpkins for the whole winter. As the friend got up to leave, 'Me Malebohang offered her guest the largest of the pumpkins. When the guest refused, saying she couldn't take one of her pumpkins, 'Me Malebohang answered, "We Basotho know that this is the way to do it. Next year I may have nothing in my field, and if I don't share with you now, who will share with me then?"

I am not suggesting we shouldn't store food — I think we must. Most Americans have only a few days' worth of food in their houses, which is potentially terribly dangerous. FEMA, the Department of Homeland Security and other authorities call for Americans to keep a supply of emergency food and water. And despite the fact that crises have occurred, most of us don't.

Thirteen million Americans go hungry every day because they are too poor to buy food — but we still imagine that we, somehow, will be magically immune. But as times get harder, support programs for the hungry will probably erode. Food pantries are already feeling the pinch. We need to store food now to protect ourselves from economic stress, bad harvests and transportation problems. Everyone reading this book should begin to build a six-month food supply. There are resources in the back of the book to tell you how to begin.

• • •

Trade cuttings and plant divisions with your neighbors.

Emphasize multiplying edibles such as Jerusalem artichokes.

• • •

But I would also request that we view food storage not as solely a personal preparation but as a collective one that enriches, rather than impoverishes, our communities. If we choose to buy from multinational corporations and big box stores, we are voting with our dollars in their favor, no matter what harm they do to our local communities, food systems and hope of sustainability. If we choose to hoard, rather than share in hard times, we know what will be our own fate if someday our neighbor has something to share. If we spend our money in a place that is already working to impoverish our local economies and extract wealth from our communities, we are not making ourselves secure, but insecure.

Thrift is not the opposite of generosity, the closed fist that holds on to what you have, but the enabler of generosity. A frugal life that does not waste and cares for what you have is what enables you to give away, to share, to open your hands and pour forth what you have preserved.

In practical terms, this means that instead of buying surplus MREs, a giant box of ramen and 50 pounds of HiC from the bulk warehouse, we need to treat our food storage the way we treat our food in general — and go for locally produced and/or organically and sustainably grown food, sacks of local potatoes in the root cellar and whole grains and beans in our storage areas whenever possible. We should look for whole, rather than processed foods, which means figuring out how to cook and eat them. Our food storage and our other stored supplies should support our values and nurture our community. That means we should be donating some of it when need arises and inviting guests to share whenever we can. It means we should be both hospitable and generous from our position of wealth and from a position of poverty.

How to Eat Cheap

When oil finally hit $100 a barrel, I won my bet with my economist friend Steve with an easy two years to spare (I was betting by 2010). This would be great news, except like everyone else I have to buy gas, so the $50 bet won't exactly offset a large investment.

And, like everyone else, I buy food too, something that is increasingly tough on the pocketbook. Food prices are up dramatically, and some staples, such as flour and milk, have doubled or more in price. I store food in fairly large quantities, so our family is still eating on older prices; but I'm not convinced that the crisis has occurred, so we will end up buying more.

How do you cut back your food budget when things get tight? Well, your friends are going to be beans, lentils and grains. They are nutritious, tasty, simple, accessible and store well. If there's any way you can come up with the money, buy them in big bags — a minimum of 10 pounds; 50 is better. Whole grains and dried beans store nearly forever (brown rice is an exception — white stores better, but is less nutritious). You say you can't use 50 pounds of beans? I bet you can — over five years. They will still be good, just need a bit longer to cook. You have to think ahead a bit and soak the beans or throw them in the slow cooker or on the back of the stove the night before.

Your other friends in the fresh food department are root vegetables and cabbage. At the grocery store, these will be among the cheapest items available. If you can get to a farmers' market or farm stand, they will be even cheaper. Again, bulk is better — my local farm stand is selling cabbage at 10 heads for 10 dollars. Even a single apartment dweller might eat cabbage twice a day — raw in a salad, then sautéed with garlic and pepper. Three heads will last two weeks sitting on the counter in a place with reasonably low heat. If you can afford your fridge, two more heads can be crammed in. The other five can be turned into sauerkraut or kimchi and will last even longer. Ten heads of cabbage could easily provide a large portion of your vegetable needs for eight weeks or more for one person.

Potatoes, beets, turnips, parsnips, sweet potatoes, onions and carrots are generally fairly cheap. Roasted vegetables make a superb cheap staple meal.

Squash are also often reasonably priced, and they have the advantage of requiring minimal preparation. Most can be baked in the oven until soft, with oil or butter, a few spices, and then spread on bread. Or puree them and turn them into soup.

What about meat? Frankly, I don't recommend buying any kind of meat that is cheap — it is almost certainly industrial meat and not good for you. But if you are accustomed to meat, other options are to learn to hunt or to raise your own. If there is one absolute rule that I recommend to everyone it is that we all stop eating industrial, confinement meat — period. The costs to our society, our health and our culture are too high. Either find a better alternative or do without.

You might buy very small quantities of healthy meats and stretch them. (My favorite ground meat stretcher is grated zucchini — you can use it 50–50 with ground beef or turkey.) Or simply use the meat as a flavoring, as many cultures do. A small bit of chicken in a stir-fry can transform it to a heartier-seeming meal. A delicious chili can be made with a half pound of beef for a large pot of beans, making enough to feed a crowd and take leftovers to work. A wonderful sausage soup can be made with cabbage, carrots, onions and a half pound of intensely flavored sausage.

Or consider talking to your local pastured poultry producer about buying the parts they often can't sell. Chicken feet make terrific soup stock, and are a delicacy in some cultures. Livers are rich in vitamin C and iron, and absolutely wonderful tasting. We love cooked chicken livers pureed and spread on toast. Bones are often discarded by butchers, and can make wonderful, meaty tasting broth. But remember, meat is not necessary to good health, and if you are poor, you probably won't be eating a lot of it. That's okay — it isn't necessary to make food taste good, either.

Use up every scrap of food. Do you have leftover garlic bread? Make it tomorrow's salad croutons. Stale bread? Bread pudding. Better yet, add some bananas gone black — either the ones you shoved in the freezer or some on the day-old table at the grocer's for 10 cents a pound.

Did you peel the broccoli stems and cook them? There's another meal there. Don't forget sprouts. Sprouting seeds bought in bulk are cheap and can cover much of your nutritional needs. What about vitamin C? Rose hips bought in bulk are cheap, but cabbage will take care of that too. Wild greens are a great source of nutrition, and many, like plantain and dandelion, are growing in your yard or the park. (Just get them from places that don't spray.)

Cut your use of coffee, tea, sugar, salt and fat in half. You'll get used to the taste and you will be healthier for it. What's for breakfast? Oatmeal, bought in bulk. Or if you don't like oatmeal, apples are cheap in the fall, and you can make applesauce easily enough. Then warm it up on the stove and mix in raw oats and a little cinnamon — yum! Or how about rice pudding, if you have milk or soy milk? Or what about polenta — cornmeal boiled to a thick porridge. It can be eaten with sweetener or fried with garlic and oil.

If you have children under three, please nurse them. The US makes breastfeeding enormously difficult. We provide little support, little time and often separate infants and mothers very quickly. But it is worth trying hard to do this, particularly going into difficult times. Many of us watched dehydrated infants suffering in the Superdome — babies who, if they could only have been nursed by their mothers, might have been spared harm. The food you make for your babies and toddlers is the best possible food for them and can help insulate your kids from the worst results of hunger.

. . .

Enlist your neighbors in supporting your new projects, whether getting chickens or landscaping your front yard with berries and nuts. If you are doing something new, it helps to have community support.

. . .

Consider accepting dinner invitations or attending events with free food. You might dumpster dive (Google "freegans") or consider just asking politely of your co-workers as they toss half their meal, "Can I have the other half of that sandwich?" It takes courage — our society looks down on the poor so much that advertising your need seems shameful, but it isn't. The truth is that much of the growing poverty has little to do with the choices of ordinary people.

If things get really desperate, there are further options. First of all, consider applying for any poverty support programs you are eligible for. I know a lot of people resist accepting charity, and that's honorable — up to a point — but don't be foolish, and risk your health or that of your children. If you are eligible for food stamps, WIC or some other program, apply. Or consider visiting your food pantry when you need to. Healthy adults may be able to go to bed hungry once in a while — children should not. Talk to people at your synagogue, mosque, church or temple, or at your community center if you are hungry — they may know about resources or be able to offer help. The simple truth is that the times we are coming into may bring many people to desperation through no fault of their own — don't let shame prevent you from eating.

·

THIRTEEN

Health Care

*If you are going to deal with the issue of health in the
modern world, you are going to have to deal with much absurdity.
It is not clear, for example, why death should increasingly be
looked upon as a curable disease, an abnormality by a society
that increasingly looks upon life as insupportably painful and/or
meaningless. Even more startling is the realization that the
modern medical industry faithfully imitates disease in the way
that it isolates us and parcels us out. If, for example, intense
and persistent pain causes you to pay attention only to your stomach,
then you must leave home, community and family and go to
a sometimes distant clinic or hospital, where you will be
cared for by a specialist who will pay attention only to your stomach.*
— WENDELL BERRY

*"I've been in hospitals," I said. "They take away your pants.
Then they hurt you and starve you and expose you to disease.
Then they bill you for it. A lot."*
— SPIDER ROBINSON

Public Health

AS I MENTIONED IN THE FIRST CHAPTER, MANY PEAK OIL AND CLIMATE
Change activists have, as much as everyone else, tended to think that the
biggest energy consumers in our lives are the places we most urgently need to
focus our attention. This reasoning has led us to emphasize things like transportation and energy replacement. This is a reasonable assumption, of
course. We look around and think, Where do the fossil fuels go at present?

and it seems reasonable to associate large usage with the most important sectors of our society. But if we rethink the problem, and truly get our minds around the fact that the future really is going to be very different from the present, we can begin to think about it in terms of optimization — the places where we get the most quality of life out of our fossil fuel inputs. That is, I believe we have, thus far, been asking the wrong questions about what matters.

If we were to ask, Where do we need energy the most? we would get a very different answer. Perhaps the most bang for our fossil-fueled buck comes in health care. In fact, when anyone suggests moving to a much lower-energy society, the most disturbing and frightening thing for them to imagine losing is usually health care. When we talk about the changing economy, the question that most immediately jumps up is, What will we do about health insurance? The shift here — from medical care to insurance — is a telling one, because right now medical care is so costly that almost no one can afford to pay for it outright. And yet, medical care in and of itself does not have to be as expensive as it is for us. The French, who arguably have the best medical system in the world, spend only half what we do.

• • •

Begin studying herbal medicine and getting to know the herbs in your garden. Be sure you also learn when to consult a medical practitioner.

• • •

In the coming changes, the most important things will be making sure that people can live simpler, lower-energy lives without unbearable costs. That means keeping infant mortality low and lifespans long. It means stabilizing population. As we've seen, to a large degree decisions about how many children to have are based on expectations of those children's survival. In a society with a great deal of uncertainty about the future of children, we can expect rising rather than falling birthrates.

Along with access to education and basic social welfare programs such as support for the elderly and disabled and food price stabilization, I would argue that one of the most urgent projects we can engage in is finding a way to maintain the benefits of modern medicine in a low-energy society. And as I research this problem, I increasingly believe that this can be accomplished, that we have the resources to create a low-energy national health care — or, if our government will not lead on such a project, that states, regions or even communities can enable such a health care model.

I am not claiming that we can reproduce modern health care as we know it, or that the change will be without cost or difficulty, but I do believe it is possible to integrate a lower-energy health care system into our existing models, and that the project of doing so, besides preparing us for a crisis, might also improve the lives of the 40 million Americans currently without access to health care.

Now, just as I am not a demographer, an economist, a nutritionist or any of the other things I've presumed to do research on and offer analysis of, I am not a medical professional. My intent here is not to offer specific medical advice, but to jumpstart the conversation about what kind of low-impact, low-energy medical infrastructure we can have. My goal is not to end the conversation, but to begin it, and to pass on my thoughts to those who can take it further.

The Myths of Medicine

It is difficult to begin to triage the current medical system without first evaluating our assumptions about how the medical system works. I think many of us are carrying three false beliefs about medicine. They are:

1. More health care is better, and good health care must be expensive.
2. The benefits of modern medicine always outweigh the costs.
3. Social good programs like health care are things you get to later rather than sooner.

The first assumption seems fairly obvious — in a world where billions of people, including millions of Americans, don't have access to health care it would seem that if you could get all the health care you wanted, that would be better. But in fact, the data are more complex than that. For example, a recent article in *The Atlantic* by Shannon Brownlee, author of *Overtreated: Why Too Much Medicine is Making Us Sicker and Poorer,* includes the telling quote by a Dartmouth Medical School professor: "If we sent 30 percent of the doctors in this country to Africa, we might raise the level of health on both continents."

That is, even something that seems to be as obvious a good as a large number of doctors isn't necessarily so under the current system for a host of reasons, including the fact that multiple specialists attending to treatment often lead to confusion and errors, and that doctors tend to concentrate in wealthy areas, so that more doctors doesn't mean better distribution of health care.

Americans spend about twice as much money on health care as Europeans do, but our lifespans are no longer and often shorter. We take more drugs than they do, endure more medical interventions at the end of our lives, report lower levels of satisfaction and happiness with our health and suffer more from anxiety and depression than people with lower levels of health care. It is also true that our present medical system is not about "health" so much as treating disease, and that a system that actually focused on preventive care, health and wellness — all much lower-input practices than our present one — might work better with less energy.

A *Harvard Magazine* article about Dr. George Valliant, the author of *Aging Well,* describes tracking several groups of men over more than 50 years, including Harvard graduates and inner-city, lower-class Boston men, and notes that among all these groups access to health care was not the defining factor in quality of life or health in the senior years — basic self care and staying away from doctors was. That is,

> ...being able to afford better doctors, hospitals, and healthcare is unrelated to their health or longevity. "It's not economic at all," [Valliant] asserts. "People who go to hospitals are sicker than people who don't. Having better doctors and hospitals is a bit like locking the barn after the horse is out. The trick is not going to hospitals in the first place." (harvardmagazine.com/2001/03/the-talent-for-aging-wel.html)

Though it is obviously important that sick people have access to health care, at present only three out of every 100 dollars spent on health care in the US go to any kind of help in maintaining good health rather than to the treatment of medical problems. For example, midwife Kathy Breault observes that an increase in Caesarean sections is tightly linked to an explosion of gestational diabetes in women, which often causes very large babies that cannot be delivered vaginally. The increase in gestational diabetes is almost entirely a product of our industrial diet and sedentary lifestyle, and yet while health insurance will pay for a C-section, it will only rarely fund nutritional education or cooking classes and never pay for a babysitter to allow an expectant mother to cook a meal, shop at a farmers' market or get some exercise.

It is important to realize that Americans have similar lifespans to average Cubans, and higher infant mortality rates, despite the fact that Cuba is a vastly poorer nation and spends about $186 per person annually on health care — compared to $4500 per person in the US. In Kerala, a state in India, lifespans are not quite the same as in the US, but they are similar to those of inner-city African Americans. Kerala infant mortality rates are lower than mortality rates for infants in Cleveland or Baltimore's inner city. That is remarkable because Keralans use one seventeenth the resources we do to maintain health.

There are other examples of "low income, high well being" nations that spend very little on health care, demonstrating that neither energy use nor expenditure is the determining factor in long lifespans and low infant mortality. What does matter is making health care and its corollary, education (the ability to obtain and make use of health information is tied to literacy levels to a large degree), a major social priority, even to the exclusion of other projects if resources are limited.

The Amish are another important example. Amish people in the US have a number of factors that would seem to place them at risk of higher infant mortality rates and lower lifespans — they receive little preventive care, eat a high-fat diet, have no health insurance, use herbal and home remedies first, and give birth to most of their children at home, using lay midwives. And yet the average Amish lifespan is virtually the same as that of the average non-Amish American, despite their spending one fifth or less on health care.

. . .

If you are a lactating mother, maintain your lactation as long as possible — in a crisis, there may be urgent need for wet nurses for the babies of women who can't nurse.

. . .

All of these examples demonstrate the simple truth that, although hospitals and medical care are energy intensive, it is not impossible to dramatically reduce our need for expensive, energy intensive medical care by prioritizing health and general welfare.

Whenever I talk about going to lower-energy usage, a percentage of people shout out something like "But that would mean going back to the stone age, to lepers walking the streets and people throwing their feces out the window on our heads!" (Okay, I exaggerate a little for effect.) But I think it is fair to say that variations on "Without power, life would be intolerable" is a common assumption, and that it is tied to myth #2 above, that modern medicine is an unmitigated good.

Now, do not mistake me — I believe that much of medicine is good. My family and I have received enormous benefits from it, and I do not diminish those benefits. But everything comes with a price, and sometimes we simply choose not to see the price of things clearly. That is, often when we worry about the dangers of losing modern medicine and society, we see clearly the costs of not having easy access to high-technology, high-energy medical care, but don't see, because we have assimilated them, the high costs of the medicine and the society that makes it possible.

The Costs and Benefits of Modern Medicine

In considering the second myth, the first thing we need to do is establish what gains from modern medicine we have received. Our intuitive response to modern medicine is to exaggerate our need for its input in many cases, or exaggerate its benefits compared to the alternatives. By this I mean that modern medicine and modern industrial life do enable us to treat some illnesses better than others but also cause or enable other illnesses to occur more frequently. Were we suddenly to experience a catastrophic energy shortage (something I do not view as especially likely, but will use as a model here), like that which struck Cuba during the Special Period of the 1990s, we would likely see some illnesses increase and others almost wholly disappear.

Among the medical concerns we would not see, or would see infrequently in a low-energy, relocalized, sustainable society, would be death and injury from car accidents. Right now, 1 million people die annually worldwide from car accidents, and another 7 million are injured or disabled. Car accidents are the leading cause of death for people under 25.

• • •

Make sure that emergency supplies such as first aid kits and flashlights are readily available and can be easily located in the dark in a crisis.

• • •

Illnesses we would probably see less of in a low-energy society include all communicable illnesses, including things like flu, colds, SARS, and other airborne diseases, particularly those originating in other nations (fewer people traveling means less disease transmission). We would also experience fewer "lifestyle diseases" such as high blood pressure, heart disease, strokes and type two diabetes. Illnesses brought on by poor diet and sedentary lifestyle would certainly be reduced. In fact, in the aftermath of the Special Period in Cuba, a significant rise in lifespan was seen because of increased exercise and better diets.

We would also probably see fewer medically induced deaths. A study released by Health Grades, a private medical quality control group, suggested that in 2000, 2001 and 2002, an average of 195,000 people died from in-hospital medical errors. The study suggested that this number is double previous estimates. In addition, the hospital environment, including inappropriate use of antibiotics, is responsible for the spread of "superbugs" such as MRSA, which has now escaped the hospital environment and is showing up in schools. A recent study in the *Journal of the American Medical Association* suggests that the US has 95,000 MRSA cases per year, of which approximately one out of five is fatal. More people die in the US from

MRSA than die from HIV. Though it is probably too late to eradicate some of the superbugs already created, a lower input health care system, used less often, would create fewer opportunities for superbugs to evolve and escape into the general populace.

Over the longer term, much lower emissions of pollutants, industrial toxins and carbon would make a huge difference to our health in reduced levels of cancer, autism, birth defects, neurological disease, asthma and lung disease, among others. As far as I know, no one has yet run the numbers to calculate the total net gains and losses here, but I mention this mostly to observe that we pay an enormous price for our lifestyle, and yet we tend not to think of it in those terms. We tend not to think of the sudden death of a family member from a heart attack or a child's cancer as part of the cost of our society — we tend to think of it in isolation.

There would be costs, in terms of lives, in a lower-energy medical system. If we anticipate that we could manage many essential treatments, but that high-input items such as elective surgery, helicopter evacuations, defibrillators in every public building and other high-energy medical investments might be less available, some people would suffer and die. There is no question of that, and it is not something that should be minimized or elided. But it is important to remember that some people who would have died in a high-energy society would not suffer and die in a lower-energy one, and that too should not be minimized or elided.

Why Health Care Should Be at the Center of Things

The third myth is the one that says that we must focus on the economy, on rail systems, on everything but health care. Underlying this assumption is the belief that if we're headed for disaster, it is self-evident that we can't provide universal health care. After all, we don't have that now. But we cannot allow that to be a barrier.

Instead, I wish to make the case that we absolutely must focus our energies on health care — to the exclusion of other projects, if necessary. The national discussion on universal health care has focused so far only on creating "perfect" modern models — that is, systems where everyone can have as much unconstrained access to treatment of illness as they want. In fact, when universal health care is proposed, the notion that any kind of constraint of access might occur is the single most effective negative argument. How many times has each of us heard the claim that if we had universal national health insurance, we might have to wait for surgery?

But if we imagine a national health care service that focuses on maintaining health (as opposed to treating sickness), on delivering basic preventive care as widely as possible, and on investing in the health care measures with the greatest possible benefits for longevity and public health at low cost, we might be able to create a model that could co-exist with any national health insurance plan and, until/unless one is created, could serve the existing needs of the 40 million Americans currently without health care. Such a system would reduce the death rate from lack of health care access (18 million people die each year because of insufficient access to health care). Right now, many insurance programs simply will not pay for preventive measures. For example, my midwife friend Kathy Breault notes that she has difficulty getting insurance reimbursement when she vaccinates for the HPV virus, which causes cervical cancers, but no difficulty getting payment for expensive tests once a patient has an abnormal pap smear.

And if we were to look more carefully at the Amish, the Cubans, the Keralans, we might find a model of health care sufficiency that is an optimization of the best of the modern and the low tech, and we might begin to make decisions more wisely about how to expend our energy and financial resources to keep people healthy.

By "sufficiency" I mean the notion, advanced by Professor Thomas Princen, that instead of seeking out market-based efficiency solutions, we might find a principle of "enough" that can be widely applied. Some Americans have far too little access to medical care, and some have far too much. The notion of restraint and optimization in health care, up to now advanced only in the service of HMO bottom lines, might be used, instead, to create an adequate health care system that might serve people's needs rather than market needs. What Princen calls "enoughness" seems to be a real phenomenon in health care, available to us in the light of other societies that use less health care, use it differently, and still obtain the same positive results.

The examples of Cuba and Kerala, both poor places that have elected to preserve health care and social welfare above all else, even in times of crisis, should point out what is possible for us. Going into this crisis, our society as a whole is probably going to do some things to adapt while leaving others undone. I write this book in the hope that we will have a model to work on if we are left with the burden of doing the work that governments left undone, of making do from where we are, but also in the hope that we will begin to prioritize our remaining resources as Cuba and Kerala did, even if times get very difficult. Historically, that has not been the American way — when times get hard, we ration basic needs like food, shelter and health care by price, leaving a large segment of the population's needs unmet. But we could alter that.

Now, both Cuba and Kerala have roughly socialist economies, and it would be easy to leap to the conclusion that I am calling for socialism here or that socialism is a necessary prerequisite to providing health care in an increasingly impoverished society. Neither is true — I believe all useful economic models are hybrids of multiple philosophies, and I hold no particular allegiance to a single economic model. Moreover, I don't believe that using government resources to tend to the well-being of one's populace is a socialist project — any more than using government resources to support a war machine is.

If we pay taxes for any reason at all (and sometimes most of us wonder), it is that government should meet the needs of ordinary people. Right now, I think most Americans of all political stripes would agree that it is not doing so. And any analysis of health care must begin, for example, with the fact that the American military budget is twice the military budget of all other nations together, and that what we have spent on the war in Iraq would provide lavish health care many times over. Yet I've never met an American who thinks that the war in Iraq is a better investment than health. It seems self-evident to me that this is not a question of Marx versus Adam Smith, but a question whether government should serve the people or the government — something I think we can get an easy consensus on.

The Most Bang for the Health Care Buck

Much of the benefit of modern medicine has come from public health measures that are easy to continue implementing in a post-peak society, provided we plan for them. Even if we lose our access to cheap energy or experience radical Climate Change, the most important things that modern medicine has done for us have occurred in the realm of public health and are not likely to be lost — for example, the germ theory of disease, nutritional knowledge and public hygiene.

• • •

Get your animals' vaccinations up to date, and while you are at it, have a tetanus booster yourself. People who work with dirt need to have regular tetanus boosters.

• • •

That is, we are not in danger of losing the knowledge that illness is caused by viruses and bacteria, rather than miasmas and humors. Nor are we likely to lose the knowledge of how to avoid scurvy and pellagra or how to wash your hands before eating and before delivering a baby. What we do potentially face are situations that make it impossible for us to implement these things — shortages of potable water or increasing natural disasters that overwhelm public sewage and water systems.

It is important to remember that the practices associated with most public health measures are not necessarily energy dependent. For example, the Amish live as long as we do despite the fact that they have outhouses and no indoor running water. A balanced diet is something we can teach people to eat, even if nutritional supplements became unavailable. Handwashing can be done whether you carry water or turn on a tap. Oral rehydration fluids to prevent childhood death from diarrhea are still well within the budgets of most Americans, and will be for a long time to come.

• • •

Make sure you have a gravity-powered water filter that can handle both chemical runoff and disease organisms. Do not allow children, the medically compromised, pregnant women or nursing mothers to drink any unfiltered water. Ideally, don't let anyone drink it — expect water suppies to be contaminated in a crisis.

• • •

We will most need to create plans for dealing with the increasing number of system failures. For example, most of the 12 million people worldwide who die from hunger-related causes each day actually die from diseases their bodies were unable to resist because of malnutrition. So ensuring resilient local food systems, offering price supports and good security are as much health care measures as the treatment of hunger-related disease. It is always easier to prevent disease than to cure it.

Other system failures will include loss of access to water and water contamination. Because 40 percent of the US is experiencing severe drought conditions, this fact will come home quite soon for many of us, I suspect. The city of Atlanta, as I write this, is only weeks away from completely running out of water for most of its population. Unfortunately, the US has an extremely heavily contaminated water supply, and faces national water shortages in the coming decades.

One important way to reduce water contamination would be to switch the nation to composting toilets and cease putting human waste, along with all the drug residuals we excrete and other contaminants, into the water supply. This would require a certain amount of infrastructure investment and an educational campaign, but would give the nation 30 billion extra gallons of water annually, at a bare minimum. It would also allow us to replace millions of gallons of nitrogen fertilizer with high-nitrogen human urine. I mention this because as in the case of food systems, in some cases the most essential public health measures are often not thought of as health care at all. Indeed, most of the projects we are engaged in as we transition to a lower-energy lifestyle could be described as health care.

The next most important element in reducing infant and child mortality is vaccinations and antibiotics. Vaccinations tend to be controversial in the rich world, sometimes for good reason. For example, although the autism/vaccine link is not at all clear, injecting small children with proportionally large doses of mercury (used as a preservative in many vaccines until recently and still used in flu vaccines) is clearly not a good thing. The rotavirus vaccine was withdrawn after several children died of intestinal blockages linked to the vaccine. Some vaccines, including the smallpox, chicken pox and oral polio vaccines, carry the risk of transmitting a version of the illness.

To a large degree, however, American opposition to vaccines comes because even those who do not take them get the advantages of herd immunity — that is, as long as a significant majority of people receive these vaccines, those who do not receive them experience comparatively low risks. In a society where people regularly die of polio or experience heart damage from scarlet fever or sterility from mumps, we would almost certainly see fewer people unwilling to take the abstract risk of vaccines. I say this as the mother of an autistic child, a mother who is not at all happy that she was pressured into giving her son mercury-laden vaccines as an infant. But I also recognize that, statistically, many of our children would have a much greater chance of dying from a disease like measles than of being harmed by the vaccine.

That said, however, we have introduced many new vaccines in the last two decades without an appreciable lowering of our infant and child mortality rates. It seems clear that at some point, you get a decline in benefit return from vaccinating for certain diseases. It seems likely that we could raise our children with far fewer vaccines. Maintaining enough industrial infrastructure to keep these vaccines going and available worldwide would require some energy inputs, but it would be possible to prioritize our investment in renewable energy systems to synchronize with our health care infrastructure.

Antibiotics also help reduce infant mortality and resolve adult illnesses that might have long-term consequences. However, it is worth noting that more than 80 percent of the illnesses routinely treated with antibiotics in childhood would self-resolve without them. Indeed, the standard of care has changed and now many common childhood illnesses, including ear infections, are not routinely treated with antibiotics. Still, many more are than should be. Because of this, and also probably because of low levels of antibiotics in most American supermarket meat, we are seeing a steady and frightening rise in antibiotic resistance, while there are few new antibiotics in the pipeline. In addition, approximately 5 percent of all hospitalizations are connected to the overuse of antibiotics, and this statistic may be artificially low, given the radical rise, previously mentioned, of MRSA infections.

Sweden has severely curtailed its use of antibiotics, in hopes of reducing antibiotic resistance. In the US a recent report by the Centers for Disease Control (CDC) proposed drastic measures to limit the spread of resistant bacterial infection. In this case, antibiotics would be removed from all animal feeds (currently, virtually all non-organic factory meat uses low levels of antibiotics, so this would require a radical change in our food system; again, it turns out nearly everything we have to do is "health care" in a way), minimized in farm settings, and administered only in hospitals and in cases where there is real threat of death or disability. This has been proposed by physicians groups and may eventually have to be implemented. So there is a real chance, regardless of energy or economic constraints, that traditional antibiotics may not be widely available to most of us, simply because they are not good for our society as a whole.

Even if a national or state system of medical manufacture were not available, antibiotics could likely remain accessible to communities that planned ahead for their manufacture. In the presently unlikely scenario that a large part of the population could not either get or afford antibiotics, it might be possible to manufacture sulfanilamide and chloramphenicol on a local level, using high school or college chemistry labs and small quantities of renewable energies.

Neither is an ideal drug. Both have serious and sometimes fatal side effects, which is why they have been superceded. But it is reassuring to know that many of the most acute diseases of poverty could be treated with antibiotics, if not without painful consequences. Other drugs might also be made this way, particularly older ones. This would still require some fossil fuels and fueled processes, but is far less energy and cost intensive than producing tetracycline and other antibiotics. Ideally, we would reserve energy for the creation of antibiotics, as well as vaccines, to avoid such painful choices.

The other alternative is to use herbal antibiotics and medicines. These will almost certainly prove, in many cases, to be less effective than the pharmaceuticals we have become accustomed to. That said, however, less effective does not mean entirely ineffective. In his book *Herbal Antibiotics,* Stephen

Buhner documents, "Clinical studies, such as one in 1984 by Singh and Shuka, have repeatedly shown that garlic is active against strains of bacteria that are highly resistant to antibiotics." (Buhner, 34)

At least 300 such studies of garlic alone have been undertaken and many show similar results — garlic works fairly well against a wide range of bacterial agents, including MRSA. During World War I, before the invention of antibiotics, garlic was the sovereign remedy for the treatment of typhus; it remains so in much of the poor world. I have used garlic to treat routine ear infections in my children and mastitis in myself, with good and rapid results. Garlic could also replace some blood pressure and cholesterol medicines and is easily grown in the home garden. Other herbs that Buhner and others document as having clinical support for use as natural antibiotics include eucalyptus (specific for bronchial infections, according to the *Indian Journal of Medicine,* and found by Australian chemists to work well against streptococcus bacteria), licorice (which increases the production and activity of white blood cells; licorice, however, has many contraindications, so don't take this without doing considerably more research), and oregano (which according to a Cornell University study was a potent anti-bacterial against food-borne pathogens).

• • •

Many medicinal and culinary herbs are at their peak in the fall. Dry some for winter use by hanging them up in a cool, dark place.

• • •

It seems likely that some of the dangers of the loss of widespread antibiotics can be compensated for by the use of herbal antibiotics, by decreased exposure due to more localized lifestyles, by the removal of industrial meat from our diets and by lifestyle changes. That said, however, there is no doubt that many of us, particularly older baby boomers and parents will miss modern medicine if for reasons of energy or economics we are not able to make it continue.

The Beginning and the End

Two other places that medical care provides enormous returns is at the beginning and at the end of life. These areas are extremely costly and energy intensive in the US and documentably could be changed to a lower-energy infrastructure.

Pregnancy and childbirth are medically important periods of life, but many rich nations use far less medical intervention in these areas than Americans do. We are only now beginning to realize how essential wellness and preventive care are in pregnancy. Recent studies suggest that prenatal nutrition may have far deeper effects on lifelong health than anyone ever expected.

But that does not necessarily mean a large increase of investment — in fact, it may be the contrary. In many industrial nations with far lower rates of infant mortality than ours, midwife care, homebirth and a far lower rate of medical intervention is the norm. Research has shown that midwife births, except for those in very high-risk categories, are as safe as doctor-assisted births, and that outcomes that influence long-term health, such as breastfeeding initiation, are higher with midwives. Midwives offer lower intervention care, which sometimes makes an explicit difference in reducing risk. As a 1993 study reported,

> *Every study that has compared midwives and obstetricians has found better outcomes for midwives for same-risk patients. In some studies, midwives actually served higher risk populations than the physicians and still obtained lower mortalities and morbidities. The superiority and safety of midwifery for most women no longer needs to be proven. It has been well established. (Madrona, Lewis & Morgaine, "The Future of Midwifery in the United States," NAPSAC News, Fall–Winter, 1993, p. 30)*

In fact, the US's comparatively high infant mortality rate correlates strongly with the loss of midwife care and the move to medicalized birth. In 1950, the US was the tenth-ranked nation in infant mortality, and it began to decline at the same time that birth became a major specialty in medicine and the American College of Obstetrics and Gynecology began to work proactively to move childbirth into its domain. We have never broken the top ten since, while most of the top ten nations use midwives far more widely than we do. The five European nations with the lowest rates of infant mortality use midwives more than 70 percent of the time.

• • •

Save some of your baby clothes, cloth diapers and toys. Someday someone near you may need them.

• • •

The Amish, who use lay midwives (midwives trained by apprenticeship or training programs outside of traditional nursing and medical schools) for home births in a majority of cases have only a very slightly higher rate of infant mortality than the average American who delivers in a hospital.

The current model of birth is extremely energy intensive and interventionist. But a program to make midwifery, including lay midwifery, accessible to all could almost certainly reduce existing infant mortality rates, improving both prenatal care and long-term health consequences associated with prematurity and poor nutrition, reduce the cost of delivery and provide health care benefits as good or better as present rates.

Midwifery is also correlated with increased breastfeeding, which could further reduce long-term health care consequences and improve health for both mother and child, as breastfeeding is associated not only with lowered infant mortality and fewer childhood illnesses but also with long-term reductions in diabetes and obesity and with reductions in cancer rates for nursing mothers. In this case, we could only improve things by adopting lower-energy solutions.

The other place that we might consider triaging is end-of-life care. At this point, 30 percent of all medical care is provided to people in the last few years of life. Now, some of that simply makes sense — of course a person struck by a car is going to get a lot of medical care, even if they die. But some of it makes no sense at all. Often what medical care is doing is prolonging the process of dying, rather than prolonging life. I've seen this myself, working in nursing homes and when we cared for Eric's grandparents. For example, despite our express wishes and hers, Eric's grandmother, an 80-year-old woman in spinal shock with a broken neck and no hope of recovery was placed on a ventilator and endured multiple medical procedures before she was finally allowed to die, at her request and ours.

My husband's grandfather suffered severe constipation due to a medication he was taking. At the end of his life, when there was clearly no long-term hope, we still had to argue with doctors about discontinuing that medication because he might have a heart attack. At that point in his life a sudden heart attack was, in fact, a desirable ending, a better choice than a slow, painful, grinding death. The inability of our medical establishment to recognize that most people would prefer a peaceful, low-intervention death at home is one of the great tragedies of our medical system.

Much of this is driven by insurance requirements that hospice programs be applied only when a physician can make a certain diagnosis that some-one has less than six months to live — something most doctors are reluctant to do. Most insurances also require that patients give up all attempts at curative medicine before receiving at-home palliative care. The largest research program into end-of-life care in US history found that a majority of Americans die in pain, in debt, and alone — the one thing we all fear most. We are doing an almost unimaginably poor job of making death gentle — and we are doing what we are doing at enormous expense.

Study after study suggests that most Americans want to die at home, with their family, and not be in pain. Pain relief is now provided by many petroleum-based medications, often very expensive, but it need not be.

Many effective pain relievers suitable for the end of life derive from renewable plant materials like coca, marijuana and opium poppies. These are, of course, illegal, and I cannot advocate that anyone grow or use them, but were we to change our laws, two of the three can be grown in any home garden. There is no rational reason why pain relief should become unavailable in any low-energy future.

Dying at home is problematic now because so few of us are accustomed to the idea or have the skills of basic nursing. But it wasn't very long ago that most Americans died at home, cared for by family members. Community-based programs to teach home nursing and basic care of the ill and dying could enable many more people to end their lives at home.

In fact, the care of others by neighbors and family members represents an enormous potential savings in the health care system. Much routine medical care could be meted out by people trained in community programs. Even now, many rural areas rely on volunteer Emergency Medical Services. But such programs could be radically expanded to include basic palliative care, nutritional care and other treatments, even volunteer psychological support. Such a "shadow" health care system could operate cheaply, for the benefit of individual communities, or could be scaled up to the regional or national level. Millions of Americans could use such a system today.

I don't claim to have all the answers on health care — in fact, I don't know that I have any. But I do know that unless we begin meeting more of our own medical needs and preparing better to care for ourselves and each other in the future, we will suffer a great deal indeed.

PART

Six

[*Recompense*]

FOURTEEN

Abundance, Democracy, Joy

*This is what you shall do: Love the earth and the sun and the
animals, despise riches, give alms to everyone that asks, stand up for the
stupid and crazy, devote your income and your labor to others,
hate tyrants, argue not concerning God, have patience and indulgence
towards the people, take off your hat to nothing known or unknown.*
— WALT WHITMAN

These fragments I have shored against my ruins.
— T.S. ELIOT

Scared? Duh!

I WAS AT A CONFERENCE RECENTLY, AND I DID SOMETHING THAT CONFERENCE
speakers aren't supposed to do. I admitted that I was afraid. Conference
speakers are supposed to be inspiring, and admitting your fear is high on the
disheartening meter. But it is true, and I doubt I'm the only one.

The thing is, I think most people have a choice when confronted by a
reality like Peak Oil and Climate Change — either they develop a thick skin
for at least some things, or they deny. We're all aware that denial is the most
popular choice, and why not — denial is a very happy place to live, as long
as you don't mind the cost. But there is a high cost — we can't begin to
mend the damage we've done from a position of denial.

I'm an optimist by nature, and I've also got a lot of practice laughing
rather than weeping. Or I wind up my computer and type out my outrage
hoping to break through someone else's denial and make them as angry as
this stuff makes me, so that maybe we can do something to stop it. But I'm
less practiced at dealing with my own fear. I've been dripping with outrage

at the world's injustices pretty much since I was old enough to have a political conscience, sometime in my early teens. But I haven't been particularly scared, because my own blood was never in the game. I was always outraged on someone else's behalf, and of course, that's an easy emotion.

I have, as we all know, four little hostages to fortune and at least the average person's fear of suffering, death and inconvenience. I'm scared for my kids and scared for myself. Some of the time I desperately wish this would all just go away and I wouldn't have to think about it anymore. Sometimes I wish denial were an option.

But mostly, I'm glad I know even the bad, hard stuff. Because I honestly have no doubt that being prepared is better than not being prepared. I'm not even always sure I want more time. Part of me does, but part of me believes we are better off going through our depletion crisis sooner than later — soon enough that we still have money and resources to make some major infrastructure changes, soon enough that we may avoid the worst of catastrophic warming, and that there might be enough oil left for future generations for some wind power and vaccinations. And I can't wish my knowledge would go away because it is my job to protect my kids, and my desire to protect the next generations in general — I don't want to dump this burden on my sons or on other people's children. I don't think that's the proper work of parents who love their kids.

> • • •
> Resolve family conflicts whenever possible. The truth is that you don't have time for the same old battles over again, and you are likely to depend on each other in the future.
> • • •

John Adams once said that he was a soldier so that his son could be a farmer, and his grandson a poet. I'm no soldier, and if this were war (it isn't) it would be won by farmers and perhaps by poets too. But I share the sentiment. I'm going to do this work and face this as head on as I possibly can so that my children may someday choose other work. That's what moms do. Now, the thing they don't tell you about parenting when you become a mom or dad is this: being a parent doesn't make you a better person.

That is, when you become a parent, if you are going to be any good at it, a certain amount of selflessness and self-sacrifice is mandatory, but you do not, as some people seem to think, immediately become the sort of person who enjoys self-sacrifice and wants to be selfless. The ugly truth is that you are still the same greedy, lazy, selfish person you were before. (Okay, maybe you aren't, but I am.) If you were the sort of person who would rather read a novel on the couch than answer "What does this spell?" 78 times, nothing about parenthood, or even love for your kids, will transform you magically into the kind of person who finds having your novel interrupted every two minutes delightful.

I know the world is full of better people than I am, but the truth is that a lot of us are still the same ordinarily rotten people we were before we had kids. We just don't have the option of indulging our rottenness. That is, parenthood requires not that you be a good person or that your better nature predominate, but that you suck it up and do the unselfish thing anyway, even when you don't want to, even when it is damned hard.

The same is true about our present situation. We've got bad news, and it is appropriate to feel bad about it. There's no reason we have to be fearless here — frankly, the only way I can imagine being fearless is to be stupid. But we do have to be brave — that is, we don't have to feel brave but, like the Cowardly Lion, like the mom who doesn't really want to get up for the two am feeding, we have act the right way, to pretend as hard as we can that we have, as the Cowardly Lion's song says, the nerve. And the amazing thing about pretending hard is that sometimes — not always, but just sometimes — you become, as Kurt Vonnegut put it, "what you pretend to be."

The only antidote to fear I know is good work. I learned in pregnancy, facing labor (all of my labors were very, very, very long), to simply screw up my nerve, accept that the only way out is through, and to go forward into the pain. We're in the same situation now — the way out of this current crisis is through it, to go forward from where we are, with what we have and who we are. It isn't required that we not be afraid or that we don't spend a lot of time grumpily wishing that someone else would do the work and leave us alone with our book. But it is required that while we curse fate, previous generations, the current administration, G-d and the Federal Reserve, we get to work.

What work? Tikkun Olam, if you are a Jew, or even if you find the metaphor compelling. *Tikkun olam* means "the repair of the world." In my faith, that is why we are here — to fix what is broken, repair what is damaged, to improve what can be improved. As the saying goes, it is not required of us that we complete the work, but it is not permitted for us not to try.

I do not come from one of those religious faiths where you put aside the lesser emotions like fear and selfishness — in fact, as far as I can tell, the right to whine is a sacrament in Judaism. So I'd hardly be the person to tell anyone "Don't be afraid." Instead, I suggest we all be afraid. Nor do I suggest any of us fail to whine about it — that, after all, is what the Internet and best friends are there for.

But let us whine while we hammer, moan while we cook, sigh in outrage while we write and march and yell and build and fight our fear with good work and the pretense that maybe we'll become better people while we're pretending that we already are. There's too damned much to do to do it any other way. I may be a coward at times (and trust me, I am), but I've got work to do anyway.

Abundance

As I write this, we are getting ready for Purim at our house, and being a story teller and former teacher of stories I find myself reflecting on the story that goes with the holiday. Someone or other once pointed out that pretty much all Jewish festivals can be described as "They tried to destroy the Jewish people. They were foiled. Let's eat." And so it is — Purim celebrates the biblical tale of Esther and the preservation of the Jewish people.

Esther didn't particularly want to be a heroine. She was pleased to get to be queen, and there is no real indication in the story that she was displeased to have assimilated into non-Jewish culture. She concealed that she was a Jew because her uncle feared that the king would not take her as a wife, but she didn't seem much troubled by it. Esther is first and foremost the story of acceptance by and of the dominant culture, of not making too many waves. But what separates Esther is her refusal (and Mordechai's) to allow her investment in the dominant culture to shape her moral thinking.

When Haman called for the people of King Ahasuerus's realm to murder all the Jews and plunder their goods, Mordechai called upon Esther to plead with the king. Esther was understandably frightened both to reveal herself as a Jew and also to go before the king without his summoning her, as the penalty for that was death. She told Mordechai if she tried to speak to the king, she would die. Mordechai's answer was decidedly un-avuncular. It was this: "Do not imagine that you, of all the Jews, will escape with your life by being in the king's palace. On the contrary, if you keep silent in this crisis, relief and deliverance will come to the Jews from another quarter, while you and your father's house will perish. And who knows, perhaps you have attained to your position for just such a crisis."

Mordechai had raised Esther as a daughter, but he did not fail to speak harshly to her of her duty. So she risked death twice, first by going to the king and then by asking that he spare his queen and her people. And of course (or we would not be celebrating) he did. Esther ended up all right in the end, but she did so by recognizing that if she came to power in the dominant culture, it did not absolve her of moral responsibility but heightened her obligation.

Peter Parker said it too: "With great power comes great responsibility." I think most of us have no idea how powerful we are, and thus, how responsible we are. Virtually all Americans command power and wealth unimaginable to most of the people in the world. We have, as James Kunstler has pointed out, the equivalent of 200 slaves working for us — but instead of human slaves, we have energy slaves that wash our clothes, wash our dishes, make the clothes, carry us about. Most of us have more education — even if we graduated only from high school — than a majority of the world's population. It doesn't feel that way when you are in debt and struggling economically, but most middle-class Americans are richer and more privileged than kings in most of history.

Because we do not see ourselves as powerful and rich (we view ourselves mostly in comparison to our neighbors who are similarly powerful and rich), we are all caught up in our struggles; we do not tend to think that we are the very people who have great responsibility in the world. Other people are powerful. Other people can change things, not us. We are merely getting along, we do not have time, we do not have energy, we do not have money enough to spare.

• • •

The winter lull is an excellent time to get involved with public affairs.

Engage, stand for office,

attend meetings or volunteer.

• • •

But if we do not, who on earth has the time and the money, the energy and the power to change the world? Who will you ask to do it for you? Will you ask someone poorer and weaker and less privileged? In many cases those people are already doing this work — all over the world, the poor have spoken up about Climate Change and world trade, land reform and sustainability. I have read analyses of global warming and the WTO written by 12-year-olds from Nicaragua and India that put the writing of professional adults to shame.

The world is full of people who work harder than you and I, who have harder lives, fewer electronic slaves, and whose very lives are set at stake by the changes in our world, yet who still have time to stand up and speak out.

I have written this elsewhere, but I repeat it, and will keep repeating it as long as necessary: almost all that is good in human history over the past three centuries has been accomplished by oppressed and frightened, impoverished and angry people who have stood up to those that did them harm, who mortgaged their futures and endangered their lives and said "No More." Overwhelmingly, they succeeded in winning, despite lack of things you and I have plentifully — power, money, education, comfort. Our own national history includes, along with its dark side, a remarkable and courageous tradition of not counting the cost to do what is right. And every single person who has ever stood up in resistance has been less well educated, less wealthy, less privileged, less safe, less comfortable than you and I are today. How can we do less?

Most of us are not living up to our moral responsibilities or using our privilege and wealth to create justice. We, like Esther, are afraid. We are afraid of change, afraid of doing without, afraid of being different. The thought that we might have to give up all the things we are accustomed to and change to something entirely new is frightening. So mostly we are silent.

But Mordechai's words "Perhaps you have attained your position for just such a crisis," should speak to us all. Whether you believe in God or good fortune, the randomness of everything or some sort of intentionality, perhaps if we are very lucky, it is because our good fortune enables us to bring about change. Perhaps we are meant to lead, no matter how little we like the work, how frightened we are of the consequences or how comfortably we are ensconced in the dominant culture.

• • •

Make a list of your goals for the coming year and the coming five years. Keep a record of those goals, and don't forget to write down when you accomplish them.

• • •

We are like Esther. We are afraid of what it would mean to reveal ourselves, to stand forth from the culture and demand that it change. We are comfortable in our palaces and happy with our embroidered robes. And we, like Esther, are tempted to act only if we can foresee happy consequences for ourselves. But as Mordechai rightly points out, sometimes what happens to us isn't really the point — sometimes what matters is that we, in our power, have done the right thing, without counting the cost to ourselves. It takes courage. And that is not in over-great supply. But I suspect there is more of it out there than we like to admit, even to ourselves.

Am I Romanticizing Poverty?

Someone who reads my blog recently e-mailed me that my writings are merely a call for us all to return to poverty, and that I'm intentionally romanticizing subsistence agriculture. And I started wondering, am I?

The answer, I suspect, is a little bit, in the sense that I don't think anything is served by my saying, "Your future and the future of your children is drudgery and misery." I think it is certainly possible that I elide some difficulties

— or rather, that I prefer not to focus on them. Some of that is the optimist in me. And part of it is that ultimately most of the things that will necessarily get harder aren't the things I value most. That is, I suspect our physical loads will get heavier. On the other hand, I suspect that will be good for my overall health and wellbeing, so I choose to look at it as mostly a positive.

Some things about a life low on the economic food chain, I think, really are better. For example, poor agrarian societies generally have stronger social ties. In many cases, people who live in simpler economies, enticed with fewer things they can't have, report themselves to be happier. And the things about contemporary, wealthy society that really matter are mostly things that we can continue to have — if we are very careful. The things that wealth has given us that I value are these: basic medical care, including birth control and preventive care; social support networks for the elderly, the disabled, the very poor and other vulnerable people; good education; access to information; access to clean water; safe food and secure shelter; personal freedom; and a just society. And what is fascinating about all these things is that they aren't very expensive. A good education, up to and including college doesn't have to cost 30K a year. Basic public medical care including vaccinations, preventive medicine, midwifery, simple palliative care for the dying, many basic medications, birth control and some hospital care doesn't have to cost us what it does. Neither do libraries, public services and support programs for the poor.

Most of the most important things in my life are items that are not depleted or in short supply. As Richard Heinberg has put it,

> *Are there some good things that are not at or near their historic peaks? I can think of a few:*
> *— Community*
> *— Personal autonomy*
> *— Satisfaction from honest work well done*
> *— Intergenerational solidarity*
> *— Cooperation*
> *— Leisure time*
> *— Happiness*
> *— Ingenuity*
> *— Artistry*
> *— Beauty of the built environment* (Peak Everything, *14*)

The blunt truth is that an abundance of the things above is enough to compensate for the loss of other gifts.

It is worth remembering that when the Soviet Union collapsed and stopped supplying oil to Cuba, crashing the economy and everything along with it, the Cuban government did exactly the opposite of what the American government does in hard times — it kept up the social support programs. Instead of taking much-needed funds out of education, social welfare, programs for the elderly and poor, it kept those up. It opened new university campuses and more clinics because people couldn't travel as far or as easily for medical care and education. That's a choice we can make too — if we want to.

On the other hand, am I going to deny that our wealth has been extremely pleasant? Heck no. I've enjoyed all sorts of things other people can never imagine. I've traveled. I've had pretty things. I have a home of my own. I have a computer to write on and the Internet. Right now I'm sitting here on a 15-degree day, two sleeping dogs at my feet, in a warm house typing and listening to The Little Willies. Would I prefer to be outside, hand pumping icy water into buckets and carrying it?

If that were my life, if I were hauling water in the cold instead of writing here, would I be unhappy? Maybe momentarily, but generally speaking, I don't think so. I like personal comfort as much as anyone else, but, as trite as it seems to say so, the things I really care about don't depend on my not having to grow food or haul water.

Our perceptions drive our sense of what is work more than the actual work does. How many people can remember doing some now-unthinkable job when they were young and poor, and now say, "But I was happy." I've met people who walked in the snow to their outhouses, who boiled laundry on coal stoves, who hung their dripping, freezing laundry off a fourth-story balcony. And I've hauled a month's worth of laundry half a mile on my back in a sack, carried my groceries for a mile, stood outside in the cold waiting for a bus every morning, walked four miles to work. And when I look back at every one of those activities, it really wasn't that big a deal.

We look back on what we used to do and think "Amazing. We were happy. All that work didn't impinge on our enjoyment of life." But what's amazing is what we've forgotten — that work really doesn't impinge on enjoying life when it is our life. We take on our labor savers as though they are miracles, but the life we had before them was usually not so very bad. The miracle, if you can call it that, is that they've reshaped our memories so that our pasts are untenable, and untenantable, to us — we begin to think we can't go home again.

Do I romanticize subsistence agriculture? Maybe a little. I like farming, and someone who doesn't might not agree with me. And I tend to think that if we're going to have to do something (and I have little doubt that we will have to), we might as well go into it excited, treating it as an opportunity to optimize and improve our lives, rather than as a tragedy to be endured.

But I also note that I'm happier since we moved here. And I think this might not be a purely personal preference. Some of you may have watched the PBS documentary series *Frontier House*. Like all such things, it was imperfect in its creation, to some degree more about the personalities than the work. It was originally intended to debunk the myth of *Little House on the Prairie*, offer counterweight to the romanticism of subsistence agriculture. And in the end, it failed to do so — in fact, it proved that that romanticism wasn't entirely misplaced.

. . .

Create household routines that are simple and not dependent on wealth or fossil fuels. Bedtime routines, the morning cuppa, a candlelight meal once a week — these things can provide reassurance and a sense of stability even in changing times.

. . .

At the end of six months without any of the amenities of 21st-century life, without indoor plumbing or refrigeration, thermostats or grocery stores, seven adults and six children came out of the experience changed. A majority of the adults and all the children overwhelmingly found that they preferred their frontier lives to the ones they returned to. One of the men actually moved back to live in his old cabin and help out on the ranch where the filming had occurred. Another child experienced serious depression because she missed the life she described as more "real." Overwhelmingly, the kids on the show said that they missed having chores, they missed taking care of animals, and they missed being with their parents all the time. (This included multiple teenagers.) A wealthy woman building a 5000-square-foot house admitted that her house felt too big, and that in a 400-square-foot cabin, six people had never felt crowded.

Now, *Frontier House* was television, but what matters about it is how thoroughly it failed to do what it set out to do. The producers had assumed that the physical hardships would overwhelm every other part of the experience. They did for a short adjustment period, and then the emotional, spiritual and personal benefits of the life overtook the transitory concerns of physical work, and again, life was good.

So maybe I'm a little romantic. But I draw hope that if we may not be more comfortable, we might still be having fun.

The One Thing We Did Right

I've been watching the rerelease of *Eyes on the Prize*, which I haven't seen since high school. I recommend to everyone that you watch it too. Not only is it a brilliant representation of our history and one of the best documentaries of all time, it is also an inspiration for the future.

Peak Oil is not about petroleum geology or economics when you get right down to it. Climate Change is not about ice cores and meteorology. Those things matter, but they aren't the center of things. Peak Oil and Climate Change are about justice, plain and simple. They are about fairness, morality and integrity — we in the rich world have chosen to steal from the poor in our own country and other nations, and from our children and grandchildren, and we need to stop it right now.

• • •

Consider joining a religious community even if you aren't very religious — liberal Quakers, Reconstructionist Jews and Unitarians among others aren't particularly doctrinaire, nor will they enquire into your faith. Religious communities are one of the few sources of real community we have left.

• • •

The stakes are very simple: our children's lives, other people's lives, the food in their mouths and the medicine that keeps them from dying unnecessarily. If we keep consuming resources as though there is no tomorrow, there will be no tomorrow, and those who are too young or too weak or too powerless to demand anything be saved for them will die. They are dying right now, today, in poor world countries as we in the west extract $38 billion of wealth from them every year.

And that is a drop in the bucket compared to the number who stand to suffer and die because of Climate Change, Peak Oil and economic disruption. It can't always be someone else. It will be my kids and yours. We have to make deep changes, and we have to make them now.

If you believe we can't find the strength and courage and commitment to give up our cars, our heat or air conditioning, or our jobs that produce nothing and give wealth to the corporations we pretend to deplore, go watch *Eyes on the Prize* right now. Watch a 65-year-old woman with diabetes and varicose veins tell with pride how she walked eight miles round trip to her job scrubbing floors every day for more than a year, and never, ever took a ride on a bus no matter how tired she was. Watch a seven-year-old girl walk past a row of people screaming obscenities at her and throwing things, just to go to school. Watch an old man face death threats to walk into a courtroom to testify to the truth. See people face dogs and firehoses and men with guns who want to kill them and link arms and march forward. We all know people did this, because we read about it in our history classes, but what this documentary does better than any other single source is show how ordinary those actions are.

Those people were no different than you or me under the skin. They were ordinary people with ordinary fears and an extraordinary degree of courage. And I do not believe for one moment that those remarkable people, or the remarkable young men who faced death in World War II, or any of the heroes of history are any different than you and I. We too can have courage. We too can have justice. We too can do what has to be done.

What would the world look like if all of us who worry about Peak Oil and Climate Change showed true integrity? What would it look like if the millions of people who know what is coming refused to go on warming the planet and burning fossil fuels, and pledged to find another way? What would happen if we had the courage of our convictions and stood up and said "I will no longer steal from the future and the poor. I will live only on what is mine by right and in justice." There is no doubt in the world we could do this, because people like us already have. I'm trying to find out how to get there. I hope you will too.

> *These are people who are capable of devotion,*
> *public devotion, to justice.*
> *They meant what they said and*
> *every day that passes, they mean it more.*
> — WENDELL BERRY

·

Things You Can Do to Get Ready for Peak Oil, Climate Change and Difficult Times

- Plant a garden and grow some of your own food. Even apartment dwellers can grow lettuce and dwarf cherry tomatoes in window boxes, or participate in community gardens. The rest of us can transform our yards into food-producing areas.

- Order enough seeds to last you at least three years if you can. That way if you lose a crop or cannot get replacement seed, you'll be able to continue growing.

- Check out a local animal shelter and adopt a dog or cat for companionship, protection and pest control.

- Take advantage of yard sales and auctions. Buy used goods like shoes and clothes for your children to grow into as well as bedding, futons, extra towels and other basics in case you find yourself sharing quarters with friends or family.

- Rethink your seed-starting regimen now. Instead of depending on bags of purchased potting soil, electric grow lights and plastic flats, consider making use of more sustainable options like hotbeds heated by composting manures, homemade wooden flats, your own compost.

- Your local feed store has chicks in spring. Check with your local zoning board, and consider advocating to change the laws if chickens are not permitted in backyards.

- The real estate "season" begins in the spring. If you are planning a move, now is the time to research markets and find that country property or the urban duplex with a big yard. Remember that an acre is quite a large space. Smaller, intensively managed properties can be enormously productive.

- Once pastures are flush, last year's hay is a bargain. Manure and old hay are great soil builders for your new garden.

- Now is a good time to buy boots, winter coats, down comforters and other resources for keeping warm.

- As things green up in the spring, get a good identification book, and see what food is growing free around you. Eat dandelion salad from your lawn, daylily shoots and the green tips of nettles. Try a new springtime food you don't usually eat — ramps, fiddleheads or something else.

- Set up barrels or cisterns and begin harvesting spring rains from your roof for irrigation or washing.

- Grow an ornamental and useful garden full of flowers that have value as medicinal, dye and fiber plants, seasoning herbs, natural cleaners and pest repellents, such as dye hollyhocks and coreopsis, soapwort, hip roses, bee balm, bayberry and Johnny jump ups.

- Start walking and biking more. There are bicycles for every sort of rider: recumbent bikes for people with bad backs, adult trikes for older folks and the disabled, trail-a-bikes so kids can safely ride with their parents, and even bikes that people in wheelchairs can use, attached to the bike of someone who can pedal.

- Use spring holidays and the subject of rebirth and freedom to bring up the subjects of Climate Change, Peak Oil and the future with family and friends.

- Join a CSA if you don't garden, and learn to enjoy the bounty of a seasonal diet.

- Eggs and greens are at their most plentiful and nutritious in spring. Enjoy them. And you can add ground up cooked eggshells and ground dried greens to flour to increase its nutritional value.

- Start baking your own bread.

- Start a compost pile outdoors or begin worm composting indoors. Everyone can and should compost their food scraps, because putting them in landfills wastes needed fertility and produces methane, a powerful greenhouse gas.

- Use spring rhubarb, parsnips or dandelions to make wine. Wine doesn't just come from grapes!

- New houses are being built and old ones renovated. Ask permission to scavenge free building materials, cinder blocks, old windows and scrap wood for your own projects.

- Get comfortable with the spring weather. Go outside, turn down your heat or bank your fires, put on your sweaters one more time and adapt your body to the temperature.

- Sheep shearing takes place in the spring. Now is a great time to buy fleece and learn to spin with a drop spindle.

- Trade cuttings and plant divisions with your neighbors. Emphasize multiplying edibles such as Jerusalem artichokes.

- Take up beekeeping. Even if you don't have space in your yard, perhaps someone nearby would welcome bees to their garden.

- Visit nearby colleges at the end of the term, and scavenge in the dorm dumpsters. College students often leave behind astounding amounts of stuff.

- Can't afford health insurance? Many community colleges and state universities have low-cost, subsidized health insurance available to anyone who pays for a class.

☉ Early spring was famously the "starving time" when stored supplies ran out and people went hungry. As you look back over the food you stored and preserved last year, would there have been enough if you had needed it? Plan next year's food production to take into account early spring limitations.

☉ Assemble directions to family and friends if you had to evacuate. Keep them with your emergency supplies along with good maps.

☉ Put in a composting toilet and stop wasting good drinking water. Composting toilets don't smell; some of them flush; and they need not be expensive. You can find plans to make your own by downloading the Internet version of Joseph Jenkins's *The Humanure Handbook.*

☉ Make sure that emergency supplies such as first aid kits and flashlights are readily available and can be easily located in the dark in a crisis.

☉ Acquire a good first aid book, and read it now. There won't be time when you need it.

☉ Enlist your neighbors in supporting your new projects, whether getting chickens or landscaping your front yard with berries and nuts. If you are doing something new, it helps to have community support.

☉ Choose breeds of poultry that can set and hatch their own replacements. Orpingtons, Cochins and most Bantams are wonderful mothers.

☉ Grow some food in your garden for your animals. Alfalfa, root crops, even wheat can be sowed in garden beds.

☉ If your community doesn't have a food co-op, start one, focusing on local foods.

☉ Talk to your kids about sex, birth control, responsibility, your values and what you expect of them. Have this conversation early and often, and combine it with a discussion of the future, so that children understand what the implications of early sexual activity might be in a poorer world.

☉ There is enough baby equipment on the planet already. Check out freecycle or yard sales, and don't buy new. If you ask around, all the cute baby clothes you could ever imagine will magically appear.

☉ Invest in a small cart that you can pull behind you so that you shop and carry your purchases on foot. Or add a trailer to your bicycle so that you can run errands while biking.

☉ Create household routines that are simple and not dependent on wealth or fossil fuels. Bedtime routines, the morning cuppa, a candlelight meal once a week — these things can provide reassurance and a sense of stability even in changing times. The bedtime routine may be done by flashlight, the morning cup of tea may be mints from your garden, but stable routines say, "Although some things have changed, the essentials remain the same."

☉ Honeybees and native pollinators are in a dangerous decline. Plant drifts of native plants, encourage pollinators like orchard mason bees, and leave grass long for bumblebee habitats. We need our pollinators in order to eat!

- ☼ If you don't have a lot of space but are trying to grow much of your food, grow root crops like potatoes and sweet potatoes.

- ☼ Urine is mostly sterile, and safe to add to plants. A person's yearly output can fertilize more than one quarter acre. Dilute the urine in a 10 to 1 ratio, and use it on your garden.

- ☼ Encourage useful plant volunteers and learn to propagate more plants by layering, taking cuttings and grafting.

- ☼ Apprentice yourself to a local senior citizen to learn some useful skill — gardening, preserving, quilting, knitting or crocheting. Many seniors suffer from isolation while many young people need the skills seniors have. Build the connection.

- ☼ Switch to cloth menstrual pads or reusable menstrual cups like the Diva cup or the Keeper. They are both more pleasant than the disposable versions and more environmentally sound.

- ☼ Encourage your religious community to reconnect with the agrarian roots of your faith. Every religion has special harvest and planting rituals, and traditions about generosity and sharing, spring and rebirth. Plant a garden for your food pantry, or plant special festival foods and invite the community to share them.

- ☼ Many unusual fruit trees have few pest or disease issues, unlike some of the best known trees. Consider adding paw paws, Asian pears, medlars and quinces to your orchard along with peaches, plums and apples.

- ☼ Encourage your children to start their own small home businesses, perhaps managing animals or growing food and selling it. Treat what they do seriously, and validate them for contributing to the household.

- ☼ Expand your library by buying books at yard sales, library sales and used bookstores. Besides books on gardening, farming, building, cooking and other useful skills, add light reading to distract your mind from difficulties, material on history and politics to help you understand what is going on, and plenty of books, educational and pleasurable, for children to learn from.

- ☼ Consider joining your local volunteer fire department, ambulance corps or first responders group. The skills you learn and the contribution to your community will be invaluable.

- ☼ Domestic violence gets worse in times of stress. Support your local shelter for battered women, and keep an eye out for women in danger.

- ☼ Winter items like boots, coats, woodstoves and insulating curtains go on sale in the spring. Think ahead to your needs for next year.

- ☼ If you live in a hot climate, put up food in the spring for the hot, dry season ahead.

- ☼ Take advantage of lush pastures and plentiful organic milk to try out simple cheese making.

- ☼ Consider having your vet show you how to give vaccinations and do animal emergency care yourself.

☼ Track your local weather. Climate Change is making it hard for us to anticipate based on old patterns, so see what the new ones are. Track rainfall, temperatures, wind patterns and when the birds, animals and leaves appear. These may be the most reliable signs we have in our new climates.

☼ Learn about your local watershed, and encourage local water conservation efforts.

☼ Cut up old sheets or towels to use as reusable cloth toilet paper or baby wipes.

☼ If you have a diesel vehicle, consider locating a source of waste vegetable oil to power your car.

☼ Consider having a midwife delivery or training as a midwife or childbirth assistant (doula) to serve families in your area.

☼ Say a blessing, a prayer, or just be happy and thankful for spring, the season of rebirth.

☼ Learn to preserve food. If you don't garden, check out your farmers' market at the end of the day for large quantities of produce they want to get rid of.

☼ Firewood and heating supplies are at their cheapest in summer. Invest for winter.

☼ Buy hay for your animals direct from farmers all at once, rather than gradually over the winter.

☼ Teach kids how to ride a bike and about basic bike safety.

☼ Consider adding a solar-powered attic fan to cool your house.

☼ Don't go on vacation. Stay home and transform your house into a paradise instead.

☼ Throw a barbecue or open house and get to know your neighbors.

☼ Summer is a good time to have a yard sale, declutter your house and make a little extra money.

☼ Be prepared for summer blackouts. Have emergency supplies, water and lighting at hand.

☼ Talk to your landlord about making energy-saving improvements on your rental. Offer to do them yourself in exchange for a rent reduction.

☼ Build a solar dehydrator and dehydrate tomatoes, peppers and berries for your winter meals.

☼ Minimize air conditioning usage. Take a cool shower, put your feet in water, use ice packs, and set the thermostat as high as you can tolerate.

☼ Get together with neighbors and create an at-home summer camp for your kids. It saves money and kids can learn useful skills!

☼ Consider adding some tropical plants to your garden, even if you live in a cool place. Citrus, figs, even bananas can be grown indoors in the winter and set out during the summer.

☼ As summer reaches its midpoint, it is time for northerners to plan fall gardens. Don't just plant once in May. You can grow an enormous amount of food into the fall even in very cold climates — peas, broccoli, kale, Brussels sprouts, spinach, carrots, beets.

☉ Put up a clothesline! And consider hand washing your clothes outside in cool water in the summer, as everyone will enjoy getting wet anyway.

☉ If you have a finished basement, consider putting a small stove, woodstove or hot plate down there to avoid heating the house when you cook.

☉ Go fishing. Eat your catch if you have access to safe waters, otherwise, practice catch and release.

☉ Encourage pick-up sports in your neighborhood. Help kids learn to enjoy athletic activities without adult direction.

☉ Have your teenager (or a neighbor's) help you clean out your closets and attic. Let them sell the stuff you find in exchange for the extra hands.

☉ Buy a hand-pushed lawn mower and get some good exercise.

☉ Practice extreme water conservation during hot weather. Mulch gardens to reduce the need for irrigation, use gray water from sinks and showers to irrigate gardens and flush toilets, bathe less often and use less water.

☉ Summer is a good time to toilet train children. Let them run around naked outside, where accidents won't be a worry. You'll do less laundry in the winter if you get this done now.

☉ Consider replacing some or all of your lawn with something that doesn't need to be mowed — native groundcovers, vetch, mints, moss, chamomile or wildflowers.

☉ Learn to use a scythe. Cut and dry your lawn grass for animal feed or mulch, and cut weeds and brushy areas without power.

☉ Have a gardeners' potluck. Invite friends and neighbors to bring produce and enjoy a meal together.

☉ Consider a community pool if there are no beaches in your area. Public resources for keeping cool are important.

☉ Make sure you have a gravity-powered water filter that can handle both chemical runoff and disease organisms. Do not allow children, the medically compromised, pregnant women or nursing mothers to drink any unfiltered water. Ideally, don't let anyone drink it — expect water supplies to be contaminated in a crisis.

☉ Take a nap. Accidents are caused by people working too hard with too little sleep.

☉ Keep an eye out for unharvested fruits and nuts. Many suburban and rural areas have fruit bushes that no one harvests. Take advantage and preserve the food for next winter.

☉ Get ready for hurricane season, if you live where this is a danger. Have an evacuation plan and all necessary materials to safely stay put. Remember to isten carefully to weather reports, and get out when necessary.

☉ Dehydrate the outer leaves of cabbage and broccoli and use them to thicken soups.

☉ Getting ready for back to school? Reconsider transportation. Can your kids walk? Bike? Carpool? Could you walk with them or hire a neighborhood teenager to help them walk or bike safely?

⊛ Fleas and lice are common when people aren't able to bathe regularly. Know how to get rid of both without toxic chemicals.

⊛ Have you considered homeschooling? It is legal in every state, and can be enormously satisfying. Even if you don't homeschool, consider "afterschooling" — teaching your kids useful skills and providing a critical perspective they won't receive in most schools.

⊛ Invest in several solar shower bags. In summer they can be hung in the sun and give you fossil-fuel-free pleasure. In the winter hang them behind the woodstove or by the radiator and use them in the bathroom.

⊛ Draw attention to your local watershed and your vulnerabilities in that regard. As the world gets hotter and dryer, where will your water come from? Will you be competing with other communities? Are there areas of waste that could be dealt with? Wetlands to be preserved? Make safe, clean and reliable water a community priority.

⊛ Children, the elderly, the ill and the disabled are especially vulnerable to "appetite fatigue" or sharp changes in diet that result in nutritional deficits. Adapt your family to a fresh, local diet based on whole grains, beans and local produce.

⊛ Breastfeed your child. The World Health Organization recommends that women nurse until "at least" two, and the worldwide average age of weaning is four.

⊛ Hire a neighborhood teenager to work with you on your garden, a building project, an energy-saving program. Listen to them talk about their lives, and treat them with respect. Teenagers need meaningful work and to feel that adults care about them and have confidence in them.

⊛ During heat waves, check regularly on elderly and disabled members of your community, and know the signs of heat exhaustion and heat stroke. Consider inviting vulnerable neighbors to stay with you for a few days if the weather is especially bad.

⊛ Start a community theater company, a local orchestra, a blues band — art and music don't have to go away when the cheap oil does.

⊛ Keep hydrated. Cut back on caffeine and sugary beverages, and drink lots of water.

⊛ Plant high-vitamin C fruits like Aronia, seaberry and hip roses.

⊛ Up your charitable donations. Sometimes we get more by what we give away than what we do for money.

⊛ Get to know local farmers, and ask them to grow things that you'd like to get locally. A farmer might consider adding wheat or dried beans or an unusual vegetable to their crops if enough people ask them.

⊛ Keep a gas can filled with stabilized fuel if you have a car, so that you can evacuate in an emergency.

⊛ Join your local garden club or street beautification society and encourage the groups to replace street trees and public landscaping with edible trees and shrubs.

- Make compost tea out of your weeds. Most weeds contain valuable fertility (which they took from your garden) and trace minerals. Dump them in a bucket of water, let it sit for a few days and then pour it over plants.

- Add vinegar to your laundry to soften towels and jeans that dry "crisp" on the line. They won't be the same as dryer dried ones, but you'll get used to it.

- Grow only open-pollinated seeds that reproduce themselves exactly. Practice saving seed.

- Use shredded newspaper or dried leaves to make animal bedding.

- Get your animals' vaccinations up to date, and while you are at it, have a tetanus booster yourself. People who work with dirt need to have regular tetanus boosters.

- Dwarf goats and miniature sheep are suitable even for suburban lots. Consider persuading your neighbors by showing them how cute these animals are, and offering to let them graze on messy, weedy areas or brush in the neighborhood.

- Pack a picnic when you travel, so that you won't have to stop for fast food.

- Talk to your kids about your values. Begin explaining early on that "local food is better, because it doesn't use so much energy, so let's go ask where these carrots are from." As they get older, you can offer more information. "The reason we don't want you to have those clothes is that they come from a company that forces kids like you to do work for them. Would you like to help me write a letter to the company and do some Internet research about labor practices?"

- Do your grocery shopping, library trip and hardware store stop all at once. Keep a running list of places to go, and think about what stops you can make that will save you a trip later.

- Rest often as you bike, walk, garden and do other summer work. Rising temperatures and pollution mean that it is essential that you take care of your body, drink and rest when necessary.

- Now is a great time to discuss telecommuting with your boss.

- Planning a family vacation or road trip? Consider consolidating with friends or family and renting a van to transport all of you while saving energy.

- Begin studying herbal medicine and getting to know the herbs in your garden. Be sure you also learn when to consult a medical practitioner.

- Brew your own beer, or seek out local microbrewers.

- Grow an extra row of your garden for the local food pantry or soup kitchen. Encourage neighbors to do the same.

- Add some agricultural charcoal to your soil to help it maintain fertility. Research terra preta.

- If you are single, consider looking for a partner on a green or sustainability-oriented website like greensingles.com. Meeting people who have similar visions of the future can save you some trouble.

- Consider building a summer kitchen or screen room for cooking and sleeping in hot weather. It can double as a woodshed in winter.

- Acquire a Kill-A-Watt to measure electric usage. Find ways to eliminate high-usage appliances or to disconnect phantom loads. "Always-on" appliances can account for up to one third of your total energy usage.

- Use a solar box cooker instead of your stove. You will save energy and keep your house cooler. Plans for homemade solar cookers can be found online.

- Switch to propane or wood cooking for picnics, use reusable plates and cups and compost your scraps. Charcoal barbecuing is a big greenhouse gas contributor.

- Remember, preserving food isn't just canning and freezing. You can dehydrate, ferment (e.g., sauerkraut, kimchi and "kosher style" pickles), preserve in salt, wine or sugar, smoke and cool store in a root cellar. Do some research into the most nutritious, palatable and efficient way to preserve each food.

- Take time to enjoy the leisure, the warmth, the lush bounty of summer.

- Stock up for winter as though the hard times will begin this year. Besides storing, don't forget season-extension techniques for your garden, such as cold frames, row covers or a greenhouse.

- Go "leaf rustling in the fall." As your neighbors bag up their leaves, grab them and use them to build soil in your own garden.

- Thanksgiving sales tend to offer the lowest annual prices on staples like flour, baking spices, canned pumpkin and cooking oils. Stock up on ingredients for your traditional holiday foods. In hard times, any kind of celebration will be welcome.

- Hit the last yard sales of the summer and back-to-school sales and buy a few extra clothes (or fabric to make them) for growing children, and a pair of extra shoes for everyone. They will be welcome if prices rise or availability falls.

- Consider allergy shots, as a long-term solution.

- The best time to build new garden beds is in the autumn. Cover the area you want to grow in with cardboard or newspaper, pile on compost and mulch, and by spring the bed will be ready to go.

- Plant a last crop of spinach in early fall to overwinter and enjoy for late fall and spring greens.

- Fall is a great time to try out the 100 Mile Diet or the Bull's-eye Diet.

- Consider planting a beautifying, edible bulb garden. Tulip bulbs are edible, as are daylilies.

- Most storable foods are low in accessible Vitamin C. Harvest wild or tame unsprayed rose hips, and dry them for tea to ensure long-term good health.

- Discounts on alcohol are common between Halloween and New Year's. This is an excellent time to buy some wine for pleasure and vodka to make your own vanilla.

- Gardening equipment, including rain barrels and garden tools go on sale in the fall. Plan ahead for next year's needs. Seed companies also often have fall sales.

- Local honey will be at its cheapest right in the fall, so get your honey for the year. Consider making friends with the beekeeper and perhaps taking lessons yourself.

☉ Throw a "work bee" and get neighbors together on a community project. This could be anything from a barn raising to a charitable cooking project.

☉ Most cold-climate houses either have or could have a "cool room" for storage of food in winter. This could be as basic as a corner of your basement or a vented, insulated closet. Use your cool space instead of a fridge in the winter.

☉ Most local charities get the largest part of their donations in November and December. Consider spreading out your charitable donations year round to help charities keep up with community needs.

☉ Turnips and beets placed in buckets of damp sand will send up fresh greens with little light, even in west or east facing apartment windows.

☉ Many medicinal and culinary herbs are at their peak in the fall. Dry some for winter use by hanging them up in a cool, dark place.

☉ Consider planting a bed (or a field) of winter wheat. Your poultry can even graze it lightly, and in the summer you can harvest it with a scythe and enjoy home-grown bread.

☉ Fall is the cheapest time to buy livestock either to raise or to butcher. Many 4-H projects need a home now, and farmers may not want to keep animals over winter. If you are prepared to do your own butchering, animals sometimes sell for far less than their meat.

☉ Start a local gleaning program! Gleaners harvest food missed by mechanical harvesters. Some programs donate the results to food pantries; others provide food for the pickers and their families.

☉ Play "heater chicken" — compete to see how long you can go without turning on the heat or starting a fire.

☉ If you don't hunt, learn. Deer and turkey make excellent meat, and in many areas, herds desperately need thinning. Consider learning to catch small game like squirrels and rabbits as well.

☉ More children are born in the summer or early fall than at any time of year, which suggests that some of us are doing more than chopping wood to keep warm. If you don't want your family size to increase, now is a good time to update your birth control.

☉ Learn a skill that can be done in very low light conditions. Knitting, crocheting, whittling, rug braiding, leatherworking can all be done mostly by touch with little light, and give you something useful to do while relaxing in the evenings and conversing.

☉ Learn meditation and biofeedback to help deal with pain or stress.

☉ Hard cider and cider vinegar are easy to make out of fresh apple cider.

☉ Create local educational systems. Resist regionalizing schools and advocate for neighborhood school and library systems.

☉ Make an emergency plan for meeting with family if a crisis happened while everyone was at school or at work. Decide who checks on whom, where to meet and where to go, and choose a relative or friend to leave connecting messages with.

⊛ Save some of your baby clothes, cloth diapers and toys. Someday someone near you may need them.

⊛ Make "window pop-ins" out of rigid board insulation covered with cloth — these can be placed in windows at night to hold in heat.

⊛ Consider training your dog to "go with" your children as an added measure of security.

⊛ Invite someone new to your home every month. Expand your social circle and your community regularly.

⊛ Don't forget to plant garlic and multiplying onions for spring!

⊛ Consider working with your neighbors to create a local currency that keeps money in town.

⊛ Build an in-law apartment in unused space or consider setting up your home so that older family members can live with you when the time comes.

⊛ Keep a six-month supply of all prescription medicines (unless they will spoil before that) and extra copies of all prescriptions. If you are taking prescription medicines for non-life threatening conditions, consider trying to wean yourself off of them or finding an herbal, dietary or lifestyle change solution instead.

⊛ Celebrate the harvest! Winter comes soon enough — get together with friends and family and delight in the richness of the season.

⊛ Take advantage of people who want to teach their skills. Your local adult education program almost certainly has something useful and interesting — woodworking, crocheting, music, CPR, herbalism, vegetarian cooking.

⊛ Get serious about redesigning your landscape. Sit down and think hard about how you can get the most food, fuel and fiber from your yard.

⊛ The winter lull is an excellent time to get involved with public affairs. Engage, stand for office, attend meetings or volunteer.

⊛ Now is the time to prepare for illness. Keep a stock of remedies at hand, including useful antibiotics, painkillers, and tools for handling injury and illnesses yourself.

⊛ Most schools and homeschool groups would be delighted to have volunteers talk about conservation, gardening, livestock, ham radio, home-scale mechanics, or any other skill you have.

⊛ If a holiday gift exchange is part of your life, consider having a $100 holiday this year, and making most gifts.

⊛ Talk to people about Peak Oil and Climate Change, and encourage them to prepare.

⊛ Now is the time to convince your business, school, church, mosque, synagogue or community center to add a garden on that empty lawn. If you start the campaign now, you can be ready to plant in the spring.

☼ Stock up on rodent traps and non-toxic pest repellents.

☼ Consider giving farm stand gift certificates or healthy food gifts as holiday "tips" — many people are struggling to get by, and food is a good gift.

☼ Get out and enjoy the winter weather. It can be hard to adapt to a lowered thermostat if you spend all your time huddled in front of the heater. Ski, snowshoe, sled, shovel, have a snowball fight, go winter camping, but get comfortable in the cold, snowy world around you.

☼ Have your chimneys inspected and learn to clean your own, and to build a fire without creating creosote. Make sure your house has fire extinguishers, smoke detectors and carbon monoxide detectors with long-life batteries.

☼ Grow sprouts on your windowsill for winter salads.

☼ Reconsider how you are using your house. Could you add a roommate? Share with a family member? Work from home? Do projects more efficiently? Add a greenhouse? Work with what you have to make space more useful.

☼ Do a "preparedness" dry run in the middle of winter. Turn out the power, turn off the water and the heat, and see how things go for a few days. Use what you learn to improve your preparedness.

☼ Learn to mend and patch your clothes, including sock darning.

☼ Write letters to people. Letters are a rarity now, but the post is the most efficient way to communicate, and letters can be treasured forever.

☼ If someone wants to buy you a present, request something useful. Consider giving useful gifts as well — solar-crank radios, LED flashlights, long underwear and cast iron pans are appreciated regardless of your plans for the future.

☼ Make a list of your goals for the coming year and the coming five years. Keep a record of those goals, and don't forget to write down when you accomplish them.

☼ Don't heat your bedroom. Make a four poster bed — heavy coverings on the top and sides keep body warmth in.

☼ Clean and organize your house and get rid of anything you don't need. For things you store for the long term, box them and keep lists of what is in each box.

☼ Stock up on commonly used nails and screws, pins, hinges, latches, shoelaces, twine, tacks — if it holds one thing to another, you'll want it. Don't forget the duct tape!

☼ Resolve family conflicts whenever possible. The truth is that you don't have time for the same old battles over again, and you are likely to depend on each other in the future.

☼ Make sure your local emergency responders and utility companies know if there is someone in your family who is elderly, ill or disabled. Generally speaking, utility companies will not shut off heat or power, even if you are unable to pay, if you must have these things to keep an ill or disabled person safe.

☼ Acquire snowshoes or ice-gripping clip-ons for your shoes so that bad weather doesn't keep you indoors.

☺ Pay attention to your marriage/partnership. Stress is a probable for many marriages and is likely to increase in hard times. Make sure you have healthy, enjoyable ways of dealing with each other, and that your partner knows that you love him or her and are committed, even when things are hard.

☺ If you are knowledgeable and committed to doing it well, a small home business breeding animals can be a productive cottage industry — consider breeding working dogs, excellent mousers or meat rabbits.

☺ Don't entertain your children all the time. Even older babies (1 year +) can be expected to amuse themselves for periods of a half hour or so, assuming their basic needs are met. Help older kids learn to guide and watch out for younger ones.

☺ Winter is fire season. Take special care if you are using candles or kerosene lamps, or heating with wood around children or pets. Children should be taught fire safety rules early on, and young children should never be left alone with a stove going.

☺ More than half the people who undergo trauma experience depression, anxiety or post-traumatic stress disorder. Know the signs, provide support and watch children especially carefully. Expect it to take some time before things settle down again.

☺ Attend zoning meetings and consider running for zoning board. Work to amend local zoning laws to encourage green building, composting toilets, clotheslines, small livestock, mixed-use housing, front lawn gardens and other future essentials.

☺ Spay and neuter any animals you don't intend to breed. Hard times are tough on animals, so don't let yours contribute to the problem.

☺ There is no need for children to know all the bad news. Make adaptation fun — talk about how nice the new way of doing things is, or discussing living like people did long ago. Older children need more truth than younger ones, but don't rush it — or overprotect them.

☺ Think about how your family would get around if the town was unable to plow the streets in winter. Consider a set of skis, studded bike tires and even a sleigh, if you have horses.

☺ Wear a hat to minimize heat loss, and enable you to keep house temperatures low.

☺ If you are a lactating mother, maintain your lactation as long as possible — in a crisis, there may be urgent need for wet nurses for the babies of women who can't nurse.

☺ Start early seedlings in January or February and have the first tomato on your block.

☺ Sleep more in winter — our bodies are adapted to respond to darker nights and cooler temperatures by resting. Become more in touch with natural rhythms.

☺ Learn astronomy and enjoy the winter night sky.

⊘ Encourage your kids to get involved with political and social issues they care about. Help them raise money or awareness, and help them understand the role of citizens in hard times.

⊘ Winter is a great time to take apart broken items and see if you can fix them.

⊘ If you can't afford heating, check out local fuel-assistance programs. Also, some states will subsidize insulation as well.

⊘ Shelters need food, blankets and warm clothing in winter more than ever — give what you can.

⊘ Once babies weigh ten pounds, healthy infants can sleep in quite cool rooms; indeed, cool sleeping environments are associated with lower risk of SIDS.

⊘ Make sure livestock living mostly outside get enough feed to keep them warm and healthy.

⊘ Practice cooking with whole grains and beans — these are the cheapest of all healthy foods, but many people don't know what to do with them.

⊘ Practice winter wood safety — learn to use your chainsaw safely and chop wood carefully.

⊘ A pocket knife makes an excellent gift for a child of eight or nine.

⊘ Consider joining a religious community even if you aren't very religious — liberal Quakers, Reconstructionist Jews and Unitarians among others aren't particularly doctrinaire, nor will they enquire into your faith. Religious communities are one of the few sources of real community we have left.

⊘ Eat a little less over the holidays and donate the cost of what you are not eating to your local food pantry.

⊘ Winter is a time of contemplation, rest, restoration and the return of light to our lives. Delight in it!

·

The Best Books About Nearly Everything

Peak Oil, Gas, Coal and Related Concerns

Darley, Julian. *High Noon for Natural Gas: The New Energy Crisis.* Chelsea Green, 2004. This is a surprisingly interesting book that details the difficulties to come in our gas supply.

Deffeyes, Kenneth. *Beyond Oil: The View From Hubbert's Peak.* Hill and Wang, 2005. This book is quite technical, but also very readable, even funny at times. Its most valuable contribution is the explanation of the mathematics of the Hubbert curve in terms anyone with high school algebra can understand. Useful for those who are not content to take anyone's word for it.

Goodell, Jeff. *Big Coal: The Dirty Secret Behind America's Energy Future.* Houghton Mifflin, 2006. As yet there are no books on coal that take into account the information we now have about coal's peak. But Goodell's book is an excellent exposé of the coal industry and the difficulties entailed in relying on coal.

Heinberg, Richard. *The Party's Over: Oil, War and the Fate of Industrial Societies.* New Society Publishers, 2003. The first book on Peak Oil, it remains among the very best.

Heinberg, Richard. *Peak Everything: Waking Up to the Century of Declines.* New Society Publishers, 2007. The fourth of Heinberg's books in as many years, this one brings together the threads of Peak Oil with Climate Change and other crises of depletion to give a more nuanced picture than past books.

· Kunstler, James Howard. *The Long Emergency: Surviving the Converging Catastrophes of the Twenty-First Century.* Atlantic Monthly Press, 2005. Kunstler is a brilliant writer, funny, perceptive and furious. His book was the very first to bring together Climate Change, Peak Oil and the coming financial crisis.

Climate Change

Kolbert, Elizabeth. *Field Notes from a Catastrophe: Man, Nature and Climate Change.* Bloomsbury, 2006. Absolutely fascinating and readable, this book's only weakness is the lyrical, quiet style of the author, which sometimes seems to understate the terrible news she is giving us. Still, a beautiful, troubling book well worth reading.

Monbiot, George. *Heat: How To Stop the Planet from Burning.* Allen Lane, 2007. Monbiot, a journalist with the London Guardian, has, I think the clearest view of the problem of any writer. His solutions are often troubling, in part because he buys the old public–private distinction, but he tries to do what no other climate writer dares to — to find a real means of reducing emissions fairly. A superb book.

Romm, Joseph. *Hell and High Water and What We Should Do.* William Morrow, 2007. Romm, former assistant secretary of the Department of Energy, offers a bleak assessment of what the US can expect facing Climate Change and suggests a host of moderately useful policy proposals. This book perhaps most clearly lays out the effects of Climate Change on the USA, and thus, has the potential power to move people who don't believe that Climate Change applies to them.

Pearce, Fred. *With Speed and Violence: Why Scientists Fear Tipping Points in Climate Change.* Beacon Press, 2006. This respected scientific journalist has done a clear eyed and coherent examination of the reasons that scientists are so much more afraid of Climate Change than the average person. Reading this book is essential to understanding the issues fully.

Agriculture and our Food System

Kimbrell, Andrew, ed. *Fatal Harvest: The Tragedy of Industrial Agriculture.* Island Press, 2002. There are two versions of this book. One is all essays; the other, much more expensive, includes photos. Though the essays are enormously valuable, make sure you see a copy of the whole book, complete with images. There are some things that must be seen to be understood.

Lappe, Frances Moor, Joseph Collins, Peter Rosset and Luis Esparza. *World Hunger: Twelve Myths.* Grove Press, 1998. Most of us probably believe in our hearts that we understand hunger. Most of us are wrong. A deeply useful book.

Menzel, Peter, and Faith D'Alusio. *Hungry Planet: What the World Eats.* Material World Books and Ten Speed Press, 2006. This is another book that has to be seen to be understood. The authors photographed families around the world with a week's worth of food in front of them. The impact of the stories here cannot be over-estimated.

Nestle, Marion. *Food Politics: How the Food Industry Influences Nutrition and Health.* University of California Press, 2002. Nestle's great revelation is the simple truth — the food industry has enormous power over dietary recommendations, nutrition and health in the US, and we are not being told the truth about our food.

Pollan, Michael. *The Omnivore's Dilemma: A Natural History of Four Meals.* Penguin Press, 2006. This brilliant and enormously influential book exposes the fast food industry and the limits of industrial organic agriculture. Though Pollan never quite goes far enough to advocate for a real, sustainable agriculture, the book is hugely important, well researched and fun to read to boot.

Shiva, Vandana. *Stolen Harvest: The Hijacking of the Global Food Supply.* South End Press, 2000. Shiva speaks in the voice of the poor world, describing the horrors of the industrialized food system for those who are its chief victims. Enormously important.

Singer, Peter, and Jim Mason. *The Way We Eat: Why Our Food Choices Matter.* Rodale

Press, 2006. Singer is a professor of philosophy and perhaps most famous as an animal rights activist. Though I don't agree with all his arguments, he's applied the tools of ethics and reason to making good food choices and along the way reveals a great deal about the evils of our present food system. Don't let his background in philosophy scare you — Singer and Mason are fun to read and fascinating.

Economics, Consumption, Poverty

Davis, Mike. *Planet of Slums*. Verso, 2006. In one of the most disturbing books you'll ever read, Davis describes what mass urbanization has gotten us all over the world. Unless we change things, this is a vision of the world's future.

Ehrenreich, Barbara. *Nickel and Dimed: On (Not) Getting By In America*. Henry Holt, 2001. Ehrenreich's insights into the lives of the US's working poor give us a vision of what most of us face.

Kozol, Jonathan. *Amazing Grace: The Lives of Children and the Conscience of a Nation*. Crown Publishers, 1995. The best book I know of about what poverty in the US really looks like.

Menzel, Peter. *Material World: A Global Family Portrait*. Sierra Club Books, 1994. Like Hungry Planet by the same author, this book shows rather than tells us the truth about consumption and inequity, as people from all over the world stand in front of the sum total of their possessions. See also the wonderfully detailed *Women in the Material World*.

Schor, Juliet. *The Overspent American: Why We Want What We Don't Need*. Harper Perennial, 1998. Schor puts our present problem of overconsumption in a historical and political context. Very enlightening.

Seabrook, Jeremy. *The No-Nonsense Guide to World Poverty*. New Internationalist, 2003. British journalist Seabrook does a better job than anyone I've ever seen at explaining the root causes of poverty in the world.

Politics and History

Egan, Timothy. *The Worst Hard Time: The Untold Story of Those Who Survived the Great American Dust Bowl*. Houghton Mifflin, 2006. Understanding what it was like when we were poor and in the midst of an environmental disaster once before may be essential to understanding the future. Very engaging and readable.

Johnson, Chalmers. *Nemesis: The Last Days of the American Republic*. Henry Holt, 2006. Johnson's analysis of the economic and military empire we've created is well worth reading, as are the other two books in his trilogy.

Klein, Naomi. *The Shock Doctrine*. Henry Holt, 2007. Naomi Klein's masterpiece describes the destruction of our democracy and the growth of disaster capitalism. An absolute must-read.

Norberg-Hodge, Helena. *Ancient Futures: Learning from Ladakh*. Sierra Club Books, 1991. If we are to grasp the limits of industrial society, we must see it from the outside. Norberg-Hodge, who lived in Ladakh as western culture broke over its shores, has a remarkably clear-eyed view.

Orlov, Dmitry. *Reinventing Collapse: The Soviet Example and American Prospects.* New Society Publishers, 2008. Readable, funny and wise, Orlov offers a remarkably clear-eyed vision of our future and the historic parallels with the last great empire collapse.

Schenone, Laura. *A Thousand Years Over a Hot Stove.* W.W. Norton, 2003. One of the best books ever written about women's history in the US. Schenone ties life in the domestic economy to women's social history. Very enlightening, enormously readable, good recipes.

Schor, Juliet B. *The Overworked American:* The Unexpected Decline of Leisure. Basic Books, 1992. One of the most important things we can learn from this is what a high price we've paid in leisure time.

Population and Limits

Diamond, Jared. *Collapse, How Societies Choose to Fail or Succeed.* Viking, 2005. We need to know what happened when we did this before. Diamond tells us.

Ehrlich, Paul. *One With Ninevah: Politics, Consumption and the Human Future.* Island Press, 2005. Ehrlich may be one of the "old men," but he is also wise and engaging.

Hynes, H. Patricia. *Taking Population Out of the Equation.* Institute Publishing, 1993. Hynes's critique is essential to understanding the limits of our population discussion.

Meadows, D.H., Jorgen Randers and Dennis L. Meadows. *The Limits to Growth: The 30 Year Update.* Chelsea Green Publishing, 2004. An important book. What you think you know about this book probably isn't true.

Shiva, Vandana, and Maria Mies. *EcoFeminism .* Zed Books, 1993. Don't let the title scare you — this is an important book, that explores the way ecology and women are tied together.

Tainter, Joseph. *New Studies in Archaeology, The Collapse of Complex Societies.* Cambridge University Press, 1988. Tainter's best insight is his description of the ways that complexity limits our choices — fascinating.

BOOKS TO FIX WHAT IS BROKEN

New Visions for Society

Bennholdt-Thomsen, Veronika, and Maria Mies. *The Subsistence Perspective: Beyond the Globalized Economy.* Zed Books, 1999. This underrated, under-read book proposes a real and meaningful alternative to conventional Marxist/Capitalist debates.

Berry, Wendell. *The Art of the Commonplace: The Agrarian Essays of Wendell Berry.* Counterpoint, 2002. Berry is the greatest agrarian writer of this century, and all of us should be familiar with his writings.

Dreher, Rod. *Crunchy Cons: How Birkenstocked Burkeans, gun-loving organic gardeners, evangelical free-range farmers, hip homeschooling mamas, right-wing nature lovers, and their diverse tribe of countercultural conservatives plan to save America (or at least the Republican Party).* Crown Forum, 2006. Dreher makes the case for a conservatism of conservation, moving right and left together to the sustainable center.

Heinberg, Richard. *Powerdown: Options and Actions for a Post-Carbon World.* New Society Publishers, 2004. Heinberg takes a serious look at what the possibilities are going into Peak Oil.

McKibben, Bill. *Hope, Human and Wild: True Stories of Living Lightly on the Earth.* Milkweed Editions, 2007. Other places in the world have managed to navigate some of these problems. McKibben tells us how.

Princen, Thomas. *The Logic of Sufficiency.* MIT Press, 2005. Wise and imaginative, Princen dares to propose an alternative vision to our present economy and culture of "efficiency."

Shiva, Vandana. *Earth Democracy: Justice, Sustainability and Peace.* South End Press, 2005. Shiva draws the link between environmentalism and democracy quite clearly.

Low-Energy Life

Brende, Eric. *Better Off: Flipping the Switch on Technology.* HarperCollins, 2004. A lovely, poetic account of the author's experience living with a minimal level of technology.

Coperthwaite, Wm. *A Handmade Life: In Search of Simplicity.* Chelsea Green, 2004. Coperthwaite has spent years developing a democratic way of living — homes that can be afforded and achieved by even the poor, an axe and a chair that anyone can make. This is a beautiful and useful book.

Savage, Scott, ed. *The Plain Reader: Essays on Making a Simple Life.* Ballantine Books, 1998. From the practical to the philosophical, this book offers a vision of people all over the country living imaginative, plain lives.

Homesteading and How to Do Nearly Everything

Emery, Carla. *The Encyclopedia of Country Living: An Old Fashioned Recipe Book.* Sasquatch Books, 1994. If you could only take one book from this list, this would be the one. Carla tells you how to grow food, cook it, eat it, preserve it, and how to do a million other things. It truly is an encyclopedia of sustainability, and despite the word "country" in the title, everyone can use this book.

Farallones Institute. *The Integral Urban House.* Random House, 1982. This older book is a wonderful tool for a whole host of things, for city dwellers and rural ones. The emphasis, however, is on urban dwellers and enabling them to live sustainably.

Logsdon, Gene. *The Contrary Farmer.* Chelsea Green, 1994. This book has no peer, except perhaps all of Logsdon's other works. No one is as wise and funny and readable, and has as many ideas. No one is as willing to admit his own flaws and limitations, and no one has as few.

Seymour, John. *The Self-Sufficient Life and How to Live It.* DK Publishing, 2003. A beautiful book that covers how things were once done in Britain, Seymour offers a real sense of the scope of self-sufficiency. The emphasis is on country and rural life.

Stein, Matthew. *When Technology Fails: A Manual for Self-Reliance and Planetary Survival.* Clear Light Publishers, 2000. This book takes you clearly through what you need to know about every imaginable subject in a sustained crisis, and gives clear, solid information and lots of further references. When I want to know something about something I know nothing about, I often go here first.

Permaculture, Design, Landscaping

Creasy, Rosalind. *The Complete Book of Edible Landscaping.* Sierra Club Books, 1982. The emphasis here is on food plants that are beautiful enough to be used even on covenanted lawns.

Hemenway, Toby. *Gaia's Garden.* Chelsea Green, 2000. If permaculture is a new concept to you or you are attempting to begin transforming a small area on permaculture principles, this is the best book out there. In fact, I'm tempted to say this is the best book on permaculture out there — period. Though others may cover more territory, none of them is as clear, thoughtful and beautifully written as this one.

Holmgren, David. *Permaculture: Principles and Pathways Beyond Sustainability.* Holmgren Design Services, 2002. Holmgren, the founder of permaculture, has a full grasp of the application of permaculture to a lower-energy world. Lots of great information here.

Mollison, Bill. *The Permaculture Design Manual.* Tagari, 1988. I'm not sure reading Mollison is always a good idea — he can be as obfuscatory as he is enlightening. But he's a genius, and there's always good stuff to be had in genius. But if it gets irritating after a while, no, it isn't just you.

Toensmeier, Eric. *Perennial Vegetables.* Chelsea Green, 2007. Toensmeier has managed to produce an admirable book of reasonable scope with a great deal of helpful information about how you can eat without replanting all the time. Toensmeier and Dave Jacke have also written an enormous, two-volume tome about forest gardening in temperate climates. Both are valuable, but the giant encyclopedia is representative of an anality so profound it puts my own to shame.

Adapting Your Home

Harley, Bruce. *Insulate and Weatherize.* Taunton Press, 2002. Widely recommended.

Hasluck, Paul N. *The Handyman's Book: Essential Woodworking Tools and Techniques.* Ten Speed Press, 2001. Most woodworking books emphasize power tools — this is a refreshing change, showing you how to build and use hand tools.

Home Energy Magazine, eds. *No-Regrets Remodeling.* Energy Auditor and Retrofitter, 1997. Green remodeling that actually works.

Reader's Digest. *The Reader's Digest Complete Do-It-Yourself Manual.* Readers Digest Association, 1973. A friend of mine with much experience in the building trade noted that he could build an entire house with just this book.

Robinson, Ed, and Carolyn Robinson. *The "Have-More" Plan.* Storey Books, 1983. More than 50 years old, this book still hasn't lost much of its relevance. The original homesteading design book, re-released.

Warde, Jon, ed. *The Backyard Builder: Over 150 Projects for Your Garden, Home and Yard.* Random House, 1994. Includes plans for a compost drum, orchard ladder, root cellar storage bins.

Waste and Water

Campbell, Stu. *The Home Water Supply: How to Find, Filter, Store and Conserve It.* Storey Books, 1993. Water will be one of the great problems of the coming decades. We all need to know more about our water systems.

Jenkins, J.C. *The Humanure Handbook: A Guide to Composting Human Manure.* Jenkins Publishing, 1994. What we do with our outputs is at the heart of how we adapt. This is a very important book.

Playing with Fire: Heating and Cooking

Aprovecho Research Institute. *Capturing Heat* and *Capturing Heat II.* Aprovecho Research Institute, 1996. These two pamphlets show how to build a high-heat, low-fuel-use rocket stove, solar oven, masonry stove and other valuable heating and cooking resources.

Bushway, Stephen. *The New Woodburner's Handbook.* Storey Press, 1992. If you are going to heat with wood, be sure to know what you are doing. This book is definitive.

Denzer, Kiko. *Build Your Own Earth Oven: A Low-Cost, Wood-Fired Mud Oven.* Handprint Press, 2000. A wonderful, clear book on how to cook cheaply. Great bread recipe as well!

Gardening and Small-Scale Farming

Ashworth, Suzanne. *Seed to Seed.* Seed Saver's Exchange, 1991. If we are to have truly sustainable food systems, we must save seed. This book tells you how.

Bartholomew, Mel. *Square Foot Gardening.* Rodale Press, 1981. No one garden book covers everything, but for new gardeners, there is no better single volume.

Coleman, Eliot. *The Four Season Harvest: Organic Vegetables From Your Home Garden All Year Long.* Chelsea Green, 1999. How to eat fresh food all year with minimal inputs — a necessary and well written book.

Duhon, David. *One Circle: How to Grow a Complete Diet in Less than 1000 Square Feet.* Ecology Action Publications, 1985. David Duhon actually lived on what he could grow in a very small space, and describes what crops and diet can enable us to grow our own food.

Hartung, Tammi. *Growing 101 Herbs that Heal.* Storey Books, 2000. The best book I know about growing medicinal herbs.

Jeavons, John. *How To Grow More Vegetables and Fruits, Nuts, Berries, Grains, and Other Crops Than You Ever Thought Possible On Less Land Than You Can Imagine.* Ten Speed Press, 2002. Technical and deep, this book may have more to do with saving our lives than any other. Jeavons shows how to produce enormous amounts of food in small spaces. The tables in the back alone are worth the price of the book.

Lovejoy, Sharon. *Roots, Shoots, Buckets and Boots.* Workman Publishing, 1999. There can be no more essential work than teaching the next generation to garden. A wonderful, inspiring book for everyone who loves a child.

McGee, Rose Marie Nichols, and Maggie Stuckey. *The Bountiful Container.* Workman Publishing, 2002. This is the best single book about container-based food gardening.

Reich, Lee. *Weedless Gardening.* Workman Publishing, 2001. A good introduction to mulch gardening and the science behind it.

Smith, Edward C. *Incredible Vegetables from Self-Watering Containers.* Storey Publishing, 2006. Self-watering containers can produce enormous yields, expanding our food production capacity.

Medicine

American Red Cross Society and Kathleen Handal, M.D. *The American Red Cross First Aid and Safety Handbook.* Little, Brown, 1995. This represents the absolute minimum an ordinary person should know about first aid.

Bickley, Lynn. *The Bates Guide to Physical Examination and History Taking.* Lippincott, Williams and Wilkins, 2007. This is a highly technical and extremely expensive book, but also very important. Knowing how to examine someone and take a medical history is essential to providing even basic community medical care.

Burns, A. August, Ronnie Lovich, Jane Maxwell and Katherine Shapiro. *Where Women Have No Doctor.* Hesperian Foundation, 1997. An essential resource for those who may have no access to women's medical care — either today or in the future.

Coffee, Hugh. *Ditch Medicine: Advanced Field Procedures for Emergencies.* Paladin Press, 1993. This is the book you hope you never have to use. But in the meantime, make sure someone in your community, ideally several someones, have read this book.

Davis, Elizabeth. *Heart and Hands: A Midwife's Guide to Pregnancy and Birth.* Celestial Arts Publishing, 1997. Several of the midwives I've met recommend this book as one of the best books on home birth and midwifery. Everyone in a community must have someone who can safely deliver a baby if it is needed.

Dickson, Murray. *Where There Is No Dentist.* Hesperian Foundation, 1983. Millions of Americans have no access to dental care right now. This book fills an enormous gap in our culture.

Werner, David, Carol Thuman and Jane Maxwell. *Where There Is No Doctor: A Village Health Care Handbook.* Hesperian Foundation, 2002. Everyone should own this book, read it, and be familiar with its information. This book was designed for people in rural areas who might not have access to medicine, but represent a powerful blueprint for communities in the US who may also struggle to get the medical care they need.

Herbal and Alternative Medical Care

Brinker, Francis. *Herb Contraindications and Drug Interactions.* Eclectic Medical Publications, 1998. This highly technical work is essential for people using herbs. It provides exhaustive lists of potential problems.

Bulmer, Stephen. *Herbal Antibiotics: Natural Alternatives for Treating Drug-Resistant Bacteria.* Storey Publications, 1999. The wild growth of MRSA and other antibiotic resistant infections make this book absolutely essential.

Duke, James A. *The Green Pharmacy: New Discoveries in Herbal Remedies for Common Diseases and Conditions from the World's Foremost Authority on Healing Herbs.* Rodale Press, 1997. Duke is one of the world's foremost herbalists, and this is an alphabetical (by ailment) guide to the use of herbal medicine.

Green, James. *The Herbal Medicine Maker's Handbook: A Home Manual.* Crossing Press, 2000. Most books on herbalism assume that you will buy your remedies at the store, but this one offers real strategies for those who want to make the transition from garden to medicine cabinet.

Pizzorno, Joseph E., and Michael T. Murray. *The Textbook of Natural Medicine.* Churchill Livingston, 2007. Very expensive and highly technical, this is not a layperson's guide, but valuable for anyone who wants to go beyond ordinary lay knowledge.

Cookbooks

Dragonwagon, Crescent. *The Soup and Bread Cookbook.* Workman Publishing, 1992. It is a very simple concept — recipes for soup made of everything imaginable, and some bread and salad recipes to accompany them. The soups are the centerpiece. A definite keeper — under lock and key, if necessary.

Lewis, Edna. *The Taste of Country Cooking.* Knopf, 2006. Lewis was one of the great figures of American cooking. She grew up in a community of farmers, African American descendents of freed slaves, and this book is an evocative and delicious link to that culture and its cuisine. This is real, seasonal, delicious country food, along with lovely narratives of what the life was like. The food is simple, but if you don't grow your own, you are unlikely to understand what is so beautiful about her emphasis on the natural, real flavors of food.

Longacre, Doris Janzen. *The More With Less Cookbook.* Mennonite Central Committee, 2000. One of a series of four, all focusing on staple foods, meat used as a treat or seasoning, and accessible recipes. Great for basic, staple American-style recipes. *Extending the Table* provides authentic ethnic recipes and stories from around the world. *Simply In Season* focuses on seasonal eating. The fourth is a children's cookbook with the same title.

Robertson, Laurel. *The Laurel's Kitchen Bread Book.* Random House, 1984. If you are going to grind your own grain to make bread, you need this book. There's definitely an old-fashioned, 1970s complete-proteins-and-carob-cookies feel to it, but who cares? There are hundreds of recipes for bread products using every kind of grain, and it is well worth having.

Wolfert, Paula. *Mediterranean Grains and Greens.* Harper Collins, 1998. One of the more fascinating cookbooks I own. It is 350 pages of recipes using mostly whole grains and fresh greens. Most Americans would hardly believe it was possible to write such a cookbook, but it is not merely possible, but glorious.

Yin-Fei Lo, Eileen. *From the Earth: Chinese Vegetarian Cooking.* MacMillan, 1995. There are lots of recipes in American storage cookbooks for mock meat made from tofu and gluten. Most of them, frankly, suck. They don't taste anything like meat, and they don't taste particularly good, either. On the other hand, if you've ever eaten Chinese Buddhist cooking, you will realize that there exists the perfect fruition of fake meat cookery. It is very good. So if you think you may have to make do with soybeans and wheat for dinner any time soon, this is the cookbook to have.

Local Food Systems

Flores, H.C. *Food Not Lawns: How to Turn Your Yard Into a Garden and Your Neighborhood into a Community.* Chelsea Green, 2006. Funny and smart, with a strong leftist agenda, this is not so much a garden book as a food systems book.

Kingsolver, Barbara. *Animal, Vegetable, Miracle: A Year of Food Life.* Harper Collins, 2007. Lyrical and funny, wise and brilliant, if you read only one book about food, make it this one.

Nabhan, Gary. *Coming Home to Eat.* W.W. Norton, 2002. The first of the local food books, it remains one of the best, and is particularly useful for those looking to eat local in the West.

Smith, Alisa, and J.B. MacKinnon. *Plenty: One Man, One Woman and a Raucous Year of Eating Locally.* Harmony Books, 2007. Smith and MacKinnon had the disadvantage of their book coming out in the same year as Kingsolver's, but both books are important and worth a read, offering different gifts.

Parenting

Louv, Richard. *Last Child in the Wood: Saving Our Children from Nature-Deficit Disorder.* Algonquin Books, 2006. Details the horrific damage we are doing to our children as we destroy the natural world.

Steingraber, Sandra. *Having Faith: An Ecologist's Journey to Motherhood.* W.W. Norton, 2001. No woman should enter the journey to motherhood without understanding what industrial society has done to her body and her capacity to create life. A beautiful and disturbing book.

Homeschooling and Ecological Education:

Friere, Paolo. *Pedagogy of the Oppressed.* Continuum Publishing, 1993. A classic. First, they tell you that what you know doesn't matter — this is the truth that underlies much of the difficulty in our educational system. Every teacher should read this book.

Gatto, John Taylor. *Dumbing Us Down: the Hidden Curriculum of Compulsory Schooling.* New Society, 2005. Gatto, a former teacher, sees little hope for "the system" but a great deal of hope for new ideas.

Illich, Ivan. *Deschooling Society.* Marion Boyers Publishing, 2002. Like all Illich's books, wonderful, radical, inspiring, ultimately hopeful.

Orr, David. *Earth in Mind: On Education, Environment and the Human Prospect.* Island Press, 2004. David Orr is wise and wonderful, and more fully grasps the problems of creating an ecological education than anyone I know of.

Index

About the Author

SHARON ASTYK IS A WRITER, TEACHER, blogger and small farmer. A former academic, her unfinished doctoral dissertation focused on the ecological and demographic catastrophes explored in Early Modern Literature. Abandoning Shakespeare to work on the ecological and demographic catastrophes of the 21st century, she began by running a small CSA and right now seems to write books. In her copious spare time, she raises vegetables, fruit, livestock, children and havoc with her husband in rural upstate New York.

If you have enjoyed *Depletion and Abundance*, you might also enjoy other

Books to Build a New Society

Our books provide positive solutions for people who want to
make a difference. We specialize in:

Sustainable Living • Ecological Design and Planning
Natural Building & Appropriate Technology
Environment and Justice • Conscientious Commerce
Progressive Leadership • Resistance and Community • Nonviolence
Educational and Parenting Resources

For a full list of NSP's titles, please call 1-800-567-6772 or check out our web site at:

www.newsociety.com

NEW SOCIETY PUBLISHERS